No Battle...No Victory

Scarborough Football
1998 - 2009

By Steve Adamson

Published by:
Yore Publications
12 The Furrows, Harefield,
Middx. UB9 6AT.

British Library Cataloguing-in-Publication Data.
A catalogue record for this book
is available from the British Library.

ISBN 978-0-9557889-8-7

Printed and bound by:
QNS Printing Ltd.
Newcastle upon Tyne

ACKNOWLEDGEMENTS

The author wishes to especially thank Derek Megginson for his tremendous help in the compilation of this book. Thanks are also extended to the various other people who have helped or contributed in any way, including James Hunter, Charles Place, Ian Scobbie, Sean Hunter, Keith Crowe, Mitch Cook, Neil Thaler and Mark Dawson. Most of the photos in this book are reproduced by courtesy of the Scarborough Evening News, but some others were taken by Derek Megginson, James Hunter or Stuart Canvin. Apologies to any person or organisation should copyright have inadvertently been infringed. Finally, thanks to Dave Twydell of Yore Publications, for all his expert help and advice.

THE AUTHOR

Born in Scarborough in November 1957, Steve Adamson started watching his local team, aged 11 in 1969 and has been a keen supporter ever since. He has contributed to the club programmes for over 20 years, including seven seasons as editor, and has published numerous books on the subject of local football, including The Official History of Scarborough Football Club, published by Yore Publications in 1998. Married to Eileen, he has three children, Tracey (28), a teacher in Kings Lynn, Norfolk, Michelle (22), a full time mum with two young children, and Paul (20), a Lance Corporal in the 2nd Bttn. Yorkshire Regiment, who have just deployed to Afghanistan as this book went to print. Steve has worked for Royal Mail for 31 years and hobbies other than football include travel, reading, philately, watching cricket and spending time with his grandchildren.

DEDICATION

This book is dedicated to all the players, officials, supporters and willing helpers, who contributed their time and efforts to ensure the survival of Scarborough Football Club over so many years.

Foreword

Having been involved with the fortunes of Scarborough football for more than 20 years, one thing can be said with total certainty - there is never a dull season. And that's never been truer than over the past decade following the end of Boro's 12-year tenure in the Football League.

Following the last-day heartache of relegation from the League in 1999, most of the drama has occurred off the pitch. Other then Boro's glorious FA Cup run in 2003-04 which culminated in that battling defeat against the Premiership might of Chelsea, little has gone right on the playing side.

While Boro have failed to make many headlines with their football, there has certainly been plenty of major stories with their off-the-field problems. Demotion from the Conference, the liquidation of the club and the loss of the McCain Stadium all came in rapid succession, spelling the end of Scarborough FC after 128 years of history. But from the ashes, within two seasons, we have seen the birth of two new clubs with both formed on the back of local support.

Scarborough Athletic and Scarborough Town are proudly flying the flag for the town in lower league football and, as ever, the future will be fascinating. Will the two clubs eventually combine forces and will Scarborough ever have a new ground in the town which has the potential to be the base for a club playing at a decent level of non-League football?

Past experience suggests the outcome will not be straight-forward and that Scarborough football will not do things the easy way.

Charles Place
Scarborough Evening News
Sports Editor

INTRODUCTION

Scarborough Football Club may have only been a small club in the grand scheme of things, but it was a club that boasted a rich and glorious history. Formed in 1879, they experienced long periods of struggle as well as spells of great success during their long history. Some of the highlights included winning the Midland League championship with a record points total in 1930, a league and cup double in the North Eastern League in 1963, three FA Trophy final wins at Wembley in the 1970's, and winning the Conference championship in 1987, to become the first non-League club to achieve automatic promotion to the Football League.

Twelve seasons were spent in the League, during which a number of notable cup runs were embarked upon, and the promotion play-offs were reached on two occasions. For a town with a population of under 55,000, and an isolated geographical location on the East Coast of Yorkshire, that meant a 40-mile journey to the nearest city, the club did remarkably well to sustain Football League status for so long, before finally dropping back into non-League football in 1999, in the most unbelievable and sensational ending to any season in the history of the Football League.

The club battled on for another eight years, lurching from one financial crisis to another, before eventually collapsing under a mountain of debt in June 2007, to bring an end to 128 years of history and tradition. At the time of their demise, the club was actually older than no fewer than 65 of the 92 Football League and Premiership clubs, including such great names as Arsenal, Chelsea, Liverpool, Manchester City, Manchester United, Newcastle, Leeds United and West Ham.

Fortunately a new club quickly rose from the ashes, with the creation of fans-run club, Scarborough Athletic, who joined the Northern Counties East League, but the loss of the stadium was a massive blow, and the fan-base was split, with a second new club, Scarborough Town, also being created soon after, to leave us with the present situation of the town now having two separate clubs, playing at fairly low levels of the football pyramid, and no suitable stadium available in the town. This book tells the story of those eleven remarkable seasons, from 1998 to 2009, and tries to understand how it all went so wrong, and what the future might hold for senior football in the town of Scarborough.

Contents:

THE FIRST 119 YEARS

Scarborough Football Club was founded in the Summer of 1879, by a group of local cricket enthusiasts, keen to secure an active winter pastime. A series of advertisements were placed in the Scarborough Gazette newspaper, inviting interested gentlemen to attend sessions at the North Marine Road cricket ground each Saturday afternoon, so that association and rugby football matches could take place. With encouragement from Lord Londesborough, a benefactor and stalwart supporter of Scarborough Cricket Club, experimental fixtures were arranged against other fledgling clubs from the York and Hull areas. The first recorded game took place on 2 October 1879, under the rugby code, when Scarborough lost by one goal and three tries to one try, against a team from York. Eventually though the Scarborough club started playing association matches only, their first ever fixture in this code resulting in a 2-1 victory against a team from Bridlington on 6 November 1880.

For the first few years of the club's existence, a programme of friendly or challenge matches was arranged throughout the winter months, but the local football scene then received a big boost in 1885 with the formation of the Scarbororough & East Riding County Football Association. The new association organised an annual knockout tournament, and thus the club played its first ever competitive match, with a 5-0 win against another local team, St Mary's in the first round of the new Scarbororough & East Riding Cup in January 1886.

Interest in local soccer grew rapidly in the late 1880's, with the Scarborough club operating a second team, and several other local clubs being formed. Scarborough won the East Riding Cup for the first time in 1888, and the following year they entered the English FA Cup for the first time. Within a few years they were also regular entrants in other cup competitions such as the FA Amateur Cup and the Cleveland Amateur Cup.

In 1898 the club accepted an invitation to become founder members of the new second division of the Northern League, and in 1900, when the second division was abolished, they found themselves competing against some of the best amateur clubs in the country in the single division Northern League. Several years of struggle followed, and there was a four season spell in the Yorkshire Combination, before Scarborough finally left the Northern League in 1926, after an FA inquiry found the club guilty of making illegal payments to players. Professionalism was adopted, and after one season in the Yorkshire League, Scarborough embarked on their long association with the Midland League in 1927. The championship was won, with a record points margin in season 1929-30, but financial problems soon came to the fore, and the remaining years leading up to the Second World War were very difficult for the club, although they did register their first FA Cup win against a Football League team in 1930, with a sensational 6-4 victory over Division Three North leaders Lincoln City.

When football resumed after the War, Boro remained steady members of the Midland League for many years, occasionally enjoying a good FA Cup run or adding to their impressive record of successes in the North Riding Senior Cup. The early 1960's saw the collapse of the Midland League and Boro, led by player-manager Eddy Brown, went on to win the North-Eastern League title in 1962-63. They joined the reformed Midland Counties League in 1963, remaining there until 1968 when the club was selected to become founder-members of the newly created Northern Premier League.

Under player-coach Colin Appleton, Boro became one of the leading non-League clubs in the country during the 1970's, regularly finishing near the top of the N.P.L. as well as reaching Wembley four times in five seasons in the FA Trophy, the knockout cup for senior non-League clubs that had been launched in 1969.

1903-04 season group - Back, far left, is stalwart Club Chairman Thomas Cole, 'The Father of Local Football'

1929-30 season,
Captain Billy Clayson with the Midland League Champship Shield

Boro won the Trophy three times, and in 1979, left the N.P.L. to join the new Alliance Premier League, formed as a national league for the top non-League clubs in the country.

The Alliance Premier League Cup was won in 1984, but it was season 1986-87 that was to become the club's most successful ever, when, under new manager Neil Warnock, Boro won the championship, to become the first non-League club to win automatic promotion to the Football League. A 2-2 home draw against mighty Wolves was the club's first ever match in the League, and Boro spent twelve seasons at this level, recording a string of impressive cup successes against the likes of Chelsea, Portsmouth, Plymouth Argyle and Coventry City and also twice reaching the promotion play-offs during this time. This book takes up the story from the start of season 1998-99, a year after Boro had been beaten 7-2 on aggregate by Torquay United in the semi-finals of the Third Division promotion play-offs.

Two more memorable achievements:
(Top) Civic Reception for the Conference Champions 1986/87
(Right) Skipper, Jimmy Shoulder, with the the F.A.Trophy, won at Wenbley in 1973.

Memorable Programmes from the past:

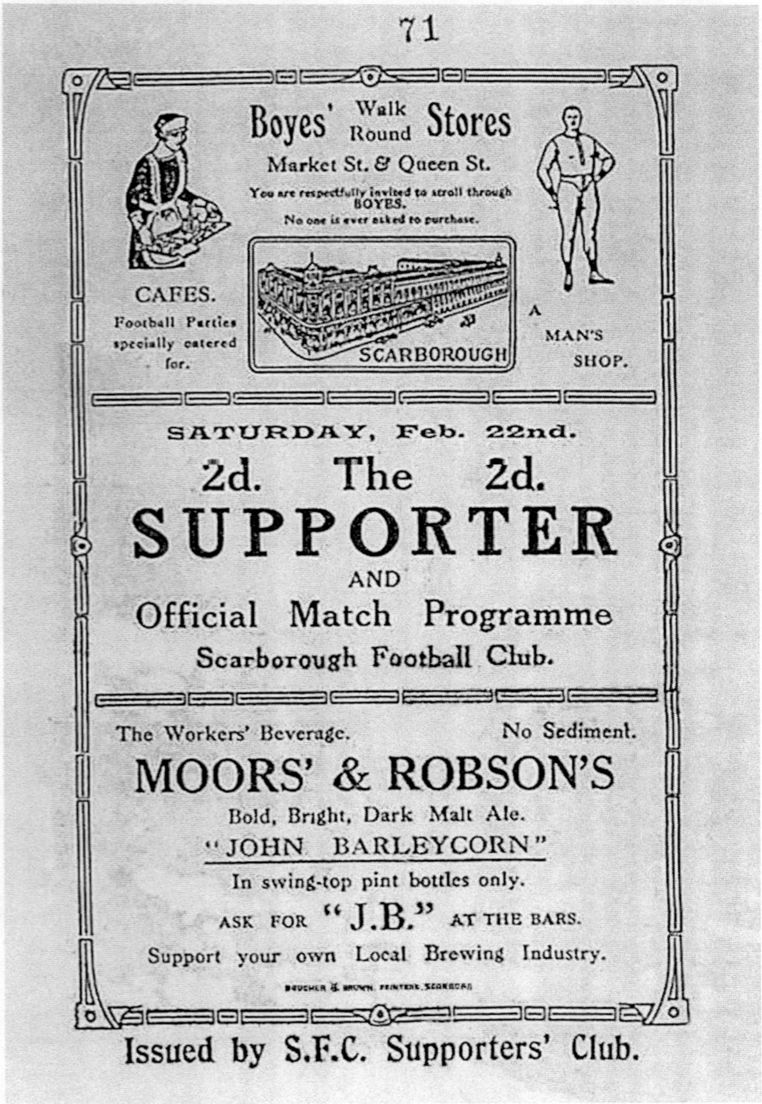
71

Boyes' Walk Round Stores

Market St. & Queen St.

You are respectfully invited to stroll through BOYES.

No one is ever asked to purchase.

CAFES.

Football Parties specially catered for.

SCARBOROUGH

A MAN'S SHOP.

SATURDAY, Feb. 22nd.

2d. The 2d.

SUPPORTER

AND

Official Match Programme

Scarborough Football Club.

The Workers' Beverage. No Sediment.

MOORS' & ROBSON'S

Bold, Bright, Dark Malt Ale.

"JOHN BARLEYCORN"

In swing-top pint bottles only.

ASK FOR "J.B." AT THE BARS.

Support your own Local Brewing Industry.

Issued by S.F.C. Supporters' Club.

The oldest known Boro programme from the 1929/30 season
Midland League vs.Newark

F.A. CHALLENGE TROPHY COMPETITION
FINAL
SCARBOROUGH
VERSUS
WIGAN
ATHLETIC
SATURDAY, 28th APRIL, 1973 Kick-off 3 p.m.
WEMBLEY
EMPIRE STADIUM
OFFICIAL PROGRAMME 10p

THE
BORO'
REVIEW
THE OFFICIAL PROGRAMME OF SCARBOROUGH F.C.
SCARBOROUGH
Saturday, January 3rd, 1976
SCARBOROUGH
v
CRYSTAL PALACE
F.A. CUP 3rd ROUND
5p
SCARBOROUGH FOOTBALL CLUB

CHELSEA
Littlewoods Cup 2nd Rd 1st Leg
SCARBOROUGH
Tuesday 19th September 1989 Kick-off 7.30 pm
Commodore
Official Matchday Magazine Price £1.00
CFC

BORO
Review
THE VOICE OF SCARBOROUGH FOOTBALL CLUB
RONSON
SCARBOROUGH FOOTBALL CLUB
NO VICTORY
NO BATTLE
THOMPSONS . BUPA BELVEDERE
COCA COLA CUP FOURTH ROUND
ARSENAL
WEDNESDAY 23rd DECEMBER, 1992. K.O. 7.30 p.m.
MATCHDAY MAGAZINE £1.00

The Anton Johnson Affair

Having gambled heavily on winning promotion in the 1997-98 season, but failing at the play-off semi-final stage, majority shareholders John and Gillian Russell stunned supporters by putting their 70% shareholding up for sale just three weeks before the start of the 1998-99 campaign. Former chairman John Russell, who had handed the reigns to Ken Ferrie at the end of the previous season, said "*We had some success last season, but to progress further we need extra investment to help get the club up to the next level. I have put blood, sweat and tears into this club over the past four years and I will not be walking away, but we do need to attract new investors into what is a well-run club that can really go places"*. Former Leeds United chairman Bill Fotherby expressed an interest in taking over, but it was Essex-based businessman Anton Johnson who eventually took control of the club, by agreeing to purchase a 51% stake in the club, with the Russell's retaining 19% of the shares.

John Russell announced, *"The reason we have sold some of our shares is so the club can move forward, and I am absolutely delighted we have now got the investment we need"*. Anton Johnson, who had previously been involved with Bournemouth, Rotherham United and Southend United was unveiled as Boro's new majority shareholder at noon on Saturday, 8 August 1998, just three hours before the opening match of the season, ironically at home to his former club Southend United. He brought with him a new chief executive in Dave Cusack and a new company secretary, Clive Purdy, while Ken Ferrie remained as club chairman and John and Gillian Russell retained their seats on the board. In his first statement to the local press, Johnson pledged to make funds available to strengthen the team saying, *"Money will be made available, but I am not putting a figure on how much. I think the reality of today is that money can buy success. I know Scarborough is regarded as a small club, but I intend to make it a big club"*.

However, despite the optimistic announcements from both Russell and Johnson, many Boro fans knew enough of Johnson's background, to have grave misgivings about what was in store for the club. A former nightclub owner, Anton Johnson had a dreadful record in his dealings in football clubs, particularly at Southend United where he had been in charge from June 1983 to October 1984; during this time the club's debts had spiraled from around £250,000 to £700,000 when he finally departed. It was never established where the money had gone despite a lengthy investigation by the Essex Police fraud squad. The Football League had banned him from all future involvement in running a football club, and he had also been declared bankrupt in June 1988. Yet, here we were just ten years later, and he was back in charge of a club in the Football League. A flamboyant, charismatic man, he certainly talked a good game, and John Russell had welcomed him to the club with open arms.

With the team making a poor start to the season, events behind the scenes were even more distressing as none of the promised funding to strengthen the playing squad was forthcoming and Johnson was rarely seen at matches. As the team slumped towards the bottom of the table, supporters were increasingly asking when the promised new signings would materialise. At a board meeting on 19 September, Anton Johnson announced that he had taken over from Ken Ferrie as club chairman. He added, *"John Russell and Ken Ferrie will remain on the board to give myself the support and backing when needed, to take Scarborough Football Club into the higher divisions. It is time to dampen all the detrimental rumours that have been circulating, and reassure the fans that there is no crisis at the club."*.But rumours of discord in the boardroom remained rife, and a marathan ten hour board meeting took place on 9 November, at which Anton Johnson was not present.

His beleagured chief executive Dave Cusack was left to try to explain what was going on, and he announced, *"It was a lengthy board meeting, very constructive and productive. A lot of things were discussed and sorted out for the well- being of the club.*

The team was struggling for goals, and a £20,000 bid to sign experienced striker Andy Saville from Cardiff City collapsed, after the player had agreed to sign, with chief executive Dave Cusack explaining, *"We had to pull out of the deal on the advice of our financial advisors because of pressing liabilities at the club"*. Former owner John Russell hit back, saying *"I am devastated and astonished at this decision. When Anton Johnson and his people came to the club, the liabilities of the Football Club were known 100% to them. My main reason for selling the club to them was to get some investors to come in and take the club on to the next level, and obviously that would involve bringing in new players to strengthen the team"*.

A fans forum, organised by long standing supporter of 40-years, Ken Hepton, was staged at The Cricketers pub on 13 November, when around 150 fans heard John Russell outline his plans to take legal action to regain control of the club from Anton Johnson, who he said, had failed to comply with the terms of his purchase of the 51% shareolding.
Asked why he agreed to sell the club to Johnson, Russell replied, *"I am sorry, it was a mistake"*.

He also explained that Johnson had inherited a £600,000 debt, which comprised of a £300,000 bank overdraft, outstanding directors loans, including £104,000 owed to Ken Ferrie for work on building the new stands, and various other short term debts, including a PFA loan and a £40,000 VAT bill. Russell added that he felt that was a manageable level of debt, and no larger than the debts faced by many other lower division clubs.

In late November 1998 the Football League announced it was launching an investigation into the club's affairs and the business relationship with the increasingly reclusive Anton Johnson. Soon after, John Russell reported that he had succeeded in regaining control of the club with his wife Gillian resuming her position as secretary, after the transfer of shares back from Anton Johnson following his breach of the terms of the sale agreement. Chief executive Dave Cusack was then dismissed, and the Russells appointed a new chief executive, 44-year old Kevin Green. Upon regaining control of the club, John Russell revealed that Boro were losing almost £25,000 a month, and said the wage bill had increased by a staggering 70% over the past two seasons, while attendances had shown a marked decline. Most supporters found irony in those comments - for it had been John Russell who had sanctioned the huge increase in the wage bill, in his unsuccessful bid to secure promotion the previous season!

Anton Johnson on his arrival

Season 1998-99 Boardroom upheaval and relegation heartache

Having splashed out the cash in a bid to win promotion the previous season, only to go down 7-2 on aggregate to Torquay United in the play-off semi-finals, chairman John Russell stepped down at the end of the campaign and put the club up for sale on the eve of the 1998-99 season.

Despite securing a lucrative sponsorship deal with Arnott Insurance, the club was forced to make drastic cuts to the wage bill, having made a huge loss of £250,000 in the previous season, and no fewer than nine senior players left the McCain Stadium, including inspirational centre-back and player-coach Gary Bennett who signed for Darlington in a £20,000 deal, former Leeds United and Everton top flight midfield star Ian Snodin who joined Doncaster Rovers as their new player-manager for a £5,000 fee and hugely popular central defender Jason Rockett who was forced to retire, aged 29, due to a crippling knee injury. Other members of the previous season's squad to move on were Troy Bennett, Simon Bochenski, Jamie Mitchell, Colin Sutherland, Paul Atkin and Michael McElhatton.

Manager Mick Wadsworth, operating with a greatly reduced playing budget, brought in a host of new signings, the most notable of whom were 30-year old French defender Alex Marinkov from French third division side Raon L'Etape, 19-year old Newcastle reserves striker Ian Milbourne, experienced York City defender Paddy Atkinson, former Barnsley and Scunthorpe midfielder Wayne Bullimore from Peterborough United and 6ft centre-back Jason Lydiate from Blackpool, all on free transfers.

With events in the boardroom grabbing the headlines, the season opened with three successive defeats, the club's worst start to a league campaign for 50 years, but then came a morale-boosting 3-0 away success over Leyton Orient, with goals from Liam Robinson, Steve Brodie and Matthew Russell. Three of the next five games were also won, including a 3-1 home triumph over eventual champions Brentford on 19 September, with Steve Brodie scoring twice, which saw Boro climb to 12th in the table, but from then on it was downhill all the way.

The board-room in-fighting continued to make the news, while on the pitch, manager Mick Wadsworth was struggling to field a settled team. Midfielder Gareth Williams, who had made 105 Football League appearances for Boro, scoring 27 goals, was transferred to Third Division rivals Hull City for a £25,000 fee and striker Neil Campbell moved to Southend United for £15,000, while experienced keeper Tony Elliott suffered a career-ending back injury in a 3-0 defeat at Darlington on 28 November.

First round defeats in all three cup competitions didn't help the cash-flow situation, and with Boro dropping into the bottom two in the table, crowds also began to dwindle. A 1-0 win away at Rochdale ended an eight-game winless run in the League, but as Christmas approached Boro were firmly entrenched in a relegation battle. The festive period brought no respite as a 3-2 defeat at Mansfield Town on Boxing Day was followed by a 4-1 home loss to Scunthorpe United two days later. Alex Marinkov hit a spot kick winner in a 1-0 home victory over Exeter City on 16 January, but when the next match resulted in a single goal defeat at Brighton, manager Mick Wadsworth resigned, to take over as Colchester United boss.

Derek Mountfield, the former Everton, Aston Villa and Wolves defender, who had joined the club in December on non-contract terms, and club stalwart Ray McHale, were appointed as joint caretaker-managers, but the team suffered successive 5-1 drubbings, away at Scunthorpe and then at home to Cambridge United, followed by a 3-1 loss to Shrewsbury Town. Former long serving club director Derek Watson passed away after a long illness, aged 72 in February. He had served on the board for 26 years before stepping down in 1985. Darlington striker Darren Roberts was signed on a free transfer, while Jason Lydiate went out on loan to Rochdale.

A 2-1 home win against Swansea City, with goals from Chris Tate and Darren Roberts was the managerial duo's last match in charge, as the vastly experienced 58-year old Colin Addison, previously manager at Derby County, Hereford United, West Brom and Athletico Madrid amongst others, was brought in and given the task of leading the club away from the foot of the table.

Addison made veteran keeper Tony Parks, a UEFA Cup winner with Spurs in 1984 his first signing, although popular French defender Alex Marinkov left to join Scottish giants Hibernians for a £30,000 fee. A Chris Tate strike earned Boro a terrific 1-1 draw at high-flying Brentford in Addison's first match at the helm, and the revival continued four days later when Tate netted twice in a 3-1 win at Chester City. A thumping 4-0 home defeat by Rotherham United was next, but a run of three wins and a draw, including a battling 1-1 draw in front of almost 14,000 fans at Hull City, and a 3-0 home success over fellow strugglers Carlisle United, lifted Boro off the foot of the table.

Confidence throughout the club was lifted, but hopes of climbing away from the danger zone were shattered as Boro slumped to five successive defeats, including a 3-0 reverse at fellow relegation candidates Hartlepool, and Boro dropped back to the foot of the table. With just three games left to play, the situation looked bleak for Boro as they trailed Carlisle United by four points and had a vastly inferior goal-difference, although they did have a game in hand on the Cumbrian side.

Bottom of Division Three

	P	W	D	L	F	A	Pts
Hartlepool United	44	13	10	21	51	64	49
Carlisle United	44	10	15	19	41	52	45
Scarborough	43	12	5	26	44	75	41

On Saturday 1 May, Boro travelled to the Shay to face play-off contenders Halifax Town, desperate for a win to stay in touch with the teams above, knowing a defeat would have been devastating to their hopes of avoiding the drop. Roared on by around 400 supporters, Boro boosted their chances of staying up by coming away with a well deserved 2-1 win, courtesy of early goals by Graeme Atkinson and Steve Brodie, while the other two relegation candidates fought out a 0-0 draw at Hartlepool, a result which ensured Hartlepool would avoid the drop.

Boro were now two points behind Carlisle with a game in hand, and they gave themselves a great chance of staying up with a convincing 3-0 home victory over Plymouth Argyle four days later. Steve Brodie opened the scoring after just two minutes, and a second half double from Chris Tate wrapped up the points. As the final day of the season approached, Boro were off the bottom of the table, and their fate was now in their own hands.

	P	W	D	L	F	A	Pts
HartlepoolUnited	45	13	11	21	51	64	50
Scarborough	45	14	5	26	49	76	47
CarlisleUnited	45	10	16	19	41	52	46

Boro entertained 9th-placed Peterborough United, managed by old adversary from his Barnet days, Barry Fry, on Saturday 8 May, knowing a win would preserve their Football League status. Even a draw or defeat could also be enough, provided Carlisle didn't better Boro's result, in their home match against Plymouth Argyle. A bumper crowd of 4769 packed into the McCain Stadium, while 7599 were at Brunton Park, Carlisle for the vital end of season showdowns.

It didn't start too well for Boro, as Peterborough took a 7th minute lead, but Darren Roberts equalised three minutes before half-time.

With the score 1-1 at the interval, the pendulum still swung Boro's way, as Carlisle were being held 0-0 by Plymouth in their game. Both matches were covered on radio five live, and a huge roar from the Boro crowd greeted the news that Plymouth had taken the lead up at Carlisle just four minutes into the second half. Surely Boro were safe from relegation now! But Carlisle equalised soon after, and Boro, who gave a surprisingly sluggish display, seemed content to settle for a 1-1 draw against Peterbororough. At the final whistle, hundreds of fans swarmed on to McCain Stadium pitch, believing Boro had avoided relegation as Carlisle were still drawing 1-1 with Plymouth. Directors Gillian Russell and Trevor Milton even appeared in the main stand, preparing to uncork a bottle of champagne to celebrate the great escape.

However, devastating news then began to filter through that Carlisle had snatched a dramatic last-gasp winning goal, with on-loan Swindon Town goalkeeper Jimmy Glass smashing home a sensational winner from a corner kick some five minutes into stoppage time, to enable the Cumbrians to scramble off the bottom of the table and send Boro back down to the Conference. It was an unbelievable ending to Boro's 12-season spell in the Football League.

Final Positions

	P	W	D	L	F	A	Pts
HartlepoolUnited	46	13	12	21	52	65	51
CarlisleUnited	46	11	16	19	43	53	49
Scarborough	46	14	6	26	50	77	48

In May 1999 Boro stalwart Geoff Bowman, died at the age of 66. His 38-year association with the club began in 1950 when he began playing for the 'A' and reserve teams, and he later had a lengthy spell as trainer and sponge man under Colin Appleton. When he retired in May 1988 he was made an honorary life member of the club.

(Above) Manager Colin Addison and (left) the story so far....Club history published by Yore Publications in 1998.

Nationwide League Division 3 Saturday, 16 September 1998
SCARBOROUGH 3 BRENTFORD 1

Teenage midfielder Neil Radigan, a product of the youth system, turned in an impressive display in his first full appearance in the senior team, as Boro shocked title favourites Brentford, to pick up their best result of a difficult season. The visitors, who had been relegated the previous season, were lying 4th in the table under new owner Ron Noades, who had installed himself as chairman-manager, and had picked up the August manager of the month award. Centre-back Jamie Bates was playing his 500th first team game for the Bees. Boro meanwhile, were down in 17th place, and were without striker Chris Tate through injury as they sought to end a run of 3 successive defeats, and this surprise win saw them climb to 12th in the table, while Brentford slipped down to 7th.

Boro keeper Tony Elliott made a superb save from a fierce Dirk Hebel shot, before Steve Brodie took centre-stage, scoring twice in the first half, stooping to head home a low cross from Gareth Williams in the 33rd minute, and then latching onto a precise through-ball from Williams to side-foot past the keeper just 3 minutes later. He almost completed a quick-fire hat trick, but Bees keeper Jason Pearcey blocked his goal-bound shot just before the interval. Brentford applied some heavy pressure in the second period, and pulled a goal back when Lloyd Owusu volleyed home on 63 minutes, but Boro wrapped up the points with a controversial penalty five minutes later. The linesman spotted an infringment, and the excellent Alex Marinkov blasted home the spot kick to secure 3 much needed points for Mick Wadsworth's team.

Scarborough Tony Elliott, John Kay, Paddy Atkinson, Neil Radigan, Jason Lydiate, Alex Marinkov, Wayne Bullimore (Ben Worrall 65), Jamie Hoyland, Gareth Williams, Steve Brodie (Neil Campbell 87), Liam Robinson (Matthew Russell 76)
Brentford Jason Pearcey, Danny Boxall, Ijah Anderson, Chris Coyne (Lloyd Owusu 46), Darren Powell, Jamie Bates, Darren Freeman, Dirk Hebel (Warren Aspinall 61), Robert Quinn (Kevin Rapley 61), Martin Rowlands, Andy Scott
Referee John Kirkby(Sheffield) Attendance 2028

Nationwide League Division 3 Wednesday, 5 May 1999
SCARBOROUGH 3 PLYMOUTH ARGYLE 0

Boro took the relegation battle to the final day of the season with this crucial win against a Plymouth side that still had an outside chance of snatching a play-off place. A splendid 2-1 away win over Halifax four days earlier had left them two points adrift of Carlisle at the bottom of the table before kick-off. A depleted Boro had John Kay, Wayne Bullimore and Paddy Atkinson all missing through injury, and Liam Robinson was also unavailable, as his wife gave birth to a baby girl that evening while Plymouth were without top scorer Dwight Marshall, but included 38-year-old assistant manager Steve McCall and on-loan Nottingham Forest striker Steve Guinan in their side.

Desperate for the points to preserve their Football League status, Boro made a dream start, scoring after just two minutes when Steve Brodie headed home a Darren Roberts cross. Plymouth fought back, but Graeme Atkinson and Matthew Russell stood out in a resolute Boro defence, while Darren Roberts fired just wide at the other end. On-form 21-year-old Boro striker Chris Tate netted twice in the space of three minutes in the second half, striking a low shot past the keeper on 74 minutes and then firing home the rebound after the keeper had saved his initial shot in the 76th minute to wrap up a much needed win which lifted Boro off the foot of the table, and left them needing to beat Peterborough on the final day of the season to be certain of avoiding relegation.

Scarborough Tony Parks, Mattew Russell (Gary Porter 80), Graeme Atkinson, Ben Worrall, Shaun Rennison, Mike McNaughton, Jamie Hoyland, Nathan Jones, Chris Tate (Andy Saville 80), Steve Brodie, Darren Roberts
Plymouth Argyle James Dungey, Paul Wotton, John Beswetherwick, Steve McCall (Brendam McGovern 70), Mick Heathcote, Simon Collins, Martin Barlow, Lee Phillips (Jon Ashton 62), Mark Sale, Ian Bastow, Steve Guinan
Referee Scott Mathieson(Stockport) Attendance 2398

Chris Greenacre in action against Exeter City, during Boro's 1-0 win in January 1999.

February 1999
Darren Roberts celebrates his goal dramatically as Boro beat Swansea City 2-1.

KEEPER'S INJURY TIME GOAL SENDS BORO DOWN

"You will never see anything like this again - ever. Believe me, words fail to do justice to the drama that engulfed Brunton Park at 5pm yesterday. Remember the name Jimmy Glass, because his part in the history books is forever assured." (Sunday Sun)

In the most amazing and sensational end to a season ever, Carlisle United retained their 71-year old Football League status when on-loan goalkeeper Jimmy Glass smashed home an amazing injury-time goal to defeat Plymouth Argyle and send Boro down to the Conference in the most heartbreaking fashion.

The Cumbrians' 2-1 home success over Plymouth, coupled with Boro's disappointing 1-1 draw against Peterborough, enabled Carlisle to climb off the foot of the table with the last kick of the season. Just seconds remained when Carlisle were awarded a corner kick, manager Nigel Pearson signalled all his players forward, including the keeper, and when Graham Anthony (who had actually played two games on loan for Boro from Sheffield United in 1996), sent over the corner, a Scott Dobie header was parried by the Plymouth keeper only for Glass to swing his left foot, and smash in a sensational last gasp winner.

The elated keeper said afterwards, "The fans behind my goal kept me in touch with the score at Scarborough. I knew we had to win, so when we won the corner in the final minute I just went up. The ball dropped to my feet and I just hit it into the net and was then swamped by about 3000 Carlisle fans". Glass became a national hero, making the headlines on TV and in all the Sunday papers, but in Scarborough, feelings of despair and disbelief were the order of the day. Boss Colin Addison commented, "The word that comes to mind is cruel, very cruel. But nothing surprises me in football. If we had survived after such a difficult season, it would have been as good as anything I ever achieved in my career. We were sitting in the dressing room waiting for the Carlisle result, and we just couldn't believe it when we heard that their goalkeeper had scored the winner in the last minute of stoppage time".

While the scenes of ecstasy and jubilation were engulfing Brunton Park, it was heartbreak and despair at the McCain Stadium.

Needing to beat Peterborough United to retain their Football League status, Boro could only draw 1-1, and were relegated after Carlisle's sensational last gasp victory over Plymouth. The fact that Carlisle's winning goal was scored with virtually the last kick of the season by an on-loan goalkeeper was incredible enough, but made even more unusual and controversial because he had actually joined the club AFTER transfer deadline day.

High profile Carlisle chairman Michael Knighton had shocked fans by selling first choice keeper Tony Craig to Blackpool on transfer deadline day, leaving on- loan Derby County goalkeeper Richard Knight as the only senior keeper at the club, and when a goalkeeping crisis at Derby led to Knight being recalled to Pride Park just a day later, Carlisle were left without an experienced goalkeeper to call upon. Fortunately for the Cumbrians, the 1988 Football League AGM had voted to allow clubs to register a new goalkeeper after transfer deadline day, if they were left without a keeper due to "injury, illness or special circumstances", and so third choice Swindon Town custodian Jimmy Glass was signed by boss Nigel Pearson.

Whether choosing to sell your regular keeper on transfer deadline day and having a loanee recalled the following day constituted 'special circumstances' was not the only controversy surrounding Carlisle's great escape act. Boro were also aggrieved at the events at Brunton Park on the final day of the season, because a mass pitch invasion had followed Carlisle's equaliser against Plymouth, causing a lengthy delay in restarting the match. This was the reason Boro's match had finished earlier than the game in Cumbria, and the Carlisle players knew Boro's result well before the final whistle at Brunton Park.

But Boro's fate had been sealed, and they were heading back to the Conference after a 12-season stay in the Football League. Perhaps the most disappointed man at the club was assistant manager Ray McHale, a member of the 1987 Conference winning team, and scorer in the first ever League match against Wolves. He commented, "The elation of coming into the League was magnificent, phenomenal. Now this is the lowest point in my career. I was just hoping that fate would give us a bit of luck today, but it wasn't to be, and I am completely shattered".

Scarborough FC: 1998-99

Tony
ELLIOTT

Kevin
MARTIN

Phil
NAISBETT

Nicky
BUXTON

Jason
LYDIATE

Alexandre
MARINKOV

John
KAY

Michael
McNAUGHTON

Matty
RUSSELL

Paddy
ATKINSON

Richard
JACKSON

Jamie
HOYLAND

Wayne
BULLIMORE

Ben
WORRALL

Graeme
CARR

Neil
RADIGAN

Stephen
BRODIE

Chris
TATE

Liam
ROBINSON

Ian
MILBOURNE

Neil
CAMPBELL

Manager

Mick
WADSWORTH

Season 1999-2000 Relative success back in non-League and title glory for the youth team.

Boro returned to the Conference after 12 seasons in the Football League with a much changed squad following a Summer clear-out by boss Colin Addison. Amongst the players to leave were the chairman's son, Matthew Russell, who moved to Halifax Town for a £50,000 fee, as did Chris Tate, for £150,000, Graeme Atkinson to Rochdale, Nathan Jones to Southend United and Ben Worrall to Exeter City. Despite dropping out of the League, Boro remained a full time club, and Addison brought in eleven new signings, all on free transfers, the most notable of whom were vastly experienced 34-year old defender Lee Sinnott, formerly with Walsall, Watford, Bradford City, Crystal Palace, Huddersfield and Oldham, who came in as the new player-coach. 23-year old keeper Andy Woods from Doncaster Rovers and 25-year old midfielder Marcus Jones from Telford United also joined. Another new signing was full back Mark Tyrell, who had changed his name by deed poll since his previous spell with Boro, between 1994-96, when he was known as Mark Wells!

The new look team made a sensational start to the season, winning 5-0 at home to Yeovil Town, as 22-year old former Carlisle striker Gareth McAlindon scored twice on his Boro debut. A 2-2 draw at Southport and a 1-0 success at Forest Green Rovers followed, and then a 1-1 home draw against Hednesford Town, but the unbeaten run ended with a 3-1 home defeat to Stevenage Borough on 28 August. Striker Steve Brodie broke his nose in a 1-0 win at Morecame on 30 August, but scored three goals during the month and was named 'Conference Player of the Month' for August by Match Magazine.

In September, chairman John Russell announced that he was in talks with a leading North East company who were interested in making a 'substantial investment' in the club. Three straight defeats saw Boro drop to mid-table, and 6ft 4ins striker Andy Morris arrived at the McCain Stadium in a loan deal from Rochdale. He scored in a 4-1 home win over Hayes, and was again on target in a thrilling 4-4 draw at Hereford. There was a big FA Cup disappointment when Southern League side Tamworth won 1-0 at the McCain Stadium in the 4th qualifying round, but in October, millionaire Insurance tycoon Brooks Mileson, chairman of Boro's shirt sponsors Arnott Insurance Group Holdings, was unveiled as the club's new benefactor, after he agreed to make a substantial investment in the club with a view to buying a controlling interest.

Unlike the previous season's Anton Johnson fiasco, Brooks Mileson arrived at the club with a good reputation for his involvement in football. Based near Gretna in Cumbria, he was a long time sponsor of the Northern League, and also of Whitby Town Football Club. John Russell remained as club chairman, and Brooks Mileson immediately made funds available for team strengthening. Colin Addison brought in powerful centre-back Paul Ellender from Altrincham for a £60,000 fee, while Gareth Williams returned from Hull City in a £10,000 deal, Chris Tate rejoined the club from Halifax Town for £60,000 (less than three months after moving to the Shay), and Matthew Russell also rejoined Boro from Halifax on a free transfer.

A good FA Trophy run saw Boro put out Ilkeston Town, Stocksbridge and Burnham before slipping to a shock 2-1 defeat at NPL side Bishop Auckland, while in the Conference Boro held a top six place for most of the season without really challenging for a promotion push. A good end of season run-in brought seven wins, three draws and three defeats to leave Addison's men in 4th position in the final table.

Keeper Andy Woods had an outstanding season, and reliable full-back Simon Betts and the centre-back pairing of Paul Ellender and young Shaun Rennison also stood out as Boro ended with the best defensive record in the Conference, just 35 goals conceded in 42 matches. Keeper Andy Woods created a new club record by keeping six successive clean-sheets in December and January, whilst defender Simon Betts became the first Boro full back to score a hat-trick in a 5-0 FA Trophy win over Stocksbridge Park Steels in January.

Neil Thompson, a member of Neil Warnock's 1987 title winning Boro team, returned to the club on non-contract terms late in the season after leaving his role as York City player-manager, and 23-year old midfielder Denny Ingram arrived on loan from Hartlepool for the final two months of the season. One of the biggest success stories though was the Youth team, under the guidance of popular manager Ian Kerr, which won the Football League Youth Alliance Division 1 (North) Merit title.

They wrapped up the championship with a 4-0 defeat of Wrexham in the last match, to finish three points ahead of Carlisle at the top of the table with Burnley in third place. Leigh Grant and French youngster Mounir Alkhatib both scored twice in that game and other star performers over the course of the season included keeper Paul Newton, Danny Brunton, Mark Swales, Alex Gildea Stewart Morris and top scorer with 13 goals, Leigh Toone.

The youth team also enjoyed a good run in the Football League Youth Alliance Cup, topping the North East qualifying group, and then beating Preston North End 2-1 at home, before losing 1-0 to an injury time goal at home to Bury in the national quarter-finals. Three of the youth team regulars, Brunton, Morris and Gildea made first team appearances in the latter part of the season.

So, it had been a relatively successful return to the non-League ranks for Boro, but there were still major financial problems at the club and the Football Association imposed a transfer emargo at the end of the season, until outstanding wages had been paid to three former players who had left the club following relegation from the Football League. The sum owed was only £4,500 and this was quickly settled, but chairman John Russell reported that the club made a loss of £400,000 in the year ending April 2000. Brooks Mileson had enabled the club to sign some top quality players, but Russell revealed, "We have bought players, and we now have a wage bill which is higher than when we were in the Football League. The fans want champagne football, but we only have lemonade income." He added that Mr Mileson's accountants were looking at ways the club could reduce its debts.

One possible boost to club funds was the news that Boro would be one of eight Conference teams invited to compete in next season's Auto Windscreens Shield, the competition for lower division Football League clubs.

Looking back on the season, and the 4th place finish, manager Colin Addison commented, "This has been a learning season for us in the Conference. It's a pity we couldn't manage third spot, but we are already looking forward to next season."

Seven players were released at the end of the season, Marvin Harriott, Kevin Martin, Mark Tyrell, Darren Roberts, Ian Milbourne, Gareth McAlindon and David Bass, and the club announced a freeze on season ticket prices for the third year in a row, in an effort to entice back some of the missing supporters, following a 27% decline in home crowds.

The season ended on a high though, when Boro was represented by former director Jim Crawford and his wife Maureen, a former club secretary, in a parade of past FA Trophy winners, prior to the Wembley final between Kingstonian and Kettering Town.

Nationwide Conference Saturday, 8 January 2000

HEDNESFORD TOWN 0 SCARBOROUGH 3

With both manager Colin Addison and his assistant Ray McHale suffering with flu, it was youth team boss Ian Kerr who took charge for 10th placed Boro's first ever visit to Hednesford. The hosts were two points and two places higher in the table, and were looking to bounce back from a 6-2 defeat at Telford United in their previous game, while Boro had lost just one of their previous 8 Conference matches.

After a fairly uneventful opening 20 minutes, Boro began to take control of the match, with the pace and skill of strike trio Chris Tate, Steve Brodie and Darren Roberts giving the home defence an uncomfortable afternoon. Tate opened the scoring on 26 minutes when he swept home a low cross from Brodie on the right. The lead was doubled two minutes later when home keeper Billy Stewart blocked a shot from Brodie, and Boro skipper Gareth Stoker chipped the rebound over the keeper's head from 25-yards. Keeper Stewart made two excellent saves towards the end of the first half, and it was one-way traffic in the second period, with Boro keeper Andy Woods hardly getting a touch of the ball. Steve Brodie fired home a low shot to put Boro 3-0 up after 57 minutes, and Stewart again pulled off some fine saves to prevent a much bigger scoreline. Hednesford midfielder Jimmy Kelly was sent off for a second yellow card nine minutes from time, as Boro returned home with a very convincing victory and a fifth successive clean-sheet.

Hednesford Town Billy Stewart, Stuart Evans(Sean O'Connor 67), Lee Colkin(Domonic Reece 46), Andy Comyn, Chris Brindley, Ian Robinson, Stewart Airdrie, Jimmy Kelly, Neil Davis, Scott Goodwin, Paul Szewczyk(John Norman 46)

Scarborough Andy Woods, Matthew Russell, Simon Betts(David Bass 84), Marvin Harriott, Paul Ellender(Marcus Jones 74), Lee Sinnott, Darren Roberts, Gareth Stoker, Chris Tate(Stewart Morris 88), Steve Brodie, Gareth Williams

Referee Steve Castle (Wolverhampton) Attendance 1057

Gareth McAlindon on the ball against Kingstonian, September 1999

New benefactor
Brooks Mileson

Lee Sinnott wins a header
in a 1-1 home draw with
Hednesford Town

(Above) Andy Morris (2nd left) and Sean Rennison challenge at a corner kick vs Rushden & Diamonds, October 1999.

(Left) Boro vs Sutton Utd February 19th 2000 final score: 3-0. Chris Tate (left) celebrates the first of his double with Stewart Morris (right).

Nationwide Conference Saturday, 15 April 2000

SCARBOROUGH 5 FOREST GREEN ROVERS 0

Boro moved up a place from 4th to 3rd with this thumping win over relegation threatened Forest Green Rovers, after a wonderful display that manager Colin Addison described as the best since he joined the club. Both Denny Ingram and Chris Tate passed late fitness tests, and former York City player-manager Neil Thompson made his first home appearance since returning to the McCain Stadium. In a sensational opening, Boro went 3-0 up within ten minutes as Ian Hodges deflected a header past his own keeper, then Darren Roberts drilled home a low shot from a tight angle, and Chris Tate lobbed the keeper after being set up by Steve Brodie.

Forest Green keeper Justin Shuttlewood made a succession of fine saves and Neil Thompson had a goal-bound header cleared off the line as the pressure continued to mount on the visiting defence. The fourth goal finally arrived after 65 minutes when a clever flick by Darren Roberts set Steve Brodie in on goal, and he expertly lobbed over the advancing goalkeeper, then on 76 minutes Neil Thompson drilled home a powerful left-footed free kick to wrap up the scoring, to equal the 5-0 victory over Yeovil Town in the first match of the season. Experienced former Aston Villa and England striker Tony Daley was in the Forest Green side, while 19-year old substitute Alex Gildea was the only Scarborough born player out of the 25 players who appeared in the Boro team during the season.

Scarborough Andy Woods, Simon Betts, Gareth Williams, Shaun Rennison, Paul Ellender, Neil Thompson, Denny Ingram, Gareth Stoker(Alex Gildea 70), Chris Tate(Stewart Morris 70), Steve Brodie, Darren Roberts
Forest Green Rovers Justin Shuttlewood, Ian Hedges, Wayne Hatswell, David Norton(Adrian Mings 62), Billy Clark (Don Forbes 73), Chris Burns, Tony Daley, Jason Drysdale, Frankie Bennett, Dennis Bailey(Paul Hunt 62), Bradley Thomas
Referee Nigel Bannister (Goole) Attendance 1636

Football League Youth Alliance
Merit League - Div One North

	P	W	D	L	F	A	Pts
Scarborough	8	6	2	0	22	5	20
CarlisleUnited	8	5	2	1	14	8	17
Burnley	8	4	3	1	16	6	15
PrestonNorthEnd	8	4	0	4	15	20	12
MansfieldTown	8	3	2	3	14	12	11
BradfordCity	8	3	0	5	9	16	9
StockportCounty	8	2	2	4	12	15	8
Wrexham	8	2	1	5	8	19	7
HullCity	8	0	2	6	6	15	2

Darren Roberts celebrates Boro's first goal with Paul Ellender (5) in the Forest Green Rovers 5-0 victory.

The end of the Russell Era

Chairman John Russell's popularity began to plummet as news of the club's mounting debts came to the fore. Since taking over the club towards the end of the 1993-94 season, he had remained a hugely popular figure with the fans, having overseen the building of the two impressive new stands at the McCain Stadium, and established a highly successful youth policy at the club. Together with his wife and fellow majority shareholder, Gillian, Russell had developed the stadium into one of the best in the Conference, and the youth policy had started to pay dividends, with numerous players progressing through to the first team. But the pressures of maintaining a full time playing squad on relatively low gates, together with the loss of income when the club lost its Football League status, led to Russell trying to sell his shareholding, which resuled in the ill-fated Anton Johnson takeover in August 1998.

Throughout the Summer of 2000 there had been strong rumours that all was not well behind the scenes, and just a week before the new season kicked-off, reports that the club could go into administration began to circulate as the players' wage cheques bounced. Russell once again made desperate efforts to try to sell his majority shareholding to bring in some much needed new investment, but the situation looked bleak when, at a board meeting on Friday, 11 June, Russell dramatically resigned as chairman and fellow director Ken Ferrie quit the board. Vice-chairman for the past three years, Trevor Milton, owner of York based Minster Carpets took over as chairman, and it was announced that Leeds based insolvency practitioners, O'Hara & Co had recommended that a creditors meeting be called, in a last ditch effort to stave off the threat of the club going into liquidation.

It was revealed that the club was around £2m in debt, with £220,000 owed to the Inland Revenue, £27,000 to Customs & Excise, £52,000 to John Smiths Brewery, £46,000 to Halifax Town for the transfer of Chris Tate, £700,000 in bank overdrafts to HSBC and Nat West, significant loans owed to directors, including £110,000 to Ken Ferrie, around £287,000 loaned by Brooks Mileson, and dozens of other smaller amounts owed to kit suppliers, advertisers, coach companies, printers and local tradesmen.

A business plan, drawn up by insolvency expert Peter O'Hara of O'Hara & Co, along with new chairman Trevor Milton and major investor Brooks Mileson was seen as Boro's last hope of avoiding liquidation, but it needed a minimum of 75% of creditors to agree to accept either part payment or in some cases shares in lieu of payment, for the club to avoid going into liquidation, in which case most of the creditors would receive nothing. The crucial creditors meeting to discuss this plan was held at the McCain Stadium on Friday, 25 August 2000, and despite opposition from the Inland Revenue and Customs & Excise, most of the small creditors agreed to the package, with former director Ken Ferrie writing off much of the £110,000 he was owed for building work his company had carried out at the ground, Halifax Town also gave the plan their support. As part of the deal, John and Gillian Russell agreed to leave the club, and transfer their shareholding to Brooks Mileson for the nominal price of £1.

After the package was agreed, insolvency expert Peter O'Hara said, *"It was close, we needed to have a 75% majority in favour, and in the end we got 79% but it really was in doubt until the end of the meeting. Now we have got this vote, Mr Mileson will take control of the club, and hopefully it can move forward. There is no doubt that John Russell has been a super chairman for the football club, but he has not been good for the creditors."* The Inland Revenue and Customs & Excise agreed to receive their debts in instalments, Brooks Mileson personally guaranteed the bank overdraft, and the creditors agreement meant that the club could now plan ahead without the immediate threat of a winding up order.

The outgoing John Russell, heavily criticised for allowing the huge debts to mount up, said much of the deficit was due to the enormous costs of building the two new stands and improving the stadium, as well as the big drop in income when Boro had been relegated back to the Conference. He also said players wages had increased from a maxium of £300 per week to £800, taking the club's monthly wage bill to a staggering £50,000. In an emotional letter to the Scarborough Evening News he concluded, *"We leave you with a fabulous stadium, a youth policy that in the next few years will provide much revenue to the club and a proper professional structure to be proud of. "We are guilty of one thing - not having enough money, added to the fact that I am a supporters' man, and tried to keep the fans happy by giving them what they wanted."* Mileson however was scathing in his condemnation of Russell's financial mismanagement of the club, he was reported as saying, *"He obviously did not look at the club's accounts for every year he was chairman. In any other business than football, it would have ceased to exist years ago."* New chairman Trevor Milton's remarks were more diplomatic when he stated; *"this club belongs to the town and to the people of the town. We have got some loyal fans who have been put through a lot of pain over the past couple of years, and now it is time for some stability."*

John Russell

A board meeting in early June saw the departures announced of chief executive Kevin Green and commercial manager Paddy Mullen, and there was a massive shock for supporters on the eve of the season when manager Colin Addison resigned midway through the pre-season period, after 18 months at the helm, later taking charge at Conference rivals Yeovil Town. The problems of travelling from his home in Hereford, together with the club's on-going financial crisis led to him stepping down, and popular former Boro full back and York City player-manager Neil Thompson was appointed as caretaker manager.

Season 2000-01 More boardroom changes, as youth comes to the fore

The change of manager, just three weeks before the start of the season was one upheaval the club could have done without, but there were even more alarming events taking place off the field, as events in the boardroom almost brought the club to its knees, until new majority shareholder Brooks Mileson gained control, and with the support of unpaid creditors, the club was able to start the Conference season - which at one point had looked increasingly unlikely.

Despite their financial problems Boro remained one of only six full time professional clubs in the Conference, and just a day before the season began it emerged that the previous month's players' wage cheques had bounced. New chief Mileson set about revamping the backroom staff, bringing in 53-year-old Keith Agar, who had vast experience in the commercial departments at Leeds United, Doncaster, Darlington and Bradford City, as chief executive, and ex Boro striker Darren Foreman as the new commercial manager. Meanwhile on the field, the team began the season with a 1-1 draw at Stevenage Borough thanks to a late Steve Brodie equaliser, and three days later there was a 2-2 draw with Morecambe in the first home fixture, as Mileson paid the players out of his own pocket. Just 24 hours after the crucial creditors meeting which secured the club's future, Boro picked up their first win as Gareth Williams netted in a 1-0 home success over Kingstonian.

Ian Kerr's youth team was involved in a sensational match away to Bradford City in the Football League Youth Alliance on 9 September. They recovered from a 4-1 interval deficit to record a stunning 5-4 win, with goals from Steve Bell, Mark Swales, Peter Fitzsimmons, David Henderson and Anthony Ferguson.

Four successive wins in late September sent Boro soaring up the table, but pre-Christmas form was poor as just one of the next ten Conference matches was won, and there were defeats in three cup competitions, including a hugely disappointing 4-3 home loss to Leigh RMI in the 4th qualifying round of the FA Cup. Neil Thompson was appointed permanent manager in December, but he had to release a number of players to cut the wage bill, with Chris Tate transferred to Leyton Orient for a £25,000 fee, Simon Betts joined former Boro boss Colin Addison at Yeovil Town and Marcus Jones moved to Cheltenham Town. The impressive Denny Ingram earned himself a longer contract and boss Thompson blooded a number of young players from the youth team as David Pounder, Danny Brunton and Paul Atkinson all ended the season as first team regulars, while Ashley Lyth also made the step up, and was transferred to Leicester City for a £100,000 fee after just six first team appearances.

Doncaster Rovers were beaten home and away over Christmas and there was a 4-0 away success over Runcorn in the FA Trophy, before Burton Albion triumphed 1-0 at the McCain Stadium in the next round. French teenager Romain Faure looked an exciting prospect at sweeper and Cherif Diallo also gave a string of fine displays at centre-back, alongside star performer Paul Ellender, who unfortunately picked up 16 yellow cards and so missed several games through suspension, while both Steve Brodie and Cherif Diallo missed a number of matches through injury.

Simon Betts was transferred to Yeovil Town for a £10,000 fee, and as the financial situation continued to give cause for concern, chief executive Keith Agar pledged that the club would remain full time. He said, "We will remain full time. We have never even discussed going part time because we want success. To be successful you need a good team and that is what we are aiming for here. At the same time we have to run a business and try to break even, or as near as possible to that. We are a Conference club with 1000 gates, that is the reality of the situation. Manager Neil Thompson has been given a budget on the playing side which he will have to stick to very strictly. One thing is certain, there will be no inflated salaries or signing on fees in the future."

Midfielder Jason Blunt and striker Jamie Burt both signed contracts and former York City players Martin Reed and Scott Jordan both featured in the team with Boro remaining midtable as the season drew to a close. Highlights included a 2-1 away win against Nuneaton Borough, with Gareth Williams scoring both and a splendid 1-0 victory at Conference runners-up Yeovil Town in the final game, thanks to an early spot kick by player-manager Neil Thompson.

After all the off the field traumas, a final placing of 10th was regarded as very satisfactory, and the number of promising young players emerging from Ian Kerr's youth team gave great hope for a brighter future. The youth team recorded a number of excellent victories, including beating Hartlepool 7-0 in the Youth Alliance Cup, with goals from Leigh Toone 2, John Keegan 2, Adam Jewell, David Henderson and Mark Swales.

However, there were yet more boardroom changes as the season drew to a close, with majority shareholder Brooks Mileson, based almost four hours away in Cumbria, rumoured to be interested in taking over at his local club Carlisle United. Two potential new investors watched as Boro drew 1-1 at home to Telford United on 10 April - a game that drew an alarmingly low crowd of just 723, and at the final home fixture against Hednesford Town on 28 April, 34-year old Halifax businessman Darrell Littlewood, managing director of a debt management company, and 29-year old Mick Taylor, a millionaire lottery winner, also from the West Riding, were unveiled as Boro's new owners, having bought a 63% shareholding from Brooks Mileson for a nominal fee.

Littlewood took over as club chairman, with Trevor Milton stepping down from the board, and the new chief said he was keen to make Boro a fan-friendly club, with supporters represented on the board. He said, "We are just two guys who are football fans. Two football nuts who have bought a football club and want to do our best to make it a success. We are new to this, and intend to pay a lot of attention to what the supporters want. It is still their football club, their team. Mick Taylor has been a friend of mine for a long time. He scooped £4.1 million on the lottery last year, but I don't want the fans to get too euphoric and start thinking we have got millions to spend on the club, we havn't. We must look at alternative streams of income."

So, just eight months after taking over from John Russell and saving the club from folding, Brooks Mileson was on his way out of the McCain Stadium, although he pledged to continue to help financially. He said, "I have achieved my aim, which was to prevent the club from going into oblivion. That gives me a lot of satisfaction, but it was very difficult because of where I live and my business commitments, to give the club the time that it requires. Darrell Littlewood will give the club full time commitment.

"He and Mick Taylor are young men, very enthusiastic and have a lot of ideas. I will continue to help the club in any way I can, and will guarantee the bank overdraft. I have a moral responsibility to clear that, and it will not land in the laps of the new owners."

Chief executive Keith Agar left the club and the new owners brought in 43-year-old banker Ian Davidson to replace him, whilst also appointing local builder Andy Borrie to the board of directors as a fans representative. Players released at the end of the season included Stewart Morris, Alex Gildea, Matthew Russell and Cherif Diallo, while midfielder Gareth Williams turned down the offer of a new contract. There was sad news of the death of former long serving club director Bob Whelpton, at the age of 87 in May, and the Football League Annual General Meeting rejected a plea from the Conference for a two up, two down promotion and relegation system.

Chairman
Darrell Littlewood.

Nationwide Conference   Saturday, 16 September 2000
SCARBOROUGH 4 NORTHWICH VICTORIA 0

Just 4 days after a 3-0 home defeat by table toppers Rushden & Diamonds, midtable Boro bounced back in great style to register their biggest win of the season against a Northwich side that had drawn 1-1 at Chester in midweek. Marcus Jones failed a late fitness test, and manager Neil Thompson handed French youngster Romain Faure his senior debut, with teenager David Pounder partnering Steve Brodie up front, while Northwich had veteren 41-year old former Northern Ireland International Jimmy Quinn leading their forward line.

Watched by a sparse crowd, almost 300 down on the previous home game, Boro made an excellent start, as David Pounder connected with a Paul Ellender pass, to send a low shot crashing into the net off the post in the 13th minute.. Andy Woods then made a terrific save to keep out a Quinn thunderbolt, but on 22 minutes Northwich went down to ten men when Malcolm Bailey was sent off for a second bookable offence, and within two minutes Steve Brodie latched onto a poor back pass to fire Boro into a 2-0 lead. David Pounder made it 3-0 after 57 minutes, finishing off a one-two with Brodie before slotting past the keeper, and Brodie completed the scoring in the 71st minute, smashing home following a cross from Gareth Stoker. With youngsters Alex Gildea and Stewart Morris coming on as substitutes, Boro finished the game with five teenagers on the pitch.

Scarborough Andy Woods, Matthew Russell, Danny Brunton, Denny Ingram, Paul Ellender, Romain Faure, Gareth Williams (Alex Gildea 80), Simon Betts, Chris Tate (Gareth Stoker 55), Steve Brodie (Stewart Morris 80), David Pounder
Northwich Victoria Malcolm Rigby, Malcolm Bailey, Neil Ellis, John Robertson, Wesley Simpson, Mark Devlin, Richard Norris, Peter Holcroft (Carl Laurie 61), Jimmy Quinn (Steve Walsh 75), Gary Fletcher (Ged Kimmins 75), Darren Vicary
RefereeP. Robinson (Hull)   Attendance 845

Nationwide Conference   Saturday 16 December 2000
MORECAMBE 4 SCARBOROUGH 4

Hosts Morecambe had beaten Third Division Cambridge United in the FA Cup in their previous game, to set up a plum home tie against Premiership side Ipswich Town in the third round, while Boro had gone down 3-1 at Stoke City in the LDV Vans Trophy in their last match. With Simon Betts serving a one-match suspension, Matthew Russell returned from injury to take his place at right-back, and Morecambe included their two recent signings, experienced midfielder Steve Walters and 22-year-old former Everton trainee striker Mark Quayle, who had scored the winner in the cup victory over Cambridge. (Quayle was to join Boro 3 years later, when he again proved to be an FA Cup hero, scoring the winner against Southend, to set up Boro's fourth round meeting with Chelsea in 2004)

Both sides had hat-trick heroes in what turned out to be a thrilling game, with Boro showing a never-say-die attitude to twice come from two goals down to snatch a point. Morecambe went in front in the 4th minute when on-loan Boro keeper Phil Priestley parried a Quayle shot, only for Gary Thompson to slot home the rebound, and two minutes later Mark Quayle pounced on some slack defending to fire the home side 2-0 up. Steve Brodie pulled one back after 22 minutes, stabbing his shot under keeper Mark Smith, but within a minute Quayle restored Morecambe's 2-goal advantage with another clinical finish. On 52 minutes a Neil Thompson free kick was volleyed into the net by Cherif Diallo to make it 3-2, and Boro were level on the hour when Diallo sent a defence-splitting pass for Brodie to fire home. Once again Morecame went ahead, just 2 minutes later, when John Norman headed across goal, and Quayle headed home to complete his hat trick. However, Brodie restored parity, and completed his hat trick, when he poked the ball into the net following a low cross from Stewart Morris, five minutes from time.

Morecambe Mark Smith, Andy Fensome, David Perkins, Dave McKearney, John Hardiker (Paul McGuire 78), Steve Walters (Michael Stringfellow 26), Gary Thompson, Stuart Drummond, Mark Quayle (Phil Eastwood 62), John Norman, Ryan-Zico Black
Scarborough Phil Priestley, Matthew Russell, Neil Thompson, Shaun Rennison, Paul Ellender, Denny Ingram, Gareth Williams, Gareth Stoker (Danny Brunton 27), Cherif Diallo (Stewart Morris 78), Steve Brodie, Dave Pounder

Referee A. Canadine (Rotherham)   Attendance 2023

Season 2001-02 Financial problems again... And Russell Slade pulls off the great escape.

New chairman Darrell Littlewood instigated several cost cutting measures ahead of the new season, with all the club's highest earners placed on the transfer list. The first to leave was reigning player of the year Paul Ellender who moved to Conference rivals Boston United for a £30,000 fee on the eve of the season. A further blow to manager Neil Thompson's plans, was the broken leg suffered by young full back Danny Brunton in a pre-season North Riding Senior Cup tie against Middlesbrough.

The Conference campaign opened with a 1-1 home draw against Forest Green Rovers, striker Darryn Stamp netting a late equaliser for a Boro side that included two debutants, trialist former Grimsby and Scunthorpe full back Ashley Fickling and 17-year old YTS wing back Peter Fitzsimmons, while 31-year old former Boro star Christian Short was also in the side, having enjoyed a successful League career with Notts County, Sheffield United and Stoke City since last playing for Boro 11 years earlier. Further 1-1 draws against Northwich and Barnet followed, before a 1-0 home defeat by Margate on 27 August, watched by just 886 fans.

A fans forum attended by 70 fans heard Littlewood report that the club was still in financial difficulty and losing around £30,000 a month. He said, *"We are in a tight squeeze financially and the only way to get out of it is through more support and the backing of the local business community."* The first win of the season came on 1 September when a Darryn Stamp double earned a 2-1 away success over Woking, but only two points were then collected from the next seven matches and news broke that the players' wage cheques for August were two weeks late. A 2-0 home defeat by Morecambe on 18 September attracted only 616 supporters, the club's lowest home league crowd for 15 years. The situation was starting to look bleak, both on and off the pitch.

Manager Neil Thompson handed in his resignation on 21 September, striker Steve Brodie went out on loan to Swansea City, later signing for a £5,000 fee, and both Christian Short and Jamie Burt walked out on the club as the financial uncertainty once again flared up, with the PFA stepping in with a loan to make sure the players' wages were paid. Departing boss Thompson said, *"I leave today with my head held high, knowing that I have worked tirelessly for the cause, in very trying circumstances."*

Youth team coach Ian Kerr was handed the managerial reigns, with assistant boss Ray McHale taking over the youth team role, with the help of school of excellence director Mitch Cook. There were also changes on the administration side, with chief executive Ian Davidson, who lived in Hertfordshire, making way for Keith Agar to return to the club as general manager.

Darryn Stamp and Gareth Stoker scored as Boro let slip a 2-1 lead to lose 4-2 at Dagenham & Redbridge in Ian Kerr's first match in charge, but a stoppage time winner from Shaun Rennison secured a 2-1 home success over Chester City in the next game. Denny Ingram left to join Northwich Victoria, but former Darlington midfielder Stuart Elliott came in, and made his debut in a 2-2 draw at high-flying Boston United in which six teenager six played for Boro, including 19-year-old Andrew Windross who scored his first goal for the club.

A 6-0 thrashing at Hereford United was not the ideal preparation for a local derby FA Cup 4th qualifying round trip to face Unibond Leaguers Whitby Town, managed by old Boro favourite

Harry A Dunn, and an already grim season sunk to even lower depths as Boro gave a dismal performance to crash 3-1, and lost the chance of a much needed £20,000 windfall from the FA Cup prize-fund.

Next came a humiliating 5-2 home defeat to Leigh RMI to send Boro to the foot of the Conference, but behind the scenes, chairman Darrell Littlewood had lined up a potential new investor, saying, *"I am looking at completely transferring all my shareholding and that of Mick Taylor's to new people, in order to give the club a fresh start."*

A 3-0 defeat at Telford United left Boro stranded at the bottom of the table, with 13 points from 19 matches, four points adrift of nearest rivals Hayes. Relegation was looking a certainty and debts had crept back up to £300,000 and a large overdraft, but it was announced that yet another change in ownership had taken place, with 51-year old Sewerby based businessman Malcolm Reynolds taking over from Littlewood. He immediately appointed former Notts County boss Russell Slade as Boro's third manager of the season (and it was only November). Ian Kerr reverted to his role as youth team manager, and Ray McHale again became assistant manager.

New manager Russell Slade.

In his first interview since taking over, Malcolm Reynolds said, *"I have managed to give Scarborough Football Club a stay of execution, but there is a lot of hard work ahead for us. The main task over the next few months is to keep this club alive, and at the same time make it attractive enough for other interested parties to get involved. We need stability here, and a positive infrastructure to build on."*

New manager Slade brought in a number of new faces on non-contract terms, including veteran former Bolton and Sheffield United midfielder Mark Patterson who joined as player-coach, keeper Mark Smith from Eastwood Town, ex Middlesbrough defender Steve Baker and 18-year-old striker Dene Shields on loan from Sunderland.

Young striker Andy Windross struck the winner as Slade's reign began with a 1-0 home win over Farnborough Town, but it then emerged that keeper Smith had been ineligible to play in the game against Farnborough, and Boro were docked three points, later reduced to one on appeal.

Loyal clubman Ray McHale left Boro to take up a post as chief scout at Oldham Athletic, 32-year-old defender Richard Dryden came in on loan from Luton Town and young defender John Keegan moved out to Gainsborough Trinity

A disappointing 2-1 home setback against Northwich was followed by a Boxing Day thriller at Doncaster Rovers, where Boro lost 4-3 after going 3-1 up. But this result proved to be the turning point in a traumatic season, as Russ Slade's side then went on an amazing run which saw them lose just two of their final 19 Conference matches, including a nine-match unbeaten run, to storm clear of the relegation zone. A good FA Trophy run, which included a dramatic penalty shoot-out defeat of Barnet, also brought in some much needed cash, and a final placing of 12th in the Conference was seen as a remarkable achievement. The best results of the run-in included a 3-2 win over Hereford United, a 3-1 victory over Telford, and 2-0 defeats of Southport and champions Boston United.

The youth team under the guidance of Ian Kerr enjoyed a decent season in the Football League Youth Alliance, their best result being a 5-0 away success over Grimsby Town in August, with goals from Mark Swales, Max Wadsworth, David Henderson, Andrew Windross and Craig Temperton.

It had been one of the most remarkable seasons in the history of the club, and manager Russ Slade was hailed as a miracle worker for dragging the team out of the relegation zone, and at the end of the season he signed a contract to stay at the club, saying, *"I have enjoyed my time here, and I have started something which would be nice to carry on next season. "This is just the start - we need to work harder, get fitter and move on, to make a championship challenge next season."*

Nationwide Conference Saturday, 1 September 2001
WOKING 1 SCARBOROUGH 2

Both sides had made poor starts to the season, with Boro having opened with 3 draws followed by a home defeat to Margate, while Colin Lippiatt's Woking had won their first match, but then lost 3 in a row. Boro had player-manager Neil Thompson and young French defender Romain Faure missing through injury, but trialist striker Jamie Barnwell-Edinboro, formerly with Coventry, Cambridge and Doncaster, made his debut from the substitutes bench, and there was an experimental 3-man attack, with Jamie Burt coming into the team to join Darryn Stamp and Steve Brodie up front.

On a lovely sunny afternoon, the home side took a 7th minute lead when sloppy defending allowed Scott Huckerby, younger brother of Man City's Darren, the chance to fire home. Boro were level within 60 seconds when Gareth Stoker played the ball wide to Chris Short, whose left wing cross was headed in off the post by Darryn Stamp. The game developed into an end-to-end tussle with chances for both teams. Stamp had a header cleared off the line by a defender, while Woking's Steve West glanced a header just wide of the post, before Boro went in front on the stroke of half time,as Stamp headed in from a Jason Blunt free kick. Two minutes into the second half Stamp should have completed his hat trick, when 17-year old Peter Fitzsimmons was fouled in the area, but Stamp's spot kick was easily saved by the keeper. Jason Blunt's curling shot struck the Woking bar and Stamp had an effort saved, as both teams came close to scoring, but Boro held on for their first victory of the season.

Woking Tony Tucker, David Piper, Rob Hollingdale (Scott Steele 68), Steve West, Paul Steele, Michael Fowler (Junior Kadi 70), Jamie Pitman, Barry Moore, Roscoe D'Sane, Charlie Griffin, Scott Huckerby (Warren Haughton 82)
Scarborough Andy Woods, Christian Short, Peter Fitzsimmons, Shaun Rennison, Ashley Flickling, Denny Ingram, Jason Blunt, Gareth Stoker, Darryn Stamp, Steve Brodie (Jamie Barnwell-Edinboro 80), Jamie Burt
Referee M. McCoy(Hampshire) Attendance 1244

Nationwide Conference Tuesday, 16 April 2002
SCARBOROUGH 2 BOSTON UNITED 0

Boro began this match just 5 points above the relegation zone, while Steve Evan's Boston United were top of the table on goal-difference from Dagenham & Redbridge, and on course to win the title and gain promotion to the Football League. Neil Thompson, who had begun the season as Boro player-manager returned to the McCain Stadium in his capacity as Boston United's assistant manager, while ex Boro centre-back Paul Ellender featured in the Boston team and around 400 travelling fans also made the trip. Fit again defender Steve Baker was recalled to the Boro side by manager Russ Slade, and David Pounder replaced Darren Connell up front. There was sad news on the eve of the match, after former Boro player and manager Billy Ayre died of cancer, 3 weeks short of his 50th birthday.

In a rousing, highly competitive game, Boro turned in their best display for many months, taking the lead with a stunning goal after 23 minutes, when Steve Baker's free kick was headed on by Darryn Stamp, for David Pounder to smash home a fierce 15-yard volley which flew past the keeper. It was a fiery, action-packed game with both teams creating and spurning chances, before Boro increased their lead three minutes into the second half, as Darryn Stamp seized on a poor back-pass and rounded the keeper to score his 13th goal of the season. Andy Woods made terrific saves to deny both Ross Weathersone and Daryl Clare, and in injury time Boston's Simon Rusk was sent off for violent conduct following a melee, in which he pushed Darren Connell in the face. Despite losing, Boston remained top of the table as Dagenham & Redbridge went down to Hereford, while the win for Boro, along with Stalybridge Celtic's defeat at Northwich, ensured their safety from relegation.

Scarborough Andy Woods, Scott Jordan, Mark Hotte, Phil Salt, Shaun Rennison, Steve Baker, Jason Blunt, Mark Patterson, Darryn Stamp, Ryan Sugden, David Pounder (Darren Connell 83)
Boston United Paul Bastock, Mark Clifford, Andy Lodge (Mark Angel 21), Paul Ellender (Ross Weatherstone 46), Peter Costello, Jim Rodwell, Mick Brown (Jamie Cook 49), Anthony Elding, Daryl Clare, Simon Weatherstone, Simon Rusk

Referee T. Green (Leicestershire) *Attendance 2228*

Players released at the end of the season included Romain Faure, Marcus Jones and Whitby-born Paul Atkinson. There was good news from the Football League AGM, when member clubs agreed to two up-two down promotion and relegation with the Conference, giving a second club a chance of promotion via four- team end of season play-offs.

Former Boro centre-back Billy Ayre, sadly died of cancer aged 49 in April 2002. One of the stars of the great Colin Appleton teams in the 1970's, Billy played in the 1976 and 1977 FA Trophy finals at Wembley, and he later had a brief, but unsuccessful spell as manager in 1994.

Season 2002-03
A much improved season, and plans for a ground move announced

Boro's debt to the Inland Revenue had risen to around £260,000 and chairman Malcolm Reynolds said the only way the club could survive would be to sell off the McCain Stadium, and move to a new ground which would incorporate community facilites such as a multi- purpose sports hall, fitness centre and all weather playing surface that could be hired out to generate income. He hoped that the Council would lift the covenant on the ground, restricting it to sports use, so that the club could move to a new purpose-built site, which he felt could be ready as early as the start of the 2004-05 season. Former chairman Geoffrey Richmond had earlier suggested this route to secure the club's future in the Summer of 1990, when he had hoped to build a new stadium on Dunslow Road at Eastfield.

Boro player from the 1950's and early 1960's, Colin Smailes, died, aged 67 in July, and the club announced a 7% increase in season ticket prices for the new season, while ground admission charges for adults increased by 50p to £8-50 for the new campaign.

Manager Russ Slade gathered together a strong-looking squad, with the arrival of some experienced new signings, including new player-coach Nicky Henry, the 33-year-old former Oldham, Sheffield United and Tranmere midfielder. Also joining the club were 34-year-old target man Keith Scott from Dover Athletic, 33-year old centre-back Richard Dryden who had played briefly on loan from Luton the previous season, Middlesbrough midfielder Anthony Ormerod, striker Neil Campbell who returned after a spell with Doncaster Rovers and 25-year-old French midfielder Olivier Brassart from Yeovil Town. The reserve team was reinstated after a one year absence, and competed in the Pontins League Division One East, where they finished bottom of eleven teams with a record of 3 wins, 1 draw and 16 defeats.

Striker Darryn Stamp was transferred to Northampton Town in a £45,000 deal on the eve of the season, and Darren Connell and Danny Brunton were also allowed to leave at the end of the pre-season period. Despite the influx of experience, Boro made a slow start to the season, Karl Rose scoring in a 1-1 draw at Burton Albion, but the opening six matches produced just four draws and two defeats. Two African trialists, 24-year-old Nigerian forward Bimbo Fatokun and 26-year-old midfielder Mohammed Sillah from Sierra Leone both came in and made good impressions, with Fatokun scoring twice as a first win was secured in a 4-1 home success over Kettering Town, and he added another in a 1-1 draw at Farnborough in the next match. A 2-0 home win over Leigh RMI on 24 September in which both Fatokun and Sillah got on the score sheet, lifted Boro into the top half of the table for the first time.

Long serving youth team coach Ian Kerr left the club in October to take up a position as director of youth football at Third Division Hartlepool. In his eleven years at Boro, originally joining as football in the community officer in June 1990, later replacing Glyn Snodin as youth team coach in August 1998, he had been a great servant to the club, even having a brief spell as first team boss after the departure of Neil Thompson in 2001. He was replaced by another loyal clubman, as former player Mitch Cook added to his roles as director of Boro's school of excellence and football in the community officer, to take charge of the youth team.

However, the youth team was scrapped soon after and withdrawn from the Football League Youth Alliance in a cost cutting measure. Prior to their resignation, the Boro juniors had enjoyed a good run in the FA Youth Cup, beating Whitley Bay 6-2 and Chadderton 4-0, before losing 3-2 at home to Burscough.

In the FA Cup, a 4th qualifying round win over Arnold Town was rewarded with a home tie against Third Division Cambridge United in the first round proper, and Boro were unlucky to go down 2-1 after extra time in a replay after a 0-0 draw at the McCain Stadium. League form was reasonably good, and 3 successive wins in the run-up to Christmas had supporters dreaming of the play-offs.

But a 5-2 home defeat by Doncaster Rovers on Boxing Day put a jolt to those dreams, and although Burton Albion were beaten 4-1 on 4 January, Boro never quite managed to find the consistency to challenge for the top five, and a place in the play-offs. 21-year-old defender Shaun Rennison suffered a career-ending cruciate ligament injury in a 1-0 win at Hereford, and new arrivals included striker Ryan Mallon, on loan from Sheffield United, and ex Bolton and Watford defender David Holdsworth.

In early December, shortly after Boro's FA Cup defeat by Cambridge United, chairman Malcolm Reynolds spelt out his vision for the club's future in a programme article : *"The game of football has an uncanny knack of bringing you down to earth with a bang and the day after the Cambridge replay saw me visit the Inland Revenue in Sussex for further negotiations on the club's historic debts which were inherited from the previous owners. What is clear now is that our relocation plans are the only way forward for Scarborough Football Club. We must operate from facilities that earn us an income 365 days a year. I have been very hopeful of support from Scarborough Borough Council in our plans, and you will have seen the club's announcements in the press. For those of you who live in the Scarborough area, I strongly urge you to contact your elected representatives, to seek their support on Council."*

In mid January, with the club £350,000 in debt plus the large overdraft, a bid to enter voluntary administration was granted by the High Court in Leeds. Mark Loftus of insolvency specialists BKR Haines Watts was appointed as administrator.

He said, *"We are looking at the possibility of restructuring the club's finances, which may involve an injection of additional external finance, and putting together a proposal which will hopefully be acceptable to the creditors."* Manager Russ Slade announced his resignation, but retracted it following talks with chairman Malcolm Reynolds. Boro were lying 6th in the Conference, one place outside the play-off positions, but the uncertainty behind the scenes had an adverse effect on results, and a run of eight games without a win put an end to all hopes of a promotion bid and also included an FA Trophy exit to Southern League side Dover Athletic.

More bad news came in the form of a transfer embargo, imposed after the club went into administration, while leaving the McCain Stadium was striker Keith Scott who moved to Leigh RMI in a £5,000 deal. An agreement to get the embargo lifted was secured, and there were 3 debutants in a 3-0 defeat at Barnet on 22 February, 19-year-old strikers Gary Cohen from Watford, Cleveland Taylor, on loan from Bolton and Oldham midfielder Danny Hall. There were yet more comings and goings in the final weeks of the season as Boro's promotion hopes frittered away. Defenders Dave Ridler, formerly with Wrexham and Macclesfield Town and Michael Price from Hull City plus 19-year-old Middlesbrough midfielder Keith Gilroy were drafted in, while former Boro full back Ashley Lyth, back on trial after his release from Leicester City, suffered a broken leg in a reserve team match against York City at the McCain Stadium.

There was a poignant moment before the last home match of the season against Nuneaton Borough, as a minute's silence was observed in memory of 24-year-old Royal Marine Christopher Maddison from Scarborough, who was killed in action in Iraq two weeks earlier. Boro won the match 4-1, but the season ended with a 3-1 defeat at Margate to leave Boro 7th in the final table, eight points short of the play-offs. Released at the end of the season were Olivier Brassart, Bimbo Fatokun and Neil

Campbell, while defenders Richard Dryden and Paul Dempsey turned down the offers of new contracts.

Tony Smith, the popular Boro reporter for the Scarborough Evening News died suddenly, aged 56 in April. On a brighter note, the Supporters Club, led by chairman Stuart Canvin, once again played a leading role in backing the club, both physically, in organising transport to away matches, and financially. With the club still experiencing severe financial difficulties, the Supporters Club donated £2500 for physio equipment, £500 to upgrade the PA system, £300 in two match sponsorships and a further £2000 in sundry donations.

Boro exited administration, and the Conference announced plans to get tough on clubs who go down that route in the future, with a 12-point deduction planned for any club going into administration, and they also imposed a salary cap on member clubs in an effort to promote financial responsibility.

Gareth Stoker left Boro to join Forest Green Rovers and keeper Andy Woods moved to Northwich Victoria. Adult admission prices for next season were increased from £8-50 to £10, with concessions rising from £4-50 to £5, but the cost for juniors went down from £2-50 to £2.

Nationwide Conference Saturday, 7 September 2002

SCARBOROUGH 4 KETTERING TOWN 1

With a record of 4 draws and 2 defeats from their opening six matches, Boro were lying 3rd from bottom of the table, while visitors Kettering were one place lower and also winless with 3 draws and 3 defeats. Boro boss Russ Slade had Jason Blunt and Steve Baker injured, and Mohamed Sillah and Nicky Henry both suspended. Nigerian born striker Bimbo Fatokun, signed from Belgian club Royal Antwerp, made his home debut, and assistant manager Mark Patterson was also brought into the side, as Boro looked to get their season up and running against the newly promoted Poppies who had two former Boro players in their team, defender Brad Piercewright and midfielder Shaun Murray.

In the opening seconds Bimbo Fatokun had a powerful shot saved by the Kettering keeper, and on 5 minutes Fatokun was bundled down in the area, and Paul Shepherd opened the scoring from the penalty spot. It was all Boro, with Keith Scott shooting narrowly over, but Kettering drew level on 13 minutes when Craig Norman headed home, but Boro were soon back in control, and regained the lead after 37 minutes when Fatokun headed in from a Brassart corner. Just two minutes into the second half Anthony Ormerod, who had replaced the injured Neil Campbell at the break, sent over a low cross and Fatokun shot home to put Boro 3-1 up. The win was wrapped up through Richard Dryden's diving header following a cross by Shepherd on 72 minutes to seal a highly impressive first win of the season which lifted Boro to 15th in the table.

Scarborough Andy Woods, Scott Jordan, Mark Hotte, Paul Shepherd, Shaun Rennison, Neil Campbell (Anthony Ormerod 46), Olivier Brassart, Bimbo Fatokun (Karl Rose 78), Mark Patterson (Gareth Stoker 75), Richard Dryden, Keith Scott
Kettering Town Ian Bowling, Gary Hughes, Mark Haran (Danny Walsh 77), Martin Matthews, Craig Norman, Richard Butcher, Scott Goodwin, Shaun Murray (Chris Perkins 19), Gez Murphy, Brad Piercewright (Carl Shutt 62), Dale Watkins
Referee M Murphy (Coventry) *Attendance 1089*

Nationwide Conference Tuesday, 1 April 2003
DONCASTER ROVERS 0 SCARBOROUGH 1

Boro avenged two earlier home defeats by Rovers that season, including a 5-2 trouncing on Boxing Day, to put a severe dent in Doncaster's title ambitions, this defeat leaving them in 2nd place, 4 points behind leaders Yeovil Town, while Boro remained in 8th place. On a cold, rainy night in South Yorkshire, 150 travelling Boro fans witnessed a gutsy display by Russ Slade's boys, with new signing from Middlesbrough, Keith Gilroy, a Republic of Ireland U-21 International giving an inspirational performance in midfield, and Mohamed Sillah and Dave Ridler outstanding at the back. Rovers included former Boro player Jason Blunt in their side, as well as Tristram Whitman and Robert Gill who both later played for Scarborough.

A swirling wind and driving rain made conditions difficult, and chances were few and far between. For Rovers, a Paul Green header and a shot from Francis Tierney both went past the post, while Boro's best effort was a Bimbo Fatokun shot which was was deflected onto the post with the keeper beaten. The deadlock was broken six minutes after the interval when David Pounders' low corner fell to Sierra Leone born Mohamed Sillah, who drove his shot into the net from close range. With Gilroy dominating the midfield, Boro comfortably held onto their lead, although Paul Barnes lashed a shot narrowly over the bar near the end, much to the disappointment of the big home crowd.

Doncaster Rovers Andy Warrington, Tim Ryan, Dave Morley, John Doolan, Francis Tierney, Paul Barnes, Robert Gill (Don Goodman 56), Chris Beech, Paul Green, Steve Foster (Simon Marples 80), Jason Blunt (Tris Whitman 68)
Scarborough Andy Woods, Paul Dempsey, Mohamed Sillah, Dave Ridler, Michael Price, Keith Gilroy, Gareth Stoker, Scott Kerr, David Pounder, Gary Cohen (Cleveland Taylor 70), Bimbo Fatokun
Referee R.Booth (Sutton In Ashfield) Attendance 4155

7 September 2002: Bimbo Fatokun on the ball, against Kettering Town.

Season 2003-04 Record breaking FA Cup run, but inconsistent in Conference

Club officials 2003-2004:
President- John Birley
Chairman- Malcolm Reynolds
Secretary- Stephen Graham
Manager- Russell Slade
Physio- Martin Woodmansey
Community Officer- Mitch Cook
Associate Directors-
Martin Bell, Andy Borrie, Brian Ewer,
Rod Robinson, Tony Scott, Tony Stockdale

Manager Russell Slade signed several new players in the Summer, including former Northampton Town and Rushden & Diamonds keeper Adam Sollitt, ex Shrewsbury Town centre-back Matthew Redmile, 20-year-old former Sunderland full-back Steve Capper, midfielder Jacques Williams from Birmingham City,and strikers Mark Quayle, signed from Nuneaton Borough, and Chris Senior from Huddersfield Town. School of excellence director, and former Boro player Mitch Cook was pressed into action in a pre-season friendly against York City, when the 41-year old came off the bench for a cameo five minute substitute appearance due to a number of injuries.

A twice taken 89th minute spot kick by Keith Gilroy earned Boro a 2-1 home victory over Farnborough Town on the opening day, but the early weeks were blighted by injuries. David Pounder, the club's longest serving player, suffered cruciate ligament damage in a pre-season friendly, skipper Nick Henry had an ankle injury, Keith Gilroy broke a foot and Jacques suffered a serious rib injury in a 2-1 home defeat by Burton Albion (Boro's 500th Conference match), Karl Rose was concussed in a 1-0 defeat at Accrington Stanley and Ashley Lyth was still out, having broken his leg at the end of the previous season.

The Conference now had a salary cap in place, and chairman Malcolm Reynolds was concerned that, with so many players out injured, it would be difficult to bring in replacements, with the club limited to a weekly wage budget of £6,500. Former Partick Thistle striker Alex Nesovic had a brief spell with Boro, midfielder Jimmy Kelly was brought in from Chester City and Lloyd Blackman arrived on loan from Brentford.

Only two of the first 12 Conference matches were won, but Boro produced a shock 2-1 win over Second Division side Port Vale in the LDV Vans Trophy, with goals from Chris Senior and Jimmy Kelly. Former Boro boss Neil Warnock loaned Boro two of his Sheffield United players, defender Colin Cryan and pacey winger Ashley Sestanovich, and both made big impressions. Leigh RMI were beaten 4-1 both home and away, to boost the league placing, but it was in the FA Cup where Boro showed their best form, enjoying a record breaking run to the Fourth Round for the first time in the club's history, putting out three Football League clubs along the way.

Legendary former Sunderland goalkeeper Jimmy Montgomery, famous for his performance in the 1973 FA Cup final win over Leeds United, joined Boro as part-time goalkeeping coach, spending two days a week with keepers Leigh Walker and Adam Sollitt, but 22-year-old defender Sean Rennison left the club, having struggled to overcome a crippling knee ligament injury he picked up last season, to end his promising career.

In early December it was announced that the club had secured a 12-month option to buy land at Dunslow Road, Eastfield at a fixed price, with plans being drawn up for 200 homes to be built on the McCain Stadium site, and a new £1.5 million stadium being constructed at the new site. Chairman Malcolm Reynolds said, *"We need to move to a new site, clear all the debts and start with a clean sheet in a facility that's bought and paid for, and has the opportunity to generate £250,000 a year additional income outside of football.."* He added, *"Thanks to some very positive discussions with the Council, I believe we have a project that is acceptable to all concerned."*

With the FA Cup run dominating the season, the club became the centre of massive media attention in the run-up to the live televised match against Premiership giants Chelsea. A bad tempered Boxing Day derby match at Halifax Town saw four players sent off, Wayne Gill and Matthew Redmile of Boro, and Halifax pair James Dudgeon and Adam Yates.

Boss Russ Slade fielded an under strength team for the FA Trophy tie against Stafford Rangers, to rest first teamers during the FA Cup run, and the outcome was a 2-1 home defeat. Once the cup run ended, after a spirited display against Chelsea, Boro turned in some erratic performances in the Conference. February was a bad month for the club as sloppy defending allowed Hereford to snatch a 3-3 draw at the McCain Stadium, and this was followed by two heavy defeats, 4-0 away to Forest Green Rovers, and 4-1 at Shrewsbury Town, while strong centre-back Matthew Redmile left the club to join promotion chasing Barnet, and popular chairman Malcolm Reynolds had a spell in hospital after suffering a heart attack.

March was a much better month, as 23-year-old former Leeds striker Tony Hackworth and classy defender Kevin Nicholson were both signed on loan from Notts County. Boro won three matches including a terrific 2-1 away success over 3rd-placed Aldershot Town, with goals from Mauritian trialist Bertrand Ketchanke and Chris Senior, while former Kidderminster full-back Andy Brownrigg made his Boro debut. There was also a 1-0 home win against Yorkshire rivals Halifax Town, thanks to Chris Senior's 74th minute strike. Tony Hackworth and Keith Gilroy were on target in a 2-1 home defeat of Accrington Stanley, and the season ended with a 2-0 away win against Margate, with Keith Gilroy and Mark Quayle the marksmen, to leave Boro a disappointing 15th in the final table. Ironically the season ended as it had begun, with injuries decimating the Boro team. Keeper Leigh Walker suffered a groin strain in the Margate match, and was replaced by Adam Sollitt, and Karl Rose went off with concussion just three minutes into the game.

Despite the fantastic FA Cup run, which boosted the club's coffers by more than £400,000, the Conference campaign was a huge disappointment. Manager Slade used no fewer than 39 players in the 42 Conference matches - far too many to generate consistency, and at the end of the season he released a host of players, including Wayne Gill, Tommy Raw, Bertrand Ketchanke, Iain Davidson, James Sherlock, Michael Price, Andy Brownrigg, Jacques Williams and Tris Whitman. Also moving on was Boro skipper Jimmy Kelly who signed for Morecambe, and strikers Mark Quayle to Northwich Victoria and Karl Rose to Leigh RMI. Heading down to the Conference, after being relegated from the Football League were Boro's local rivals York City and Carlisle United, the club who sent Boro down on a dramatic last day of the season in 1999.

Matthew Redmile

(Above) Boro keeper Leigh Walker and defender Colin Cryan, in action vs Dagenham.

(Right) Steve Baker

(Below) Ashley Sestanovich scores the winner at Port Vale in the FA Cup second round match.

F A Cup 2003-2004: Route to the Fourth Round

Saturday, 25 October 4th Qualifying Round SCARBOROUGH 3 HINCKLEY UNITED 1

After a scrappy opening period, Boro stepped up a gear in the second half to run out comfortable winners over Southern League premier division side Hinckley United. Defender Ashley Lyth headed in a Wayne Gill corner to give Boro a 59th minute lead, man of the match Scott Kerr doubled the advantage on 76 minutes, slotting home after being set-up by Clint Marcelle, and Kerr then made it 3-0 seven minutes from time, converting a pass from Robert Gill. Hinckley snatched an 87th minute consolation when former Boro midfielder Shaun Murray was tripped in the box by Michael Price, and Jamie Lenton scored from the spot. A little piece of history was created, as for the first time in a Boro match, both goalkeepers were substituted due to injuries. Adam Sollitt replaced Leigh Walker for Boro just before half-time, and Hinckley's Tommy Whittle replaced Chris Taylor in the 69th minute.

Saturday, 8 November Round 1 SCARBOROUGH 1 DONCASTER ROVERS 0

In front of the Match of the Day cameras, a high tempo Yorkshire derby saw both sides create plenty of openings, with Scott Kerr twice going close for Boro and Karl Rose having a shot cleared off the line by Rovers centre-back Dave Morley. Gregg Blundell came closest for the visitors, but Leigh Walker produced a fine save to deny him. Mark Quayle for Boro, and Leo Fortune West for Rovers, went close in the second half, and, with the game seemingly heading to a replay, Karl Rose struck a shot from the edge of the box, and the ball struck the post before rolling into the net to give Boro their 79th minute winner. Doncaster piled forward in the last few minutes, but the Boro defence, with Matthew Redmile in superb form, held out to claim a place in the second round for the first time since 1996-97. Doncaster meanwhile, ended the season as Football League Division Three champions.

Sunday, 7 December Round 2 PORT VALE 0 SCARBOROUGH 1

Port Vale were lying 7th in the Football League Division Two and chasing a play-off place, but midtable Conference side Boro earned a memorable win thanks to a clinical finish from on-loan Sheffield United winger Ashley Sestanovich. Backed by an army of 1000 fans, Boro more than matched the high-flying home side throughout the game, with Vale keeper Jonathan Brain producing a superb save to deny Sestanovich and Wayne Gill also having a shot well saved. A terrific display from the Boro back four of Lyth, Cryan, Redmile and Hotte restricted the home side's openings, and towards the end, it was Boro who looked more likely to score. Sestanovich had a clever lob tipped over the bar, before he broke the deadlock in the 79th minute, when Scott Kerr played the ball wide, and Sestanovich burst into the box, rounded the keeper and slotted home the winner.

Saturday, 3 January Round 3 SOUTHEND UNITED 1 SCARBOROUGH 1

Roared on by over 1000 supporters who had made the 271 mile treck, Boro gave another battling cup performance to earn a replay despite going a goal down to the Third Division side after just 9 minutes, when a Mark Gower corner was headed down by Leon Constantine, for Jay Smith to volley into the net. Southend were on top for long periods of the first half, but Boro's defence, led by the outstanding Mark Hotte held firm. The second half was more evenly balanced, although Southend almost went 2-0 up, but Boro keeper Leigh Walker made a great save to deny Drewe Broughton. Ashley Sestanovich set up some dangerous moves, and substitute Tris Whitmas also impressed as Boro searched for an equaliser. It finally arrived on 74 minutes, when Marcelle lobbed the ball into the box, for Scott Kerr to smash in an unstoppable volley to level the scores, and keep alive the possibility of a home tie against Chelsea in the next round.

Wednesday, 14 January Round 3 Replay SCARBOROUGH 1 SOUTHEND UNITED 0

Russ Slade led Boro into the fourth round of the FA Cup for the first time ever, after a night of high drama at a packed Mc-Cain Stadium. In a see-saw match that saw chances at both ends, Southend's Leon Const-antine sliced a shot wide and Leigh Walker pulled off a brilliant save to deny Neil Jen-kins, while For Boro, Tris Whitman hit a shot narrowly past the post and Ashley Sestanovich curled a free kick inches wide. Midway through the second half Tes Bramble mis-hit his shot when well placed in Southend's last chance of the match,

Mark Quayle celebrates after scoring the winner.

With extra-time beckoning, Boro conjured up a memorable 83rd minute winner. Skipper Jimmy Kelly charged forward from midfield and sent over a cross to the far post, where predatory striker Mark Quayle rammed the ball into the net.

The final whistle was greeted by a mass pitch invasion, as hundreds of ecstatic fans swarmed onto the pitch to celebrate an historic vic-tory, the high-lights of which were shown on BBC 1's Match of the Day that night.

BIGGEST GAME IN THE CLUB'S HISTORY

The day Chelsea's millionaires came to town: The Build-up

Having created club history by reaching the Fourth Round of the FA Cup for the first time ever, with a dramatic Third Round replay win over Southend United, Boro were rewarded with a dream home tie against mighty Chelsea. The classic David v Goliath clash was immediately snapped up by Sky TV for live broadcast., and for the ten days leading up to the big game, the McCain Stadium became the focus of unprecedented national and international media attention. The game was declared all-ticket, with 1380 going to Chelsea and the remaining 4000 put on sale at the McCain Stadium on the morning of Saturday, 17 January, seven days before the cup clash. Tickets for season ticket holders went on sale at 10am, with the remainder going on sale at 1pm, and huge queues began to gather outside the stadium. At one point the queues stretched for half a mile, and all the tickets were soon sold, leaving hundreds of disappointed fans unable to get hold of a ticket. Unfortunately the downside of having Sky TV cover the match live was the loss of 400 seats in the main stand, and a large section of terrace, which were taken up by Sky staff and equipment, so reducing the ground capacity by several hundred.

The technical staff at Sky Television set up a headquarters at nearby Hinderwell School a couple of days before the match, as they began to prepare their equipment at the ground. With six trucks, 17 camera positions to organise, 5 miles of cable and around 100 staff, it was a massive operation, and there were also reporters and camera crews from various other TV and radio channels eager to speak to Boro boss Russ Slade and the players as the build up to the game intensified. BBC Look North, Tyne Tees TV, Yorkshire TV, ITN and all the national newspapers carried features and reports in the days leading up to the game, while the Sun Newspaper sponsored a new kit for Boro to wear, and several glamorous page three girls attended news conferences at the club and the match itself. The cup run to date had brought in £127,500 in prize money and TV revenue from two appearances on BBC TV's Match of the Day, and the club would receive a payment of £260,000 from Sky for live broadcast rights.

The Chelsea squad flew up from London to Teesside Airport, and then travelled by luxury coach to the Raven Hall Hotel at Ravenscar - the same luxury hotel that had briefly hosted the Bulgarian national team on their visit to Scarborough during the Euro 96 championships. Much was made in the press about the vast disparity in wealth at the two clubs. Boro were still in deep financial trouble and the only player in the team to face Chelsea who cost a fee was striker Mark Quayle, a £2,000 signing from Nuneaton Borough. Chelsea meanwhile, under billionaire owner Roman Abramovich, had a squad full of top class international players from all around the world. Abramovich had invested his vast fortune to turn Chelsea into the world's richest football club since taking control, and of the 13 players that featured against Boro, eleven were full internationals(for 6 different countries, England, Italy, Netherlands, Denmark, France and Iceland), and they cost a total of £76 million in transfer fees., their two most expensive signings being Jimmy Floyd Hasselbaink, a £15 million signing from Athletico Madrid, and Frank Lampard, who cost £11 million when signed from West Ham United.

On the morning of the match, which was a 12-30pm kick-off, the Scarborough town centre was awash with souvenir salesmen, offering scarves, flags, banners and commemorative tee shirts, while the crowds began congregating outside the ground from as early as 9am. The media were there in force as well, with more than 200 reporters, photographers and cameramen descending on the ground. Hundreds of Boro fans who didn't have tickets, packed into the many local pubs and clubs that showed the game on big screens, and the whole town was enveloped in a carnival atmosphere. Boro were at full strength for the biggest game in the club's history, apart from defender Matthew Redmile who was serving the last of a three-match suspension, while Chelsea manager Claudio Ranieri was without Argentine striker Hernan Crespo and French midfielder Claude Makelele, missing through injury, Romanian striker Adrian Muto, out with a virus, and Cameroon midfielder Geremi and Nigerian defender Celestine Babayaro, who were both in African Nations Cup action.

On the eve of the match, Boro boss Russ Slade was relaxed and philosophic as he looked ahead to the game. He said, "We are approaching the game in the usual way, with a set game-plan for the eleven players who are fortunate to take the field. This is our sixth game in the cup, and it is great for the fans who now have the opportunity to wander down Seamer Road to watch a bit of history in our first ever appearance in the fourth round of the cup - we hope to do them proud. There is no tension at all, because no one expects us to beat Chelsea, so I don't feel any pressure. I would like to thank all the volunteers at the club who have been a great help throughout this week, and also my staff, assistant boss Nick Henry, kitman Brian Hodgson and physio Martin Woodmansey, who have all pulled together to keep the players focused."

FA Cup Fourth Round Saturday, 24 January 2004

SCARBOROUGH 0 CHELSEA 1

Chelsea sat third in the Premiership behind Manchester United and Arsenal, while Boro were 15th in the Conference, just 6 points above the relegation zone, but the only previous meetings between the clubs, in the second round of the Littlewoods Cup back in season 1989-90, had seen Boro record one of their greatest cup victories of all time. A 1-1 draw in the 1st leg at Stamford Bridge was followed by a sensational 2nd leg in which Boro fought back from 2-0 down to win 3-2 with goals from Tommy Graham, Paul Robinson and Martin Russell (penalty). But, backed by Roman Abramovich's millions, Chelsea were now the richest club in world football, and their squad boasted some of the best players from all over the world.

Chelsea were on top straight from the kick-off and almost scored in the first minute, when England midfielder Frank Lampard crashed a 30-yard shot against the post, and Eidur Gudjohnsen drilled the rebound just wide. The star studded visitors did open the scoring in the 10th minute as a cross from Jimmy Floyd Hasselbaink was headed back across goal by Mario Melchiot to England defender John Terry, who headed into the net. Just three minutes later Boro's Steve Baker pulled a muscle and was replaced by Steve Capper. Boro midfielder Scott Kerr gave an outstanding performance against the Chelsea midfield duo of Lampard and Joe Cole, and Ashley Sestanovich created some good moves down the right flank but Chelsea keeper Carlo Cudicini was rarely troubled. Hasselbaink sent over several more good crosses for Chelsea, but it was Boro who came closest to finding the net, when Jimmy Kelly had a good effort blocked by John Terry as the interval was reached with Chelsea holding a slender 1-0 lead.

The visitors began the second half strongly, with Hasselbaink shooting just wide and Lampard's shot charged down by Colin Cryan. Boro keeper Leigh Walker made a stunning save to keep out a Gallas header from Hasselbaink's corner, and he also made two fine saves to deny the impressive Frank Lampard. Chelsea were well on top, but as the game entered the final ten minutes Boro almost drew level when substitute Chris Senior sent over a cross, Colin Cryan flung himself at the ball, but his diving header was directed straight at keeper Carlo Cudicini. The main talking point of the match then occurred just a minute later, when Steve Capper floated over a cross into the Chelsea box and defender Willian Gallas jumped to try to head clear, but his outstretched hand connected with the ball. It appeared a blatant penalty, but referee Barry Knight waved play on, and Boro's last chance of saving the game had gone. In the final minute Leigh Walker kept out a Mario Melchiot header, and at the final whistle Boro were given a rapturous ovation after a battling display, which almost earned them a lucrative replay at Stamford Bridge.

Boro boss Russ Slade said he was delighted with his players, but felt they should have been awarded a penalty, "It was an obvious penalty. I'm slightly biased, but it was clear to me, Gallas looked like he handled the ball, but it wasn't to be". He agreed Chelsea deserved to win the game, saying, "They had an enormous number of chances, but we stuck in there and gave our fans something to shout about. This match has put Scarborough on the football map, and financially it has been very good for us." Chairman Malcolm Reynolds was also happy with the team's display, saying, "I am proud and pleased to have gone so close to getting a result in this game. The players were absolutely magnificent, and we just hope that everyone who came enjoyed the game. Hopefully we can build on the tremendous enthusiasm that has been obvious to everyone in the town this week. Maybe the fans will come down in their numbers to support us, and local businesses will also get involved in sponsoring the club." Boro skipper Jimmy Kelly summed up the players' feelings when he said, "When we got back to the changing room after the game, the lads were absolutely gutted that we had lost by a single goal. I suppose it will only sink in later that we lost by a single goal to one of the best team in Europe."

Scarborough Leigh Walker, Ashley Lyth, Colin Cryan, Mark Hotte, Steve Baker (Stephen Capper 13), Ashley Sestanovich, Scott Kerr, Jimmy Kelly, Clint Marcelle, Mark Quayle, Tris Whitman (Chris Senior 71)
Chelsea Carlo Cudicini, Mario Melchiot, William Gallas, John Terry, Wayne Bridge, Jesper Gronkjaer (Emmanuel Petit 46), Frank Lampard, Joe Cole, Alexis Nicolas (Filipe Oliveira 66), Eidur Gudjohnsen, Jimmy Floyd Hasselbaink
Referee B. Knight (Orpington) *Attendance 5379*

The cup run brought in more than £400,000 in prize-money, TV revenue and gate receipts. So what happened to all the money ? Basically, it was handled by the administrators who were trying to sort out the club's financial problems. Within days of the Chelsea game, £50,000 was paid to the Inland Revenue, while the 15-man playing squad each received a cup bonus payment of between £4,000 to £5,000. The rest of the money was quickly swallowed up in running costs, interest payments and staff wages.

Chelsea's Frank Lampard fires in a shot, surrounded by Boro players, Clint Marcelle, Colin Cryan, Mark Hotte and Tris Whitman.

Boro fans at the match

Silverware for Boro

North Riding Senior Cup Winners 2004

Significent, because it was the last trophy won by Scarborough Football Club at first team level before the club's demise, the North Riding Senior Cup is an old established competition, with a history dating back to 1881. Boro had won the competition on 18 occasions, the most recent being 1992, and they began their 2003-04 campaign with an away tie against Northern League side Guisborough Town in the first round. The game took place four days after a disastrous 4-0 defeat at Forest Green Rovers in the Conference, and boss Russ Slade sent a strong team to Guisborough. On a bumpy pitch it took Boro a while to get going, but they soon took control of the game, and only a string of good saves from home keeper, John Storey, kept them at bay. The only goal of the match eventually came eight minutes from time, when Jimmy Kelly lashed in a spectacular volley after teenage midfielder Chris Batchelor had flicked the ball on.

In the semi-final, Boro faced a home match against a young York City side, and boss Slade included three trialists in the Boro line-up, the most impressive of whom was Mauritian defender Bertrand Kerchanke. Keeper Adam Sollitt pulled off two excellent saves to foil Levent Yalcin and Matthew Coad, before Boro began to dominate the game. Mark Quayle opened the scoring from the penalty spot on 77 minutes after a handball offence, and Karl Rose made it 2-0 in the 84th minute, when he netted after being set up by Quayle. Kerchanke and Ashley Lyth both flashed shots narrowly past the post in the dying minutes, as Boro progressed comfortably through to the final.

The final was held over to the eve of the 2004-05 season, when Middlesbrough Reserves visited the McCain Stadium on 24 July. Midfielder Mark Wilson was the only Middlesbrough player who had Premiership experience, but several of their team had played in the side that won the FA Youth Cup the previous season, including David Wheater and Jason Kennedy, who both scored in the 4-0 aggregate success over Aston Villa in the final. Scarborough were in control for most of the game, with Neil Redfearn shooting against the post, and Keith Gilroy and Robert Gill both having efforts saved. The only goal arrived in the 23rd minute when a through-ball from Ashley Lyth was chested down by Tony Hackworth into the path of Robert Gill, who calmly slotted in his first goal for the homesters. Middlesbrough came close to equalising near the end, with Leigh Walker pulling off a good save to deny Danny Graham, and Ashley Lyth heading a Wheater shot off the line, as Boro held out to pick up the trophy for the 19th (and last) time.

The victorious Boro team in the final was :- Leigh Walker, Ashley Lyth, Steve Baker, Mark Hotte, Colin Cryan, Scott Kerr, Tyrone Thompson, Keith Gilroy, Tony Hackworth, Neil Redfearn (Chris Senior 70), Robert Gill (David Pounder 81)

Boro's previous North Riding Senior Cup successes:

1908-09 beat Grangetown 2-0
1928-29 beat Whitby United 6-1
1938-39 beat Whitby United 2-1
1947-48 beat York City Reserves 4-0
1955-56 beat Middlesbrough Reserves 2-1
1958-59 beat Whitby Town 2-0
1960-61 beat Middlesbrough Reserves 1-0
1961-62 beat York City Reserves 1-0
1968-69 beat Middlesbrough Reserves 2-0
1972-73 beat Billingham Synthonia 4-1
1973-74 beat Middlesbrough Reserves 1-0
1976-77 beat Middlesbrough Reserves 3-2
1977-78 beat Guisborough Town 2-1 after 1-1 draw
1980-81 beat South Bank 1-0
1981-82 beat South Bank 3-1
1984-85 beat Rowntree Mackintosh 2-1
1987-88 beat York City 2-1
1991-92 beat Guisborough Town 3-2

Season 2004-05 Change of manager, unbeaten home record, and early cup exit.

Successful boss Russ Slade left the club in May to take over the reigns at Third Division Grimsby Town, but said, *"It has been a huge wrench to move on, and I go with many happy memories. There have been plenty of highs - obviously the FA Cup run and the tie with Chelsea, but there were also plenty of memorable matches in the Conference. Home and away, the fans have been brilliant, and I thank them for all their support."* Club coach Nick Henry, the former Oldham, Sheffield United, Walsall and Tranmere midfielder was named as Slade's successor, with vastly experienced Neil Redfearn appointed assistant manager. A veteran of 790 Football League appearances with 13 clubs, including Barnsley, Lincoln City, Crystal Palace, Oldham and Halifax, he had previously been assistant manager to ex Boro player and boss Neil Thompson at Boston United. To commemorate the club's 125th anniversary, the Supporters Club published a book, 'The complete A to Z of Scarborough Football Club, written by Steve Adamson.

New signings included 23-year-old centre-back Paul Foot from North Ferriby United, 23-year-old winger Tyrone Thompson from Huddersfield Town, and three players who had all been on loan at the club last season, defender Colin Cryan from Sheffield United and defender Kevin Nicholson and striker Tony Hackworth, both from Notts County. Boro won the North Riding Senior Cup in pre-season, and made a promising start to the Conference campaign as Tony Hackworth, and Neil Redfearn from the penalty spot, netted in a 2-0 home victory over Woking, but only two of the next nine matches were won and there was also a 4-1 defeat at Rochdale in the LDV Vans Trophy.

Supporters Club Committee
Chairman- Stuart Canvin
Secretary- Wendy Danby
Treasurer- Dave Metcalf
Committee- Rob Palmer, Pete McWatt, John Stabler, Mary Hellawell, Mike Price, Janet Spivey-Burton, Derek Megginson, Tony Scott

Lifelong fan Bernard Newby, aged 79, was mascot for the 1-1 home draw against Exeter City on 11 September.

The Under-19's team, under coach Bob MacDonald, assisted by Ian Blott, was entered into the Northern Youth Alliance and they romped to a 9-0 win over Darlington College in their first game, with goals from Ryan Blott (3), Michael Coulson (3), Jimmy Beadle (2) and Alistair Reid. They went on to enjoy a terrific season and clinched the title with a 2-1 win over Selby Town in their final game, with strikes from Ryan Blott and Michael Coulson.

The reserve team however was without a league and played a series of friendly matches. In a dramatic game against a Leeds United XI in September, Boro Reserves were beaten 5-4 after having led 4-1 with goals from Chris Senior (2), Ryan Blott and Paul Foot.

Tony Hackworth, Neil Redfearn, Kevin Nicholson and Chris Senior all netted in a 4-0 home win against Accrington Stanley on 23 October, but this was followed by a disappointing FA Cup exit to Conference North side Lancaster City in a 4th qualifying round replay. There were 3-0 wins against both Dagenham & Redbridge and Leigh RMI, but the highlight of the Conference season was undoubtedly the festive double over local rivals York City, as Boro won 5-1 at home on Boxing Day and then scored two late goals to secure a 2-0 win in the return at Bootham Crescent. Veteran, former Bolton, Carlisle, Preston and Chesterfield striker David Reeves joined Boro in January and another new arrival was midfielder Neil Bishop from Whitby Town. As the season neared its end, 16-year-old local youngster Michael Coulson was also drafted into the team, scoring a couple of goals from the substitutes bench, while Reeves struck a hat-trick in a 4-0 defeat of Farnborough Town. Boro ended the season 13th in the Conference, but had the distinction of being the only side to remain unbeaten at home. Unfortunately too many games were drawn (nine wins and 12 draws from 21 home matches). Boro also boasted the best disciplinary record in the Conference, with just one red card all season, Mark Hotte, for a professional foul in a 1-0 defeat at Hereford United in September.

Events off the field continued to make the headlines, as the club was still experiencing financial problems and plans to move to a new stadium were seen as the only way forward. At a fans forum in November, chairman Malcolm Reynolds reported that plans to build a new 6000 capacity stadium at Eastfield were progressing well. He said, *"Once the land is ready, it is quite quick and easy to build the stadium and it would take only two or three months. There will be a main stand seating 2000 and the rest will be covered terracing. I am hoping to have a plan or image of the new stadium ready for supporters to look at, by the middle of next month. There will be around 400 car parking spaces, with a bus service organised to the stadium on match days."*

In December it was announced that the club had signed a deal to buy a piece of land to the right of the approach road to the Seamer Carr waste disposal site. Chairman Reynolds added, *"Outline planning permission for building on the site, and for the development of the McCain Stadium will be submitted next month."* The club had entered into an agreement with London-based construction company, Scanmoor, who would build the new stadium, and then either develop the McCain Stadium site or sell it to another developer.

Nothing more was heard on the subject until April, when the chairman announced that the new stadium was still on course. He added that Scanmoor would build the stadium on 4.5 acres of the 15 acre site that the club had earmarked, and once Boro were playing there, the restrictive covenant on the McCain Stadium would be transferred to the new site. There would also be scope to incorporate a running track, health club, all-weather pitches, a sports hall and catering outlets on the site at a later date, to generate extra income for the club. Reynolds added, *" I want to stress that the McCain Stadium will not pass into anyone's hands until we have the new stadium in place. It's a fabulous deal for the football club, and any number of house builders would like to get their hands on the McCain Stadium. There are still certain issues to be resolved surrounding the planning process before we submit the planning application, and we are now probably looking at 3-4 months before any building work will start."*

John Trebble, the chief executive of Scarborough Borough Council commented, *"The Council would wish to make sure any new development was in place, before releasing the covenant on the existing site."* This was a highly significant statement, bearing in mind the eventual turn of events. In essence, the Council would not consider lifting or transferring the restrictive covenant on the McCain Stadium, until it was satisfied that a replacement stadium was already in place.

Boro midfielder Scott Kerr won four England semi-pro caps during the season, and was named 'England Player of the Year' by the Non League Club Directory. His citation read, *'Scott was an ever present as captain of the England side, and was a valuable member of an outstanding team. He showed a mature demur personality and leadership qualities, both on and off the pitch'.*

Several experienced players left the club at the end of the season, including 22-year-old striker David Pounder who was the longest serving player after five years at the club. He signed for York City, and also moving on were 37-year-old striker David Reeves and diminutive front runner Chris Senior who joined Halifax Town, while Mark Hotte turned down the offer of a new contract to join York City, and both Scott Kerr and Colin Cryan were snapped up by Lincoln City. Manager Nick Henry and 39-year-old assistant Neil Redfearn both signed new one-year contracts, with Redfearn announcing that he planned to continue playing for another year, after top-scoring with 14 Conference goals during the season.

Summing up his first season in charge, manager Nick Henry commented, *"I have been pretty happy with the way things have gone. One of the most pleasing aspects is that we completed the season with an unbeaten home league record, something only Manchester United and Chelsea have matched.*

"On the down side though was our disappointing away form. We have just not performed on our travels since the York City game at the beginning of the year, and that has cost us a play-off place."

Northern Under-19's Alliance

	P	W	D	L	F	A	Pts
Scarborough	16	11	2	3	53	18	35
Pickering Town	16	9	3	4	36	22	30
Selby Town	15	8	3	4	40	18	27
Hutton Cranswick	14	6	4	4	23	19	22
Goole AFC	16	6	4	6	22	27	22
Garforth Town	16	5	5	6	26	30	20
Glasshoughton Wel.	16	5	2	9	25	43	17
Pontefract Colls.	15	3	3	9	15	41	12
Darlington College	16	3	2	11	13	35	11

Nationwide Conference   Thursday, 26 December 2004

SCARBOROUGH 5 YORK CITY 1

Local rivals York City made their first ever visit as a non-League club to the McCain Stadium, following their relegation from the Football League the previous season. Under boss Viv Busby they were lying 17th in the Conference, while Boro were in 9th place, just three points outside the play-off places. Skipper Scott Kerr missed the game with a sickness bug, but Mark Hotte passed a late fitness test, while City included midfielder Darren Dunning in their line-up - the only Scarborough born player in either side. An all-ticket Boxing Day crowd witnessed an exciting match, with York having the upper hand in the early stages, on a mud-bath of a pitch following torrential pre-match rain.

York had lots of early possession, without creating any chances, and it was Boro who opened the scoring against the run of play on 25 minutes, when a Chris Senior shot struck a defender and Tyrone Thompson volleyed home the rebound. It was 2-0 just three minutes later as Neil Redfearn chipped over the keeper's head from the edge of the area after a poor clearance by a defender had fallen at his feet. Four minutes before half-time Chris Senior was brought down in the box, and Redfearn slotted in the spot kick to make it 3-0 at the interval. A bizarre sending-off on the hour mark, saw City defender Shaun Smith dismissed for a second bookable offence, when he took too long to take a throw-in. York fought back though, and Andy Bishop shot narrowly wide, before Lee Grant headed them back into the match in the 65th minute. Boro secured the win with two late goals, Tony Hackworth turning and striking a low shot into the net on 81 minutes, and Ashley Lyth converting a Keith Gilroy cross in the last minute.

Scarborough Leigh Walker, Steve Baker, Kevin Nicholson, Paul Foot, Mark Hotte, Keith Gilroy, Colin Cryan, Neil Redfearn (Ashley Lyth 82), Chris Senior (Robert Gill 86), Tony Hackworth (Steve Burton 86), Tyrone Thompson
York City Dave Stockdale, Steve Davis, Shaun Smith, Lee Grant, Chris Brass, Kevin Donovan, Paul Groves, Darren Dunning, David Merris, Andy Bishop, Paul Robinson (Paul D. Robinson 74)
Referee Mr S. Gate (Tyne & Wear)   Attendance 4586

Nationwide Conference Saturday, 9 April 2005

SCARBOROUGH 4 FARNBOROUGH TOWN 0

Although Boro had slipped to midtable, this final home match of the season was highly significant, because they were the only side in the Conference still with an unbeaten home record, while Farnborough, deep in relegation trouble, and with just one point from their last 13 matches, were playing their 500th match in the Conference. Boro were without two key defenders, the suspended Paul Foot, and Steve Baker, out with a calf injury, but striker Tony Hackworth was available after returning from injury, while Farborough included striker Lloyd Blackman, who had been with Boro, whilst on loan from Brentford, last season.

A powerful Boro performance gave them an easy win against the struggling visitors. Neil Redfearn thundered an early shot just past the post and then had a volley glance the crossbar. The opening goal came on 41 minutes as veteren former Bolton, Carlisle, Preston and Chesterfield striker David Reeves forced the ball home following an overhead kick by Chris Senior, and on the stroke of half-time Reeves was again on target as he netted at the second attempt after his first shot had been saved. Boro keeper Leigh Walker made a superb save to keep out a Michael Johnson thunderbolt early in the second half, but Boro soon regained control, and went 3-0 up on 68 minutes when Reeves completed his hat-trick, poking the ball home following a through-ball from Ashley Lyth. Scott Kerr rounded off the scoring three minutes from time, when 17-year-old substitute Michael Coulson flicked the ball on, for Kerr to round the keeper and tap home his first Conference goal of the season.

Scarborough Leigh Walker, Ashley Lyth, Kevin Nicholson, Scott Kerr, Mark Hotte, Colin Cryan, Tyrone Thompson, Neil Redfearn (Jimmy Beadle 88), David Reeves (Tony Hackworth 70), Chris Senior (Michael Coulson 80), Neil Bishop
Farnborough Town Andy Petterson (Jon Ashwood 46), Mark Rooney, Tony Taggart, Jay Smith, Anthony Fenton, Adam Theo, Danny Allen-Page, Scott Canham (Gavin Heeroo 18) (Robert Traynor 46), Carl Gibbs, Lloyd Blackman, Michael Johnson
Referee M. Matadar (Manchester) Attendance 1451

David Pounder in action against Leigh RMI, 12 March 2005.

Kevin Nicholson

(Below)
December 2004
Author, Steve Adamson (centre) presents Boro legends Colin Appleton (left) and Harry Dunn (right) with copies of the A-Z of Scarborough FC book

Managers Nick Henry and Neil Redfearn

Chris Senior

Tyrone Thompson

New signings in the Summer were 21-year-old Darlington midfielder Chris Hughes, 27-year-old former Lincoln City and Kidderminster defender Simon Weaver, 30-year-old ex Doncaster, Darlington and Hartlepool midfielder Ian Clark, and former Boro striker Mark Quayle who rejoined the club after a spell with Northwich Victoria. A number of loan signings were also brought in, including Gretna duo, Mark Eccles (midfield) and Brian Wake (striker), 18-year-old striker Jermaine Palmer from Grimsby Town and 19-year-old centre-back David Elebert from Preston North End. Four of the club's promising young players also signed professional contracts, having progressed through the school of excellence ranks, 18-year-olds Carl Cook and Jimmy Beadle, and 17-year-olds Michael Coulson and Ryan Blott. The reserve team was re-admitted to the Pontins League, and more than 500 season tickets were sold, 100 more than the previous season.

Season 2005-06 Dramatic struggle to avoid relegation as the season ends in confusion.

Boro opened the season with six debutants featuring in a dismal 4-0 defeat away to Hereford United, and then lost 1-0 at home to Morecambe (having gone unbeaten at home throughout the previous season!) A stoppage time equaliser from Paul Foot earned Boro their first point, a 1-1 home draw with Kidderminster, and this was followed by the first win of the campaign, when late strikes from 19-year-old Sheffield United loanee Jake Speight and Brian Wake secured a 2-0 away win against Dagenham & Redbridge.

Another new player on loan was Sheffield United's 20-year-old midfielder Adrian Harper, but only two of the next ten Conference matches were won. A 5-0 trouncing at Grays Athletic on 15 October sent Boro to the foot of the table, and when Harrogate Town won 1-0 in the FA Cup 4th qualifying round the following Saturday, manager Nick Henry was dismissed and replaced by 40-year-old assistant boss Neil Redfearn, who continued to play when he assumed the managerial role, bringing in experienced former Barnsley coach Eric Winstanley as his assistant.

Redfearn's first match at the helm ended in a 2-2 home draw with Aldershot Town and next came a 1-0 win at fellow strugglers Tamworth, with Mark Quayle scoring the goal that lifted Boro off the bottom of the table. More comings and goings followed, with Barnsley midfielder Sean McClare, Huddersfield midfielder Lee Fowler and Scunthorpe striker Andy Parton all arriving on loan, while Ian Clark was released and pacey striker Jake Speight also left following his £10,000 transfer from Sheffield United to Bury.

While the team was struggling in the Conference, the ground saga continued to drag on. In November, chairman Malcolm Reynolds announced that the club was close to concluding a deal which would see a major house-builder buy the McCain Stadium. He said this would enable the club to go ahead with the proposed 6000 capacity stadium at Eastfield, with building work expected to start on the new site midway through 2006.

He added, *"The club is currently losing £250,000 a year, and the value of the McCain Stadium has increased from £1.4 million in April 2003 to £4.1 million. The problem we face is disposing of the McCain Stadium for the right price. Building the new stadium is the easy bit, people tell me they can build the new stadium in around 4 months. Planning application will be submitted in the next few months. This is massive for the club because, how else can we improve our financial situation? We have a yearly income of £250,000 and outgoings of £500,000. We can't go on losing £250,000 each year.*

"The move will provide us with an additional 10 acres of land that could provide us with development income."

The Boxing Day derby at York was lost 3-1, but in the return match on 2 January, a 90th minute Chris Hughes equaliser salvaged a 2-2 draw. Three former Boro players rejoined the club, David Pounder upon his release by York City, Denny Ingram, after a spell with Halifax Town, and striker David McNiven, who last played for Boro in 2000, was signed from Leigh RMI. Former Morecambe keeper Ian Dunbavin was also brought in, to challenge Leigh Walker for the number one jersey, while on-loan Gretna striker Brian Wake moved on to play for Hamilton Academical. On 24 January, David McNiven, Chris Hughes and Lee Fowler netted in a 3-0 away win over Morecambe. Boro were now 17th in the table, seven points above bottom side Southport. But form collapsed after that, as only two of the last 15 Conference games were won, 1-0 at Aldershot Town thanks to a Michael Coulson goal, and a 3-0 home victory over Burton Albion, with Neil Redfearn (penalty), Tony Hackworth and Michael Coulson on target.

Some of the end of season displays were abysmal - a 5-1 defeat at Forest Green Rovers, a 2-0 reverse at lowly Crawley Town, a grim 2-1 home loss to a very ordinary Canvey Island, and a humiliating 7-2 home thrashing by Grays Athletic (Boro's heaviest home defeat for 54 years, since an 8-0 loss to Mansfield Town in the FA Cup first round on 22 November 1952). Boro faced a desperate battle to avoid relegation, although the Conference was expanding from 22 to 24 clubs, so only the bottom two would go down this season. With two matches to play the situation at the foot of the table was very tight

	P	W	D	L	F	A	Pts
Altrincham	40	10	11	19	39	66	41
Southport	39	10	8	21	34	65	38
Tamworth	40	8	13	19	31	61	37
Scarborough	40	9	9	22	38	63	36
ForestGreen	39	7	14	18	46	59	35

An unlikely escape route opened up when Altrincham were fined £1,000 and deducted 18 points for fielding an ineligible player. This meant they were certain to finish bottom of the table, so there was only one more relegation place to be decided. Unfortunately Boro slipped up at home to Cambridge United in their penultimate match, when Neil Redfearn fired them in front, but Cambridge fought back to win 2-1.

	P	W	D	L	F	A	Pts
Southport	40	10	9	21	35	66	39
Tamworth	41	8	13	20	32	63	37
Scarborough	41	9	9	23	39	65	36
ForestGreen	41	7	14	20	47	62	35
Altrincham	41	10	11	20	39	68	23 *

For the final match of the season Boro made the 300 mile treck to play 8th-placed Exeter City knowing a win would save them from relegation. Around 120 loyal fans made the long journey, including a party of 40 who flew to Exeter from Leeds-Bradford Airport. A battling display saw a last gasp Tony Hackworth strike earn Boro a 1-1 draw, but it wasn't enough, as Forest Green beat Stevenage 2-0 to climb above Boro. The final positions at the foot of the table were -

	P	W	D	L	F	A	Pts
Southport	42	10	10	22	36	68	40
ForestGreen	42	8	14	20	49	62	38
Tamworth	42	8	14	20	32	73	38
Scarborough	42	9	10	23	40	66	37
Altrincham	42	10	11	21	40	71	23 *

* (Deducted 18 Pts)

So Boro were consigned to relegation to Conference North, or were they ?

Essex club Canvey Island, who finished 14th in the table, then announced they were resigning from the Conference following the decision of club owner Jeff King to withdrew his substantial financial backing. So it seemed that Canvey Island and Altrincham were the two clubs to lose their Conference status. However, Altrincham launched an appeal against the 18-point deduction for fielding an ineligible player.

Confusion reigned, as the season had finished on 29 April, but Altrincham's appeal against the points deduction wasn't heard until 23 May. The case against Altrincham was that they played striker James Robinson in 13 Conference matches without obtaining International clearance, following a spell he had in Iceland. But they had signed him from fellow Conference club Accrington Stanley, where he had only played a couple of reserve games before moving on to Altrincham and the player did not inform the club of his stint in Iceland.

Despite massive public support, Altrincham had their appeal turned down and the points deduction stood, but Boro were still not safe as the Conference were not happy with the way the club had come out of their CVA and launched an investigation.

Several weeks after the end of the season, it was still not clear which league Boro would be playing in next season, but there was a mass exodus of players, with Leigh Walker, Kevin Nicholson, Simon Weaver, Sean McClare, David McNiven, Ian Dunbavin, Paul Foot, Lee Fowler, Steve Baker, David Pounder and Mark Quayle all released as the club planned to slash the wage bill. Chairman Malcolm Reynolds admitted, *"The wage bill this season was a record since I have been at the club, and that is something we can't afford to do next season."*

Boro's problems were put in perspective, when 18-year-old supporter Rob Manoury was tragically killed in a car accident in Gloucestershire.

Nationwide Conference Saturday, 26 November 2005
SCARBOROUGH 2 HALIFAX TOWN 0

With just four wins from their opening 17 matches, Boro were down in 18th position and facing a relegation battle, while visitors Halifax had made a much better start to the season, and were 5th in the table and on course for the play-offs. Boro had skipper Steve Baker missing through suspension after picking up five bookings, but new loan signing, Scunthorpe striker Andy Parton made his debut from the substitutes bench. Halifax included three former Boro players in their side, Denny Ingram, Tyrone Thompson and Chris Senior, while winger Rory Prendergast made his debut, having joined the Shaymen on loan from Stockport County. There was a minute's silence before the match, in memory of soccer legend George Best who had died the previous day, aged 59.

In an even first half, Halifax enjoyed long spells of possession but it was Boro who created the better chances, with Carl Cook having a shot saved, Neil Bishop having an effort charged down and Lee Fowler firing just wide, while Halifax's best opening ended with Martin Foster volleying wide. Boro made a flying start to the second period, taking a 47th minute lead when Lee Fowler blasted home a free kick following a foul on Neil Bishop. The lead was doubled after 73 minutes when debutant Andy Parton was brought down in the box by Adam Quinn and Ian Clark blasted the spot kick past keeper Adam Legzdins. Tony Hackworth shot wide after being set up by Parton near the end as Boro finished the match well on top, Manager Neil Redfearn was happy with the win, saying, "We tried to play good football, but it was a scrap. You expect that from a derby match, but we have come out on top."

Scarborough Leigh Walker, Ashley Lyth, Kevin Nicholson, Simon Weaver, Chris Hughes, Lee Fowler (Sean McClare 70), Neil Bishop, Ian Clark, Mark Quayle (Andy Parton 58), Tony Hackworth, Carl Cook
Halifax Town Adam Legzdins, Steve Haslam, Jake Wright, Tyrone Thompson (Darren Mansaram), Denny Ingram (Peter Atherton 7), Adam Quinn, Danny Forrest, Martin Foster, Lewis Kileen (Chris Senior 63), John Grant, Rory Prendergast
Referee D. Foster (Tyne & Wear) Attendance 1843

Nationwide Conference Saturday, 15 April 2006

SCARBOROUGH 3 BURTON ALBION 0

Since the 2-0 win over Halifax in November, Boro had failed to win their next eight home matches, scoring just 5 goals in the process and they had slumped to the foot of the Conference table. Relegation was staring them in the face and they were desperate for three points against 9th-placed Burton Albion if they were to have any chance of avoiding the drop. Centre-back Paul Foot was again missing through injury while former Shrewsbury and Halifax keeper Ian Dunbavin was preferred to Leigh Walker in goal. Visitors Burton Albion fielded an experienced side, including 37-year-old Darren Tinson and 31-year-old Gary Rowett in central defence.

Just four days after a 0-0 home draw with Tamworth, Boro turned on the style to record a much-needed win which lifted them off the bottom of the table, and gave them a glimmer of hope in the battle to avoid the drop. Tough tackling Chris Hughes and Simon Weaver both had excellent games for Neil Redfearn's side. Lee Fowler volleyed over the bar early on as Boro made a bright start, and they went ahead from the penalty spot on 34 minutes, when a Kevin Nicholson shot was handled in the area by Andy Corbett. The Burton defender was dismissed for deliberate handball and Neil Redfearn converted the spot kick. Jon Shaw and Chris Taylor went close to equalising, before Tony Hackworth blasted in a 20-yard power drive on 74 minutes, and man of the match Hackworth then set up Michael Coulson, to make it 3-0 six minutes from time.

Scarborough Ian Dunbavin, Denny Ingram (Sean McClare 78), Kevin Nicholson, Simon Weaver, Rob Atkinson, Steve Baker, Chris Hughes, Lee Fowler, David McNiven, Tony Hackworth, Neil Redfearn (Michael Coulson 67)

Burton Albion Saul Deeney, Andy Corbett, Aaron Webster, Darren Stride, Darren Tinson, Gary Rowett (Christian Moore 76), Chris Hall (Jon Shaw 22), Andy Ducross, Daryl Clare (Terry Henshaw 76), Shaun Harrad, Kris Taylor

Refereee D. Richardson (Halifax) *Attendance 1808*

Boro supporters at Exeter Airport for the crucial last match.

Teenage star Michael Coulson

(Above) Boro Skipper Neil Bishop (left), York Captain Mark Hotte (right) before the derby match.
(Below) Boro's Chris Hughes goes past York full back Lee Andrews.

A packed East stand for the Boro vs York City derby match in January 2006.

Malcolm Reynolds

Ashley Lyth

Demoted to Conference North

Chairman Malcolm Reynolds stood down in mid May and was replaced by director Ian Scobbie, a 43-year-old solicitor, specialising in insolvency, who had been involved with the club for three years. With the club having exited the CVA that had existed since June 2003, the Conference was not happy that Boro then appeared to approve another CVA in June, and both Malcolm Reynolds and Ian Scobbie were summoned to attend a Conference board meeting at Leicester City Football Club to explain the club's financial situation. Chairman Scobbie said, *"The Conference gave us a deadline for the administration order to be discharged, and we have met it. If we hadn't done so, then we could have been demoted. A similar thing happened to Telford United a couple of seasons ago, but we believe we have met every criteria. We had a meeting with our creditors, to extend and re-jig our existing CVA, so that we are able to pay them off in full and that has been agreed."*

At the Conference AGM in Birmingham in June, the Conference board announced their decision to demote Boro into Conference North and deduct 10 points from the start of the following season, due to 'financial irregularities' and Altrincham were therefore reprieved from relegation. The board decided that although Boro had met the deadline for exiting the CVA, the club had failed to meet certain financial criteria required by the Conference. Shocked Boro chairman Ian Scobbie promised to scour the rule books ahead of a possible appeal to the FA. He said, *"This decision has come as a great surprise. We accept that we finished in a relegation position, but to go down in this manner leaves a bad taste. We are not even sure exactly what breach of rules is alleged, and we have not been given a chance to respond. Our directors will meet this week to see where we go from here. I believe that the Conference board has viewed this as if we have entered into a new CVA, but in fact all we have done is to modify our existing agreement. We have been demoted for an alleged breach of Conference rules, but have never been charged with any such breach. We don't know how we are supposed to have contravened the rules."* Conference chief executive John Moules explained that Boro were demoted because the club had breached the Conference's articles of association, and the 10 point deduction was because they had entered into another voluntary arrangement with creditors. Moules said, *"We need to promote solvency and good management at our clubs. Plans have to add up, and selling the stadium would be like selling off the crown jewels, just to pay off debts that have been run up over years of living beyond your means."* Chairman Ian Scobbie felt the club had been singled out as Halifax Town were also in a CVA and Crawley Town on the verge of entering administration.

The Boro chairman added, *" This is a massive blow to the club, and will affect manager Neil Redfearn's plans for next season, as he has already done an incredible amount of work, speaking to players with a view to signing for a Conference National club. I have nothing against Altrincham, and we said from the beginning that their 18 point penalty was very harsh, but we seem to have been singled out here. Crawley Town and Halifax Town both face similar financial plights to us, yet no sanctions have been taken against them."* Having ended the season with the worst playing record in the Conference, Boro could have little argument about being relegated. The points deduction against Altrincham, and the resignation of Canvey Island would have reprieved them, but it seemed the Conference had lost patience with the continuing financial problems at Boro, and the club was now consigned to playing at its lowest level since 1979 when they had left the Northern Premier League to become founder members of the Alliance Premier League (later Conference).

After considering lodging an appeal against their demotion, Boro finally accepted their fate, with chairman Ian Scobbie admitting, *"We have had a lot of heated debate, but now I think it is time for a cool head. We finished bottom, we didn't have a good enough side, so really it is time to bite the bullet and move on. The cost of mounting an appeal would be in the region of £35,000, which I feel would be much better used on the pitch instead of going through the courts."*

Formation of The Seadog Trust

Boro chairman Ian Scobbie had suggested at the end of the 2005-06 season that the way forward could be for the supporters to take over the running of the club once the move to the new stadium was completed. A group of interested supporters got together to form a working party, with a view to setting up a new Supporters Trust - a democratic organisation, created to increase the influence of fans in the running of the club. An open meeting at the Royal Hotel on 22 July 2006 was attended by 55 fans as well as club chairman Ian Scobbie. There were also two guest speakers, Paul Hadjuk, chairman of the Rushden & Diamonds Supporters Trust, and Jacqi Forster, development officer of Supporters Direct, a government funded organisation, set up to help and advise fans on the formation of supporters trusts. Three Boro fans, Ben Courtney, Andy Crossland and Simon Cope also spoke at the meeting, and a vote was taken to proceed with the formation of a Scarborough FC Supporters Trust, under the title, Seadog Trust.

Long standing supporter, Simon Cope from Dewsbury was one of the driving forces behind the formation of the Seadog Trust, and he commented, *"We don't want to tread on the Supporters Club's toes. I have spoken to their chairman Stuart Canvin in great detail, and he is happy to help in any way he can. We certainly have no intention of swallowing up the Supporters Club or dividing the fan base."* Former Boro chairman, and the majority shareholder Malcolm Reynolds also approved of the formation of the Trust, providing they had the cash and know-how to keep the club going. He said, *"As far as I am concerned, they can have my shares as long as they show that they can keep the club going."* Simon Cope was elected chair of the Seadog Trust, and other members of the 'interim' committee included secretary Ben Courtney, treasurer Sandra Troughton, publicity officer Anthony Gough, membership secretary Richard Adamson, plus Stuart Keith, Andy Crossland, Matthew Flinton and Chris Rooke.

On 27 September the Seadog Trust was officially registered as an Industrial and Provident Society with the Financial Services Authority, and the committee issued the following list of aims of the Trust :-

1. To create a close working partnership with Scarborough Football Club, its supporters and the local community, to ensure that the views of the supporters and local community are fully represented in the running of the club.
2. To assist and promote Scarborough Football Club in any way that has been sanctioned by the Trust membership, including financially, in kind, and in developing partnerships to further the interests of the club.
3. To secure supporter representation on the board of directors of the club.
4. To acquire full ownership of the club.
5. To encourage the club to play football at the highest level possible, but always operating within a framework of responsible and prudent financial management.

The Trust held an official launch party at the Hotel St Nicholas on 23 November 2006, attended by 150 people including former players, Jeff Barmby, Kenny Dennis, Harry A Dunn, Steve Richards, Jason Rockett, Ian Ironside and Mitch Cook. An auction of donated sports memorabilia raised £2000 for Trust funds. Trust membership was set at £12 per year, and any supporters, aged 18 or over would be eligible to stand for election to the Trust board. A meeting between Boro chairman Ian Scobbie, Simon Cope and Ben Courtney of the Seadog Trust and Supporters Club chairman Stuart Canvin in early December agreed that there should be no animosity between the two organisations, as both were working towards a common goal, and the Trust offered to co-opt a Supporters Club official onto their committee, although this offer was not taken up. The Supporters Club maintained their role as fundraisers for the Football Club, and there was criticism from some Supporters Club members that the Trust did not make any financial contributions, as Boro continued to struggle along near the foot of Conference North. With the possibility of liquidation looking increasingly likely for the debt-ridden club, the Trust began to formulate a plan to establish a new club should Boro go into liquidation, and a major rift began to develop between those supporters who backed chairman Ian Scobbie's plan to sell the McCain Stadium and use the money to pay off creditors and develop a new ground at Eastfield, and those who had grave doubts that selling the ground and paying off debts would leave sufficient funds to build a suitable new stadium.

A Trust committee meeting on 2 May 2007 decided that "Plan B" would be activated if the club was liquidated in June, and the following statement was issued :- *The Trust is committed to the future of football in Scarborough, and as such, a plan to reform a club must be in place. However, we reiterate, this plan is to be implemented only if the current club is liquidated.*

The Seadog Trust comes into being.
(L to R) Andy Troughton, Sandra Troughton, James Freir, James Hunter, Shaun Burke, Ben Courtney. In front is Bertie Courtney

Season 2006-07 Boro struggle to overcome points deduction, club faces bleak future

After the mass clearout of players at the end of the previous season, chairman Ian Scobbie announced that the playing budget for the Conference North campaign was being slashed from £7500 per week to just £4000, the reserve side was scrapped, and no more full time players would be signed. Scobbie added, *"We have half a dozen players on full time contracts, and any new signings will be on part time terms. The way forward for this club is to expand our very successful school of excellence, under director Mitch Cook, and look to create an academy which would link in perfectly with the new ground when we move. If you have home grown players in the team it creates more identity with the town."*

Despite the drop in status, admission prices were increased from £10 to £12 for adults, Scobbie explaining, *"I explored every other possible option before increasing the prices, but we need to reduce the gap between our income and expenditure. I accept that we charge more than most clubs in our division, but I also suspect that we have the best facilities."*

Signs of discord at the club came to light when manager Neil Redfearn revealed that he, and several of the players, were still owed wages from the last season, and defender Simon Weaver, one of those released said he regretted ever signing for the club, adding, *"When I arrived at the club last Summer I was promised all sorts of things. I thought the deal I signed was fair and in pre-season I thought we would do well. But we made a bad start and the season seemed to just get worse. Nick Henry left and Neil Redfearn took over and we seemed to pick up, but players were not getting paid on time and the spirit of the club suffered. When you travel two hours to get to training, but don't get paid at the end of the month, it costs you personally."*

More off the field turmoil occurred when former chairman Malcolm Reynolds quit the board following an investigation into the club's financial affairs by the Department of Trade and Industry, who concluded that he was at fault for not placing the club into administration when he took over in 2001. Then there was another backroom bust-up, as chairman Ian Scobbie appointed Mark Patterson to the coaching staff, resulting in the resignations of manager Neil Redfearn and his assistant Eric Winstanley. Patterson had previously been at the club as assistant to Russ Slade, and following Redfearn and Winstanley's resignations, he was appointed as player-coach.

Another departure on the eve of the season was that of Boro's promising 18-year-old striker Michael Coulson, a product of the youth system, who signed a two year contract with Championship club Barnsley. Although he was on contract at Boro, no fee was involved, but Barnsley manager Andy Ritchie, a former Boro player, promised to loan Boro up to three players during the coming season.

Fans were stunned that the club's prize asset had been allowed to leave without a transfer fee being paid, but chairman Ian Scobbie explained that Coulson had been asked to stay, but insisted on going to Barnsley, who, with financial problems of their own, had been unwilling to offer a fee for him. Scobbie said, *"We could have insisted that Michael stayed with us, but both he, and his father were adamant that he wanted to go. We didn't want to stand in his way, and Barnsley made it clear that they couldn't offer us any money, so reluctantly we allowed him to go."* New boss Mark Patterson brought in a host of new faces for the new campaign, several of whom were based in Lancashire, where Patterson lived.

The pick of these were 18-year-old keeper Curtis Aspden on loan from Hull City, 24-year-old former Chorley midfielder Jamie Vermiglio, 33-year-old ex Preston, Stockport and Rochdale midfielder Lee Cartwright, 19-year-old former Bradford City winger Darren Thornton and 19-year-old striker Lee Whittington from Rotherham United, while former Boro defender Mark Hotte was also signed, after a season at York City.

The new-look team turned in some impressive pre-season performances, going unbeaten in 8 friendlies, but a big cloud on the horizon came in the form of a transfer embargo imposed by the Football Association amid claims from 13 former players that they were still owed money by the club. The amount owed was said to be £40,000, but chairman Ian Scobbie disputed the amount, although he admitted that some players were owed wages. He said he would pay a significant proportion of that money within a few days, and hoped that the Conference would send the £16,000 he claimed the club was owed from last season's share of the play-off fund.

Boro opened their Conference North campaign with successive 0-0 draws, away to Worksop Town and at home to Gainsborough Trinity, which were followed by a dismal 1-0 home defeat to Vauxhall Motors.and then draws against both Stalybridge Celtic and Nuneaton Borough. The first win didn't come until the sixth match, when Moor Green were beaten 3-0.

With just a small squad, and unable to sign new players, boss Mark Patterson was forced to draft some of the youngsters from the under-19's side into first team action, and Jimmy Beadle, Ryan Blott and Ged Dalton all made the step up. Hull City wouldn't allow on-loan keeper Curtis Aspden to play in the FA Cup, so the embargo was waived to enable Patterson to bring in former Leeds United juniors keeper Mark Wilberforce, while ex Boro striker Darren Foreman returned to the club in October as physio, to replace Martin Woodmansey. Having started the season on minus 10 points, it took Boro 13 matches to clear that defecit, when they drew 1-1 at home to Leigh RMI to move on to 0 points.

It was obvious that it would be a struggle to move out of the relegation zone (bottom three), and a 3-0 FA Cup defeat at Stafford Rangers the following week, after wins over Lancaster City and Ossett Albion in earlier rounds, followed soon after by FA Trophy exit at Rushden & Diamonds, left Boro with nothing to play for, except surviving the drop into the Unibond League (Northern Premier League), but behind the scenes, plans were progressing towards the setting up of a Supporters Trust to take over the running of the club, and talks regarding a move to a new ground were also taking place.

Boro remained near the foot of the table because of the points deduction, but they did pick up some good results, a 3-1 away win over eventual champions Droylsden in November, a 2-0 win at high-flying Farsley Celtic in December, a 5-1 romp away to fellow strugglers Lancaster City in January and a 1-0 home win against leaders Droylesden in March.. Lancaster also had 10 points deducted for entering administration in January, but they were the only side already below Boro in the table.

On Friday, 23 March Boro entertained Worksop Town, and used the occasion to celebrate the 20th anniversary of the 1986-87 Conference championship win. Neil Warnock and many of the players from that history-making Boro team attended the match as guests of the club, and witnessed a 2-1 win, with goals from Lee Cartwright and Ryan Blott.

Away form was good, with 1-0 wins at Workington and Harrogate Town, but home results were less impressive, and a 3-1 home defeat by Nuneaton Borough on 7 April left Boro on the brink of relegation to the Unibond League. Just two days later Tony Hackworth and Ryan Blott netted in a 2-1 win at Moor Green to leave the situation at the bottom of the table (bottom three to be relegated):

	P	W	D	L	F	A	Pts
RedditchUnited	37	11	11	15	56	60	44
LeighRMI	39	11	9	19	43	59	42
Scarborough	39	12	15	12	48	43	41 *
LancasterCity	39	2	4	32	25	10	00 *

(* 10 Pts deducted)

With just three matches remaining, news broke that the club was expected to fold within weeks due to mounting debts, with administrators Begbies Traynor seeking a petition to wind up the club. The gloom and despondency then transferred to the pitch, as Boro slipped to a 1-0 home defeat against Stalybridge Celtic, who scored in the 2nd minute of stoppage time, and with Redditch drawing and Leigh RMI winning, Boro were now four points adrift of safety, with just two games to play. On the morning of the home game against Leigh RMI on 21 April, a group of around 70 loyal fans marched through the town on their way to the McCain Stadium, in a public show of support for the beleaguered club. But a dismal 1-1 draw against the fellow relegation candidates confirmed that Boro would finish in the drop zone, and although they ended the campaign with a fine 1-0 win at Hucknall Town, they ended the season third from bottom. Without the 10 point deduction they would have finished 13th, but now they faced the prospect of playing Unibond League football next season, providing the club survived the winding up order. Manager Mark Patterson resigned shortly after the last match saying, *"It has been a very difficult time with all the problems the players and myself have faced, but if you look at our record throughout the season, I believe we can look back with pride. When I arrived at the club, I wasn't expecting the transfer embargo, and I think that was our undoing in the end. When it reached the latter stages of the season, we had a number of tired youngsters in the team, and needed to freshen things up, but just couldn't do it."*

Conference North, Monday, 28 August 2006
SCARBOROUGH 3 MOOR GREEN 0

Having started the season with a ten point deduction after entering administration, Boro had made a slow start to life in Conference North, failing to win in their opening five matches, four of which were drawn. They were stranded at the foot of the table on minus six points, while Birmingham based visitors Moor Green were 9th in the table with seven points from four games. Boro boss Mark Patterson was without the injured Denny Ingram, but Mark Hotte and Chris Thompson, who picked up knocks in Saturday's 1-1 draw at Nuneaton, were both passed fit to play in this Bank Holiday Monday clash. The visitors, who were ground-sharing at Solihull Borough this season, were managed by veteran Bob Faulkner who had been at the helm for a remarkable 20 years, during which he had taken charge of over 1100 matches.

In front of a sparse crowd Boro turned in a stylish display to earn a much needed, and well deserved victory. Darren Thornton and star performer Jamie Vermiglio created early openings but the breakthrough didn't come until six minutes before the interval when Lee Cartwright floated over a cross to the far post for Darren Thornton to head home. Moor Green almost snatched an equaliser straight from the kick-off, but Curtis Aspden made a point-blank save from a Danny Davidson header. The second half saw Boro on top for long periods, and the lead was doubled on 65 minutes when Chris Thompson was brought down in the area, and he blasted in the spot kick. The third goal arrived 3 minutes into stoppage time, as 18-year-old striker Ryan Blott collected a pass from Tony Hackworth and slammed his shot past the keeper to wrap up a morale-boosting first win of the season.

Scarborough Curtis Aspden, Ashley Lyth, Carl Cook, Lee Briscoe (Ryan Blott 90), Mark Hotte, Jimmy Beadle, Lee Cartwright, Jamie Vermiglio, Tony Hackworth, Chris Thompson (Lee Whittington 80), Darren Thornton (Sean Davies 74)
Moor Green Danny Lewis, Richard Scott, Phil Midworth, Lee Ayres, Andy Penny, Terry Fleming, Peter Faulds (Richard Follett 72), Darren Middleton, Danny Davidson (David Bridgewater 63), Dale Anderson (Jason Moore 14), Phil Trainer
Referee M. Horn (Lincolnshire) *Attendance 770*

Conference North, Saturday, 28 April 2007
HUCKNALL TOWN 0 SCARBOROUGH 1

A 1-1 home draw with Leigh RMI the previous week had confirmed Boro's relegation to the Unibond League, with the ten point deduction for entering administration proving too much of a handicap. The club was at an all-time low and fighting for its existence, facing the threat of a winding up order from the administrators. Manager Mark Patterson called for the players to restore some pride to the club in this final match of the season, and there was a magnificent response from the supporters, with 350 fans making the trek to Hucknall. Boro were missing the injured Darren Thornton and Lee Whittington, while mid-table Hucknall had won just two of their last 12 matches to slip down the table after a promising start to the season.

The game got off to a slow start, but Boro gradually took control. Jamie Vermiglio had two headers on goal, the first saved by the keeper and the second striking the post, while a Sean Davies effort was saved. Hucknall's best opening of the first half ended with Boro keeper Mark Wilberforce saving well to deny Paul Dempsey and then foiling David Johnson from the follow-up. Boro substitute Ged Dalton headed a Gary Ricketts shot off the goal-line early in the second half, while at the other end Dalton's powerful strike was saved by keeper Greg Smith. On-form keeper Smith then produced two stunning saves to deny both Lee Cartwright and Tony Hackworth as the Boro pressure intensified, and the winning goal finally came on 82 minutes. Tony Hackworth gathered the ball on the left touchline, cut inside and set off on a mazy dribble past three defenders before drilling a low shot into the net. It was a wonderful goal, and fittingly proved to be the last goal ever scored by Scarborough Football Club. Near the end Hackworth shot narrowly wide, and Ashley Lyth had a shot parried by the keeper as Boro ended their last ever match well on top.

Hucknall Town Greg Smith, Liam Powell (Michael Fox 70), Russell Cooke, Bobby Wilson, Martin Reeves (Liam Hearn 60), Tony Gallimore, Stephen Ackers, Paul Dempsey, Gary Ricketts, David Johnson, Ricky Hanson
Scarborough Mark Wilberforce, Ashley Lyth, Sean Davies (Ged Dalton 46), Lee Cartwright, Mark Hotte, Denny Ingram, Tony Hackworth, Jamie Vermiglio, Ryan Blott (Dominic Amos 89), Chris Thompson, Carl Cook
Referee P. Caswell (Leicester) *Attendance 646*

24 year old midfielder
Jamie Vermiglio.

Lee Cartwright
33 year old Midfielder.

Boro Solidarity March - April 2007

(Above) Boro Chairman Ian Scobie

(Right) Manager Mark Patterson.

Top goalscorer, Chris Thompson.

Ged Dalton surges past a
Redditch United defender.

Defender Mark Hotte
formerly with York City.

Youngster Jimmy
Beadle Age 18.

Liquidation - after last minute rescue plans fail

While the team was struggling to maintain its Conference North status, behind the scenes, the board was still seeking to conclude a deal to sell the McCain Stadium and re-locate to a new site at Dunslow Road, Eastfield, as they saw this as the only way the club could overcome their financial problems and start afresh, free of debt. The club issued a statement in November 2006 saying they had received an offer of £4 million for the McCain Stadium, subject to the lifting of the restrictive covenant, and the money would be used to pay off creditors and partly finance a new stadium, with extra funding expected to come from grants. However, not everyone agreed with this course of action, including well known local businessman and former club chairman Don Robinson, who urged the Council not to lift the covenant on the ground, saying, *"If the club proceeds with their plans to sell the ground and move, they will end up with a ground like Pickering Town's. The people in charge will say that it will be improved as the club progresses through the leagues, but the money won't be there, and neither will they."*

Graham Price, head of property services at Scarborough Borough Council said a letter had been received from administrators Begbies Traynor, who were trying to sort out the club's estimated £2 million debts. They were seeking the lifting of the covenant, which stated the land must be used for sporting purposes, as one of the club's main creditors, HM Revenue & Customs were seeking liquidation of the club. Council debated the issue, but decided they needed more information, and the matter was deferred for a month. Meanwhile, the Boro Supporters Club started up a petition, urging the Council to lift the covenant, and back the club in its efforts to sell the McCain Stadium and move to a new ground. Majority shareholder and former chairman Malcolm Reynolds said, *"I am very disappointed the Council did not agree to lift the covenant. We have kept this club alive for over four years, whilst seeking a solution to the large debts which we inherited. I have always said, the only solution that I can see, is to re-locate, settle the debts which are killing the club, and build a platform for the future. An incredible amount of work, time and money has gone into turning this into a reality, but at the last moment, Council opposition has scuppered the plans."*

The Council estimated that the current 'market value' for lifting the covenant was around £200,000, and once lifted, the ground would be available for building use, but as a compromise there were suggestions that the Council (which had a duty to act in the interests of ratepayers), could waive any payments, in return for being granted the freehold of the new stadium, which could then be leased to a community trust, including council representation, and sub-leased to the football club. But some local residents totally opposed any plans the Council might have to help the club, whose debt problems were seen by many as self-inflicted. One resident wrote to the local press stating that any application to build housing on the McCain Stadium site must be considered on normal planning criteria, ie development, suitability, impact on surrounding areas, traffic issues etc, and the financial requirements of the football club should be irrelevant when councillors consider the matter.

By January 2007 an internet campaign started by long time Boro fan Darren Trapps, calling for the Council to lift the covenant on the ground, had received over 12,000 names from all over the world, and club chairman Ian Scobbie also praised the sterling efforts of the Supporters Club, led by chairman Stuart Canvin, who had handed over £3,000 to the club in the past month. Scobbie added, *"I can't praise the Supporters Club highly enough. Year-in, year-out Stuart and the rest of the*

Supporters Club members have provided a huge financial boost to the club. I give them my heartfelt thanks." But some fans were starting to express reservations about the plan to sell the McCain Stadium and pay off the debts, worried that the amount left over, which some estimated would be around £1.5 million, wouldn't be enough to buy the land and build a new stadium. At a meeting of Scarborough Borough Council on 8 January 2007, council made the decision to agree in principal to the lifting of the covenant, subject to 'adequate protection being established for any available sums for the purpose for which the covenant was imposed'. In other words, they agreed that they would be willing to lift the covenant, but only as long as enough money was available to build a suitable new stadium.

In February Ian Scobbie announced that the club was on the verge of signing a deal to sell the McCain Stadium to developers for around £4 million, which he said would allow the club to completely wipe out all its debts and build a new 5000 capacity stadium at Dunslow Road, which could be ready by Christmas 2008 or August 2009 at the latest. He went on, "We *have had two offers for the McCain Stadium site in excess of £4 million, and one which is differently structured, where effectively, no money would change hands. They would build us the new stadium and also pay off our debts, in exchange for the McCain Stadium site. Already, work on the infrastructure for the new ground, including drainage work, has been carried out. The new site will also include a lorry park, with room for 30 trucks, which will bring in some extra revenue to the club."*

Everything seemed very positive, but despite lengthy negotiations with various parties, including Scarborough Council, Caddick Developments and Persimmon Homes, no deal was finalised, and in April administrator Rob Sadler of Begbies Traynor started a petition to wind up the club when the CVA ran out and no deal to sell the ground and pay off the debts had been agreed.

Chairman Ian Scobbie said, " *I am very frustrated because we want to get the ground move sorted and pay off the debts. We have been trying to get this finalised for months, but I think the administrators have run out of patience with us, and are not prepared to wait much longer before serving us with a winding up order. This is our final warning, and it's now make or break time for Scarborough Football Club."* The winding up petition was presented to the High Court of Justice, Leeds, and a statement from Begbies Traynor read, *"The club has now been served with a compulsory winding up order after failing to meet the requirements of its Company Voluntary Arrangement (CVA). Two extensions had previously been agreed to the deadline, which is now conclusive. Despite the support given to the club by Scarborough Council, HM Revenue and Customs and others, many years of financial difficulties have finally caught up."*

Cllr Tom Fox, leader of Scarborough Council said, *"The situation is very, very sad. The Council has done as much as it could to help. We agreed in principle to lift the covenant on the McCain Stadium, and this opened up the possibility of the land being used for housing or other uses. We thought a formula had been worked out to help the club get round its problems. Although the crisis has reached its eleventh hour, we remain hopeful that the club may be able to secure some bridging finance to satisfy the administrator."*

Possible late escape routes for the club, could have been to persuade a developer to pay 'up front' for the McCain Stadium, to clear the existing debts, or perhaps find a rich benefactor who would be willing to take over the club, debts and all. The situation was now desperate, but a glimmer of hope emerged when local property developer Gary Ledden of Crown Properties entered into talks about a possible deal to buy the ground. Chairman Ian Scobbie announced, *"I can confirm that we have reached an agreement which will see the ground sold to a local property developer.*

"The terms of the agreement require the purchaser to pay a lump sum in advance, sufficient to pay off our creditors. A further sum would then be paid once planning has been obtained for the new ground at Eastfield, and the club will play, rent-free at the McCain Stadium in the interim." It seemed as if the club had been saved, but Gary Ledden then announced that he had pulled out of the deal, saying, *"Unfortunately, and despite our best endeavours, talks broke down, but I understand the football club has now entered into an agreement with another party, and I wish the club all the very best in securing its long term future."*

It was all very confusing, and by now the club had been relegated to the Unibond League. Once again former club chairman Don Robinson entered the debate, suggesting that the Council should tell the administrators that they would not lift the covenant limiting its use to sporting purposes, so it could not be sold for housing, thus considerably reducing its value. The Council could then offer to buy the stadium for £500,000, which would give creditors around 25p in the £1. He believed a new football company could then be formed, which would have to play at a lower level, perhaps the Northern Counties East League, and could rent the ground from the Council.

The town would still have a football stadium and a team, albeit at a lower level, and creditors would get a percentage of their money back. He suggested the newly formed club should have a shareholding of £100,000, and offered to invest a minimum of £50,000 in the club. However chairman Ian Scobbie dismissed these plans, saying, *"My priorities are to gain the best possible deal for creditors, deliver the best possible stadium for the fans and reach a break-even situation financially. None of Mr Robinson's suggestions would achieve those aims."* Meanwhile, a district judge at Leeds High Court on 12 June gave the club until 20 June to secure a last minute deal to pay creditors, before proceeding with the winding up order.

It was revealed that the club's major creditors were the Inland Revenue, owed £1.26 million and HSBC, owed £850,000, with a further £100,000 owed to various other creditors.

Scarborough Council indicated they may be prepared to exercise their right to buy back the stadium (the covenant included a clause giving the Council first option on buying back the ground), and Council leader Tom Fox said, *"The Council has worked very closely with the football club to try to find a solution to their problems, but all the proposals they have brought before us did not satisfy the conditions required by us, with regards to securing the development of sport, and building a new stadium, whilst also relieving the club of its debts."*

Meanwhile, with the demise of the club almost inevitable, plans were in place to enter a new Scarborough team in the Northern Counties East League for next season, should the club be liquidated. Just as all options seemed to have failed, the club came up with a plan for developers to pay £2 million for the McCain Stadium, and also build a new ground at George Pindar Community Sports College at Eastfield. In a joint proposal between the football club and Pindar head teacher, Hugh Bellamy, after an emergency meeting of the school's governors, Council was asked to lift the covenant to allow an un-named developer to purchase the site for building purposes.

However, Council members felt there were too many unanswered questions, including whether North Yorkshire County Council, who owned the land, would give their approval, and who would own the new stadium when it was built. Council decided more time was needed to explore the proposal in full, and it was agreed that the matter be discussed at the next full cabinet meeting on 9 July. Chairman Scobbie added, *"I've done all I can, it's now down to the judge, I will ask for more time, but if that request is not granted, there will be no competitive football played by Scarborough FC next season."*

At Leeds High Court on 20 June, Ian Scobbie told the hearing to discuss the winding up petition, *"I am convinced that this latest proposal can work, and the football club can continue to play its role in the hub of the community. I appeal that this hearing be adjourned again until 10 July."*

Judge Stephen Greenwood rejected this appeal, stating that Mr Scobbie had been unable to convince him that a further stay of execution would save the club. He added, *"There is nothing in my view to suggest that another CVA should be approved, or would be successful. The various rescue attempts have all failed, and I wind Scarborough Football Club up."* Supporters Club chairman Stuart Canvin was distraught at the news, saying, *"Watching 128 years of history just slip away like this is terrible. All the hard work that has been done over the years is now for nothing. I am devastated."*

Stunned Boro chairman Ian Scobbie, who had worked so hard to save the club said, *"I'm so disappointed at the way things have turned out. I feel that, if the club had survived, we would have challenged for the Unibond premier division title next season. We had a very experienced manager lined up and a good sponsorship deal in place, which would have allowed us to pay up to £6000 per week on players wages. But the Council made their U-turn after agreeing to lift the covenant, and now the club has died."*

Tom Fox, leader of Scarborough Council revealed why the Pindar deal had not been approved, saying, *"We rejected the deal because it would have meant the Council lifting the covenant and also giving up its right of first refusal on buying the ground, without any guarantee that a new stadium would ever be built, or that the creditors would be paid."*

After 128 years of history and tradition, the club was now dead, although the new fans-run club was accepted into membership of the Northern Counties East League for the next season, after securing an agreement to groundshare 17 miles down the coast at Bridlington Town FC. Ironically, while Boro had been teetering along on the brink of oblivion, former club chairman John Russell was being sentenced to a 21-month prison term after being convicted of fraudulent trading during his subsequent disastrous spell as chairman of Exeter City Football Club, whom he led to financial ruin and relegation to the Conference.

He left the club almost £4 million in debt, and the judge who sentenced him said he had obtained membership of the Exeter City board of directors by deception, by fraudulently claiming he had substantial funds to invest in the club. The debts which finally led to Boro's demise mainly originated from Russell's spell at the club, in particular the huge debt to HSBC, which he had arranged while chairman of the club.

After several years of big annual losses, the club actually broke even in its final season, and had been accepted into membership of the Unibond League premier division for the 2007-2008 campaign. Former Boro midfielder Harry 'A' Dunn, who had a successful managerial record with Whitby Town and Blyth Spartans, had agreed to become Boro manager, and the clubs FA Cup and FA Trophy entries had also been accepted. They were drawn away to Bradford Park Avenue in the FA Cup 1st qualifying round, and away to Kidsgrove Athletic or Chasetown in the FA Trophy 1st qualifying round, but of course these matches were never played, as Scarborough Football Club ceased to exist. But, moves were afoot to form a new club to take their place......

R.I.P. Scarborough Football Club
1879 ~ 2007

Athletic are born, but fans are divided.

With Boro's demise looking inevitable unless the club could agree a plan to sell the stadium, settle the debts and build a new ground, the Seadog Trust had formulated a 'Plan B' to secure the future of senior football in Scarborough. Talks had been held to try to secure a groundshare arrangement at either Bridlington, Pickering or Whitby and a business plan was drawn up. Scarborough Council was informed of these plans and an enquiry made to the Northern Counties East League about the possibility of any new club being elected into membership for next season. The Trust decided that, should Boro fold and the plan be implemented, then the new club would be called Scarborough Athletic. Meanwhile, club chairman Ian Scobbie had also approached the NCEL about entering a new club which would initially groundshare at Bridlington Town, and on 11 June 2007 the League released the following press statement

"The League has been approached by two different entities representing Scarborough Football Club, namely AFC Scarborough, by club chairman Ian Scobbie, and Scarborough Athletic, by the Seadog Trust, representing the supporters club trust. These enquiries were communicated to our clubs at the League's AGM on Sunday, 10 June and their views obtained. The clubs were prepared to accept a Scarborough club into Division One as a late applicant - a Premier Division place was not available. It will be necessary for interested parties in Scarborough to organise one club application, which will then be vetted by the NCEL board to ensure adequate governance in all aspects of club management, and will have to receive County FA/FA approval. June 24th (14 days after the AGM) is the final date for our consideration of acceptance."

Scarborough Football Club was formally liquidated at Leeds High Court on 20 June 2007 with debts of £2.1 million plus a further £400,000 in administration charges. With the deadline for getting any new club entered into the Northern Counties East League fast approaching, Boro chairman Ian Scobbie decided not to proceed with his plan to form a new club, leaving the way open for Scarborough Athletic to be accepted into membership of the NCEL following a meeting at Bridlington Town's Queensgate ground on 24 June, attended by League president Frank Catt and secretary Tom Dixon. Ian Scobbie said, *"I agreed not to proceed with my application, though I did have some reservations. The Trust were not prepared to pull out and that would have meant no club. I was worried about the Trust's plans to return to the Borough of Scarborough, and also whether they may sell out to a company or businessman, but I wasn't prepared to see the town without a club next season."*

A meeting of the Trust committee took place at Falsgrave Community Centre on 26 June, also attended by Stuart Canvin, Wendy Danby and Andy Standing of the Supporters Club and Bridlington Town FC chairman Peter Smurthwaite and secretary Gavin Brampton. Terms of the groundshare at Bridlington's Queensgate ground were finalised, with the rent being £100 per home match. Subsequent meetings were held fortnightly as the new club began to take shape. The Trust committee members formed the Scarborough Athletic board of directors, with John Clarke named as secretary. Experienced, former North Ferriby United boss Brian France was appointed team manager, assisted by his son Darren, a former Hull City and Doncaster Rovers striker, with ex Boro player and Driffield Town manager Derek Exley brought in to help with coaching.

Admission charges for home matches were set at £5 adults, £2 concessions, with adult season tickets priced at £70. A double decker bus would be laid on to transport supporters the 17-miles to Bridlington for "home" matches and the club bought the new kit that the Supporters Club had organised for the old club to wear in the Unibond League next season. A vote of fans agreed that Scarborough Athletic would adopt the old club's badge, motto and nickname, and it was agreed that a new Supporters Club would be set up following the demise of the old one when Boro had gone into liquidation. The club held an open trials day at Pindar Leisure Centre, on Saturday, 7 July, with more than 80 players taking part, hoping to impress watching manager Brian France.

Trust chairman Simon Cope, who now became chairman of the club said, *"We need to get plans in place to move back to Scarborough as quickly as possible. If we don't, then the club could begin to wither and die. Maidstone United spent nine years in the wilderness of different towns until they finally found a new home stadium in their own town, and that is something we must avoid."* At a Trust board meeting on 18 July 2007 it was announced that £2140 in season ticket sales had been received to date, and the club was planning to organise merchandise as well as seeking volunteers to assist with manning turnstiles and stewarding at home matches.

However, not all Boro supporters were behind the new club, including many people previously associated with the old club and Supporters Club, who felt strongly that the Trust had in some way played a part in the club's demise. Some were highly critical of the Trust's refusal to assist Boro financially, and others felt the Trust had actively opposed Ian Scobbie's plans to get the Council to lift the restrictive covenant on the McCain Stadium, so that it could be sold for housing, enabling Boro to pay off their debts and build a new ground at Eastfield. A group of former Boro followers, who did not back Scarborough Athletic, were instrumental in helping the Scarborough FC School of Excellence become integrated into the expanded George Pindar Community Sports College at Eastfield. All the academy teams as well as the Under-19's side became affiliated to the Pindar College, which was backed by Sheffield United Football Club, and former Director of the School of Excellence Mitch Cook continued in the role at Pindar.

Despite some Boro fans opposing the new club, Scarborough Athletic's planning for their debut season in the Northern Counties East League first division continued, and at a board meeting on 30 July it was announced that only players who play or are named as substitutes would be paid. Five ground advertising boards and seven pages of programme advertising had been sold by that time, and the Trust had £16,500 in the bank.

By 10 August the Trust had over 450 paid up members, but there were still critics who accused those behind the setting up of the Trust, of playing a part in Boro's demise. Chairman Simon Cope refuted these allegations saying, *"I appreciate that a lot of people are looking to blame someone or some organisation for the old clubs demise, so they can point a finger and say, it was their fault. But the situation at Scarborough FC was very complex, and I don't think any one person was to blame. Fundamentally the problems the club faced were financial ones, accrued over a period of time, starting when John Russell borrowed £800,000 from HSBC. The club failed to deal with this debt over the intervening years, and instead of putting in place proper business plans incorporating a strategy of repayments, it allowed the debt to balloon to £2.5 million. That is the reason Scarborough FC died, not because of anything the Trust did, or didn't do."*

While Scarborough Athletic prepared for their debut season in the Northern Counties East League, ambitious plans were being revealed for a £2.5 million centre of sporting excellence to be built at Cayton Low Road in Eastfield, in a joint three-way project between George Pindar

Community Sports College, local print firm The Pindar Group, and Sheffield United Football Club. Plans drawn up included a full size football pitch, running track, large seated grandstand and spacious car park. At the same time as these plans were made public, Scarborough Council announced that it was in negotiations to buy the McCain Stadium from the administrators, and there were hopes that Scarborough Athletic could then play home matches there, until the new facilities at Eastfield were built, when the Council would then lift the covenant on the Seamer Road site, and sell it for housing or retail use.

At a Trust board meeting on 16 August 2007, it was announced that 90 season tickets had been sold, replica shirts were selling well, and the club had £21,000 in the bank. By the time the season kicked-off, more than 100 season tickers had been snapped up, and a new Supporters Club had been launched, with the following committee members, Craig Patton (chairman), Roy Dove (secretary), Joy Collier (treasurer), Mark Chamberlain, Jamie Daniel, Grace Haigh, Becky Powell and Lyn Powell, while former long serving Scarborough FC director John Fawcett accepted an invitation to become club president.

Season 2007-08 Scarborough Athletic begin life in the Northern Counties East League.

The newly formed Scarborough Athletic played seven pre-season friendlies as they prepared for life in the NCEL first division. Manager Brian France had gathered together a large squad, the majority of whom were from the Humberside area, where he lived, though several Scarborough based players had also joined the club. The club's first ever fixture was a goalless draw against Scarborough & District League champions Edgehill on 15 July, while the first goal for the club was scored by 20-year-old striker Shaun Chadburn in a 2-2 draw at Northallerton Town three days later.

The league campaign kicked-off on Saturday, 11 August, with an away match against Nottinghamshire side Teversal. More than 300 Boro fans travelled to the game, many dressed in suits, to celebrate their status as 'owners of the club'. After going a goal down after just ten minutes, Scarborough based midfielder Dave Thompson equalised five minutes into the second half, only for Teversal to snatch an 89th minute winner.

The following Saturday the club achieved their first win, with a convincing 4-1 away defeat of Leeds Metropolitan Carnegie, but then came a disappointing 1-0 extra time defeat at home to Rainworth Miners Welfare in the Wilkinson Sword Trophy. On 25 August a crowd of 591 gathered at Queensgate for Boro's first home league fixture, but a woeful display saw the team crash to an embarrassing 6-2 defeat.

Manager Brian France was gradually evolving his squad, as several players came and went in the early part of the season. Pontefract Collieries put Boro out of the League Cup after a penalty shoot-out, but there were successive league wins, 3-2 away to AFC Emley, with former Edgehill FC midfielder Gary Hepples outstanding, and 4-0 at home to Worsbrough Bridge, with Scott Phillips scoring twice. Despite the 34-mile round trip for home games, and the four division drop in status since the previous season, the level of support was excellent, with regular away followings in excess of 200, and home gates averaging more than 400 - crowds which were unheard of in the Northern Counties East League.

A 2-2 home draw against Tadcaster Albion on 6 October attracted a crowd of 486, and the following week Boro won 2-0 at Kirkbymoorside in the North Riding Senior Cup, watched by a ground record attendance of 317.

Meanwhile, administrators Begbies Traynor had put the McCain Stadium up for sale, and Scarborough Council was given first refusal on the ground, as other fixtures and fittings from the stadium, including floodlights, seats, groundsman's equipment, office furniture and club memorabilia were all put up for auction. There was also talk of Sheffield United FC buying the stadium to use as a base for their academy.

Hopes of the club achieving promotion in their first season were dashed when they were fined £300 and deducted six points by the League on 23 October for fielding three ineligible players, Joe Lightowler, Craig Hogg and Darren Phillips, while they were suspended by the East Riding County FA. News of their suspensions had not been passed on to the North Riding FA, and the players did not inform the club. Boro chairman Simon Cope said, *"Clubs are supposed to be informed of any existing or impending suspensions, so we will definitely be appealing against the decision, because we don't feel as though we have done anything wrong."* An appeal was launched, but was rejected by the FA.

A 3-0 home win against Yorkshire Amateur set off a 5-match winning run, in which 19-year-old midfielder Scott Phillips scored seven goals. He was the son of 38-year- old former North Ferriby defender Darren Phillips who played three games at the start of the season, and father and son played together in two of those games.

Ex-Scarborough FC striker Ryan Blott joined the club, and soon became a prolific scorer, including getting two in a 4-0 North Riding Senior Cup win against Fishburn Park. The loss of those six points meant Boro were unable to get into the promotion places, but they played some entertaining football and recorded a number of very good wins, including a 3-1 away success over Rainworth Miners Welfare, with Richard Medcalf scoring twice and Ryan Blott getting the other.

There was a sad event on 5 February, when Boro's number one supporter Bernard Newby passed away, aged 83. He had started following the club in 1935 and hardly missed a home match until the club's demise in 2007. He then began watching Athletic, before illness prevented him from travelling to Bridlington.

After going down 2-0 at home to York City watched by 505 fans in the North Riding Senior Cup semi-finals, Boro were unbeaten in their final ten matches of the season, picking up some impressive victories, including 5-0 away to Yorkshire Amateur and 4-1 at home to Gedling Town. On 24 March they romped to an 8-0 win against Borrowash Victoria, with Ryan Blott contributing a hat trick and the season was rounded-off with a 2-1 home victory over Staveley MW, with Graham Botham and Ryan Blott scoring the goals, watched by a crowd of 496.

Boro ended their debut campaign in 5th position in the NCEL first division, and had average home league gates of 485. No fewer than 36 different players were used during the course of the season, but as the season had drawn to a close, the makings of a very good team was starting to emerge. Skilful former Hall Road Rangers midfielder Scott Phillips won the player of the year award, and others to impress included ex North Ferriby midfielder Liam Widdowson, ex Hutton Cranswick keeper Dave Bramley, defender Dave Kemp, who had been plucked from local football in Hull, ex North Ferriby winger Mark Griffin and powerful centre-back Jamie Waltham, another former North Ferriby player. The pick of the local based players were former Edgehill duo Dave Thompson and Gary Hepples. At the end of the season, manager Brian France signed a new two year contract, and promised a determined push for promotion the next season.

As the season drew to a close, concern was expressed at the dilapidated state of the McCain Stadium, which had stood empty since the old club's demise. Administrators Begbies Traynor had applied for the restrictive covenant on the stadium to be lifted on 15 October 2007, so that they could sell the site for building purposes and pay off the creditors. However, the Council was concerned that the ground was being allowed to fall into a state of disrepair and Council leader Tom Fox said, *"The covenant requires whoever has responsibility for the ground to keep it in good order as a football ground or sporting facility."* Many football supporters had suspicions that the ground was deliberately being allowed to deteriorate, in order for it to be less likely to remain as a viable football stadium.

Scarborough Council announced in April that they were keen to buy the McCain Stadium, which could either be returned to use as a football ground or developed for housing, with a new stadium to be built elsewhere in the town. Sheffield United FC were still interested in buying the site, and a number of property developers were also keen to acquire the stadium for building purposes. So while the situation regarding the ground remained in doubt, Boro were already committed to playing at Bridlington for another season. Elsewhere though, there was news of another new club for Scarborough.

Not all followers of Scarborough Football Club had become fans of the new Scarborough Athletic FC when Boro folded in June 2007. Several people formerly associated with the old club, including president John Birley, secretary Derek Megginson and associate directors Tony Scott and Tony Stockdale, plus leading members of the Supporters Club had switched their allegiances to the club's School of Excellence, which had transferred its operations to the George Pindar Community Sports College at Eastfield. Former Boro player and the Director of the School of Excellence, Mitch Cook, along with the centre's coaches including Bob MacDonald and Keith Fletcher, had carried on their work at the new venue, and an Under-19's team had competed in the Northern Youth Alliance, playing home matches under the floodlights at Pickering Town FC.

At the end of the season it was announced that a new club, Scarborough Town FC was to be formed, as an expansion of the School of Excellence, to give the players who had progressed through the junior ranks, an outlet into senior football. Scarborough Town would be managed by the vastly experienced Mitch Cook, and had applied to join the Teesside League for the following season, initially playing their home matches at the McCains Sports & Social Ground in Cayton.

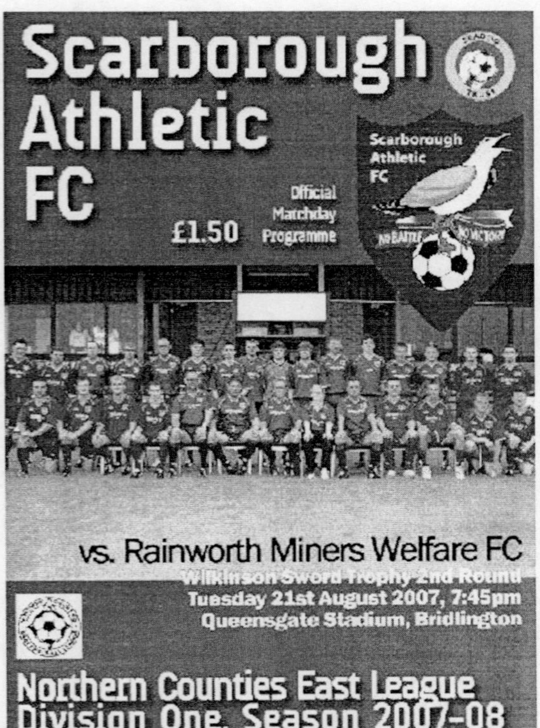

The first home game.

Northern Counties East League Div 1, Saturday, 17 November 2007
SCARBOROUGH ATHLETIC 4 ROSSINGTON MAIN 0

After a slow start to the season Boro had started to hit a run of form, and they went into this match with four successive wins behind them, in which 14 goals had been scored and only two conceded. They were 4th in the table, just six points behind top side Gedling Town, and manager Brian France was hoping for a quick double over visitors Rossington Main, following Boro's 5-1 away victory the previous Saturday. Boro were at full strength, and looking for another comfortable win against their bottom of the table visitors, who had only picked up two points from 10 league matches to date.

Boro dominated from the start, but missed a hatful of chances and also found Rossington keeper Tim Whitehouse in terrific form. Jamie Waltham had a powerful header well saved by Whitehouse, and also grazed the post with another header, and the keeper also produced fine saves to deny Ryan Blott, Richard Medcalf and Scott Phillips, while Phillips also had a shot strike the crossbar. In the visitor's best moment, Boro keeper Dave Bramley produced a double save to foil player-manager Ian Dring. On the stroke of half-time Rossington were reduced to ten men when defender Nathan Hill was sent off for appearing to head butt Mark Griffin. Boro ran riot after the interval, scoring four goals without reply. Ryan Blott drilled home the opener on 50 minutes, Richard Medcalf doubled the lead after 67 minutes and Ryan Blott added his second just two minutes later. Blott was brought down in the 70th minute, and Scott Phillips stroked home the spot kick to complete the scoring, and Blott, Medcalf and Phillips were all thwarted by the keeper near the end as Boro coasted to an easy win.

Scarborough Athletic Dave Bramley, Dave Kemp, Jamie Waltham, Carl Wood (Craig Evans 75), Mark Griffin, Scott Phillips, Gary Hepples, Liam Widdowson (Tom Barker 76), Graham Botham, Ryan Blott, Craig Hogg (Richard Medcalf 21)
Rossington Main Tim Whitehouse, Jordan Pickering, Brady Roberts, John Billups, Nathan Hill, Scott Jones, Jason Stokes, Craig Morton, Bradley Billam, Ian Dring (Jonathan Cook 50), Lee Holmes
Referee Simon Hunter (Sheffield) *Attendance 493*

Dave Thompson celebrates scoring Athletic's first ever league goal, at Teversal.

Northern Counties East League Div 1, Saturday, 15 March 2008
SCARBOROUGH ATHLETIC 4 GEDLING TOWN 1

The six point deduction for fielding three ineligible players had put a severe dent in Boro's promotion hopes and they had slipped to 8th in the table, despite picking up 13 points from their previous five matches. Visitor's Gedling however, were 2nd in the table, some 14 points adrift of runaway leaders Dinnington Town. Boro welcomed back skipper Jamie Waltham, after a 5-match suspension, and winger Ryan Morton, after a groin strain, but midfielder Dave Thompson was missing after picking up a knee injury in the 1-0 win at Tadcaster Albion in midweek.

Boro produced an outstanding team performance to thoroughly outclass the Nottinghamshire side, and get their promotion challenge back on track. After Jamie Waltham twice went close with headers, Boro opened the scoring on 8 minutes when Ryan Blott's shot was saved by keeper Louis Spriggs, only for Mark Griffin to slam home the rebound. Several more chances were created, with Morton, Medcalf and Phillips all going close, before Ryan Blott netted on the stroke of half-time, following a flick-on by Richard Medcalf. Scott Phillips was denied by a wonderful point-blank save early in the second half, before Ryan Blott converted a Medcalf cross, to fire Boro into a 3-0 lead on 61 minutes. Alan Jeffries pulled a goal back for Gedling with ten minutes to play, but Scott Phillips volleyed Boro's fourth goal in the 89th minute, and in stoppage time Gedling's player manager John Humphries was sent off for foul and abusive language.

Scarborough Athletic Dave Bramley, Carl Wood (Kevin Milner 70), Dave Kemp, Jamie Waltham, Liam Widdowson, Graham Botham, Mark Griffin, Scott Phillips, Ryan Blott, Richard Medcalf (Craig Hogg 73), Ryan Morton (Gary Hepples 55)
Gedling Town Louis Spriggs, Luke Humphries, Luke Smith, Lee Soar, Simon Labatte (Ashleigh Murdoch 28), Barry Payne (John Humphries 66), Damian Magee, Jimmy Spiers, Glyn Cotton, Alan Jeffries, Andrew Jones
Referee Jeremy Hyke (Scunthorpe) *Attendance 446*

Ryan Blott jumps for the ball vs. Dinnington Town, 6 April 2008

(Right) Athletic manager Brian France.

(Below) Boro Fans show their support.

[redacted]

Boss Brian France kept the majority of the last season's squad and brought in a handful of new signings, the pick of whom were former Whitby Town centre-back Dave Hartas and ex Tadcaster Albion midfielder Rob Ellis. A poor pre-season record of just one win in six games was followed by a slow start to the league campaign, as Boro drew 2-2 at home to Askern Villa and then conceded an 88th minute goal to go down 1-0 at Rainworth Miners Welfare. From then on however, the team suddenly clicked into gear, and went on a surging run of 13 wins and two draws in the next 15 matches to storm to the top of the table. Also included in that run were wins in three cup competitions, including a 7-1 away success over Bottesford Town in the President's Cup on 8 October, with Danny Gray scoring a hat trick. This result was bettered just six days later when Tadcaster Albion were thrashed 7-0 in the league. 17-year-old former England schoolboys captain Rob Hoyle made his debut in a 4-0 win at Staveley, and he went on to enjoy a magnificent season at full back.

In October the club announced that four former "Greats"of Scarborough FC's past had all accepted invitations to become honorary life members of Scarborough Athletic FC. Past managers Colin Appleton and Neil Warnock, and popular players Harry Dunn and Jeff Barmby were the quartet, and a club statement re"d, *"Each honorary life member will receive free entry to matches with hospitality, a certificate, and, when the club returns to Scarborough, recognition on a plaque in the clubhouse".*

The club made its debut in the FA Vase, and progressed through two rounds with wins in the North East against Birtley Town and Esh Winning, with over 200 fans travelling to support the team on both occasions.

After successive six-goal hauls, against Teversal and Yorkshire Amateur, there was a blip when Askern Villa won 2-1 in the League Cup to end Boro's unbeaten run. The team was playing some wonderful attacking football and goals were abundant. Ryan Blott struck a hat trick in a 4-1 win at Rossington Main, and hit five in the 6-1 away success over Yorkshire Amateur. Even defender Graham Botham grabbed a hat trick, including two direct from free kicks, in a 4-0 defeat of AFC Emley.

On 16 November a Queensgate crowd of 664 saw Boro win a thrilling FA Vase second round tie 3-2 against Northern League side Sunderland Nisson, with Craig Hogg scoring the winner in extra time. Three successive 6-1 wins followed a North Riding Senior Cup exit to Stokesley Sports Club, as AFC Emley and Appleby Frodingham were routed in the league, and Blackstones were crushed in the FA Vase third round. Next came a hard fought 2-0 away win against title rivals Pontefract Collieries, with strikes by Ryan Blott and Richard Medcalf, to send Boro five points clear at the top of the table, with two games in hand on the nearest challengers.

The next two matches brought yet another 6-1 win, this time against Barton Town Old Boys (hat trick for Blott), followed by a 3-0 away victory over Askern Villa. Ryan Blott was in sensational scoring form, and his two goals at Askern made it 12 goals in a run of six consecutive matches and 31 for the season thus far. On 3 January it needed an 89th minute Craig Hogg strike to secure a 1-0 home win against Rainworth Miners Welfare, and this was followed by a 1-0 defeat down in Devon against Bideford in the FA Vase fourth round, when more than 350 Boro supporters made the marathon 700 mile round trip.

After the disappointment of going out of the Vase, Boro soon got their NCEL first division promotion push on track, winning the next five matches, including a 5-3 home win against Glasshoughton Welfare (another Blott hat trick), and a 6-0 romp over Bottesford Town, when Danny Gray scored twice. Boro were now 11 points clear of nearest challengers Askern Villa at the top of the table, and also had two matches in hand.

On Tuesday, 3 March they entertained local rivals Pickering Town who were riding high in the NCEL premier division, in the quarter-finals of the President's Cup. A close match was expected, but Boro turned in a sensational display to thrash their higher ranked opponents 7-1, with both Ryan Blott and Craig Hogg scoring twice. Then it was back to league action, and a 3-1 away win against Hemsworth Miners Welfare. But the run of 15 successive league wins was halted when Boro were held to a 2-2 draw at Grimsby Borough on 11 March. Worsbrough Bridge were beaten 5-0 in the next game, but then the team suffered only their second league defeat of the season, when they went down 2-1 at Barton Town Old Boys. However, just four days later Boro travelled to Teversal, knowing a win would assure them of promotion, and despite trailing at the interval, they rallied to win 2-1 with two goals from Rob Ellis, to spark wild celebrations amongst the 250 fans who had made the trip to cheer them on.

Club Officials 2008-2009
President- John Fawcett
Chairman- Simon Cope
Vice-Chairman- Kevin Smith
Finance Director- Sandra Troughton
Directors- James Hunter, Wendy Danby, Dave Holland, Andy Troughton, Natalie Davies, Tony Brown, Richard Adamson
Secretary- John Clarke
Manager- Brian France
Assistant Manager- Darren France
First Team Coach- Derek Exley
Reserve Team Manager- Jimmy Reid
Reserve Team Coach- Andy Dorsey
Physios- Brian Waltham, Karen Hankey
Life Members- Colin Appleton, Harry Dunn, Neil Warnock, Jeff Barmby

Now that promotion had been secured, just three more points were needed to clinch the first division championship, and these were obtained when Brighouse Town were then beaten 3-0 at Queensgate, with Rob Ellis, Danny Gray and Dave Hartas scoring the title clinching goals, to set off yet more scenes of jubilation at the end of the game. The following two matches saw Boro achieve another two comfortable home wins, 6-0 against Yorkshire Amateur in the league, and 4-1 against Hall Road Rangers in the semi-finals of the President's Cup. Boro concluded their fantastic league campaign with a 0-0 home draw against Leeds Carnegie, when a record crowd of 791 gathered to watch the championship presentation and a 2-0 win at Appleby Frodingham.

But hopes of a league and cup double were dashed, when premier division side Nostell Miners Welfare snatched a 3-2 aggregate win in the President's Cup final, as Boro drew the away leg 1-1, but then slipped up in the home leg, going down 2-1, with Danny Gray notching both Boro goals in the final. Ryan Blott ended the campaign with 42 goals, while centre-back Dave Hartas played in 50 of the team's 51 matches and won the player of year award. A reserve side, managed by former Pickering Town boss Jimmy Reid competed in the Humber Premier League first division, playing home games at Hutton Cranswick. Their best result of the season was an 11-0 success against Long Riston, with striker Paul Routledge scoring five of the goals, while Michael Flinders top scored for the reserves with 15 goals during the season.

Looking back over the campaign, happy Boro boss Brian France said, *"It was a fantastic season, and winning the league was obviously brilliant for the club. We were a little disappointed not to add the President's Cup to our trophy cabinet as well, but we just didn't perform in the 2nd leg of the final against Nostell.*

"There will be no relaxing for us now though, we will be keeping ourselves very busy over the Summer as we prepare for the premier division next season.. I would like to say a big thank you to everyone who has helped me this season, especially my backroom staff of Darren France, Derek Exley, Karen Hankey, Brian Waltham and Stuart Dawes. Thanks also to the wonderful hordes of supporters who follow us everywhere, your loyal support never ceases to amaze me."

Supporters Club Officials
Chairman- Craig Patton
Vice-Chairman- Mark Hobson
Treasurer- Joy Collier
Secretary- Becky Powell
Committee- Sharon Hunter, Lyn Powell, Roy Dove, Grace Haigh, Mike Price, Sally Elwick, Ken Pattison

Northern Counties East League Div 1, Saturday, 8 November 2008
YORKSHIRE AMATEUR 1 SCARBOROUGH ATHLETIC 6

Boro had made a blistering start to the league campaign, winning 10 of their opening 14 matches to storm clear at the top of the table, while hosts Yorkshire Amateur were in 13th position with 14 points from 13 matches. Boss Brian France was without defenders Carl Wood, with a knee injury and England Under-18's star Rob Hoyle, with a foot injury, although Jamie Waltham was back in the side after recovering from his foot injury. Boro were full of confidence after thrashing Teversal 6-0 the previous Saturday, but it was just 3 weeks since they had suffered a shock 2-0 defeat against Yorkshire Amateur in a Wilkinson Sword Trophy tie. More than 180 Boro fans made the trip to Leeds, and they witnessed another scintillating performance, with ace marksman Ryan Blott scoring five times as Boro strolled to an easy win.

Blott opened the scoring after 16 minutes, taking a pass from Dave Kemp, and rounding the keeper before tapping home. The home side were level just nine minutes later when Paddy Miller scored from the penalty spot after a foul by Dave Kemp, but on 31 minutes Boro were then awarded a penalty when Simon Kirsima handled a goal-bound shot from Dave Thompson and Scott Phippips scored from the spot while Kirsima received a red card. The ten men were over-run in the second half, with Ryan Blott heading in a Dave Thompson cross to make it 3-1 five minutes after the interval. Blott then completed his hat trick on 57 minutes, sliding a low cross from Thompson into the net. Boro keeper Arran Reid saved well to deny Adam Ryder, before Blott made it 5-1, converting a Graham Botham pass after 80 minutes. Blott then completed the rout in the last minute, curling a free kick into the top corner after a foul on Mark Griffin.

Yorkshire Amateur John Gardiner, Michael Nelson, Adam Ryder, Richard Gaffey (Ajmal Arbrar 72), Jamie Hainsworth, Liam McCarthy, Simon Kirsima, Alex Wilson (Lewis Hindley 72), Patrick Miller, Allan Laud (Joe Barber 62), Daz Brown
Scarborough Athletic Arran Reid, Dave Hartas, Dave Kemp, Jamie Waltham, Rob Ellis, Dave Thompson (Mark Griffin 60), Joel Hartley, Scott Phillips (Gary Hepples 62), Ryan Blott, Rich Medcalf (Danny Gray 58), Graham Botham
Referee S. Holroyd (Sheffield) *Attendance 220*

Northern Counties East League Div 1, Tuesday, 24 March 2009
SCARBOROUGH ATHLETIC 3 BRIGHOUSE TOWN 0

Having secured promotion with a 2-1 away success over Teversal at the weekend, Boro now needed a win against midtable Brighouse to clinch the championship. Looking ahead to the game, chairman Simon Cope said, "Tonight is an historic occasion in the club's short history. As well as a time for a huge celebration of our achievements this season, it's also a time to look to the future, and realise the potential that football in Scarborough has." Manager Brian France made a few changes from the side that had won at Teversal, with Scott Phillips and Mark Griffin dropping to the bench, and Danny Gray partnering Ryan Blott up front, while Joel Hartley missed the game through injury. Visitors Brighouse had won 1-0 at bottom side Glasshoughton on the Saturday.

The game got off to a sensational start, with Rob Ellis heading in a Graham Botham corner to open the scoring after just 45 seconds. Arran Reid pulled off a good save from Wayne Crossley soon after, but Boro then took control of the game and in a frantic goalmouth scramble, Blott, Hogg and Thompson all had shots blocked. Danny Gray rose to head home a cross from Ryan Blott to double the lead on 30 minutes, then Craig Hogg twice shot narrowly wide as the pressure mounted on the Brighouse goal. In the second half, Blott, Ellis and Hepples all went close but the only goal came on the hour, when a Botham corner was flicked-on by Rob Ellis, for Dave Hartas to head in at the far post. At the final whistle dozens of fans swarmed onto the pitch to join the players in celebrating the title success.

Scarborough Athletic Arran Reid, Rob Hoyle (Dave Kemp 65), Graham Botham, Dave Hartas, Jamie Waltham, Rob Ellis (Scott Phillips 67), Dave Thompson, Gary Hepples, Ryan Blott, Danny Gray, Craig Hogg (Mark Griffin 46)
Brighouse Town Paul Brown, Jamie Fradgley, Danny Ryan, Ryan Brook, Tony Nicholson (Damian Gomersall 67), Danny Bentley (Calum Rodgers 63), Sam Talbot (David Phelps 61), Mark Brady, Wayne Crossley, Joe Pinnock, Avron Noel
Referee J. Waters (South Yorkshire) *Attendance 533*

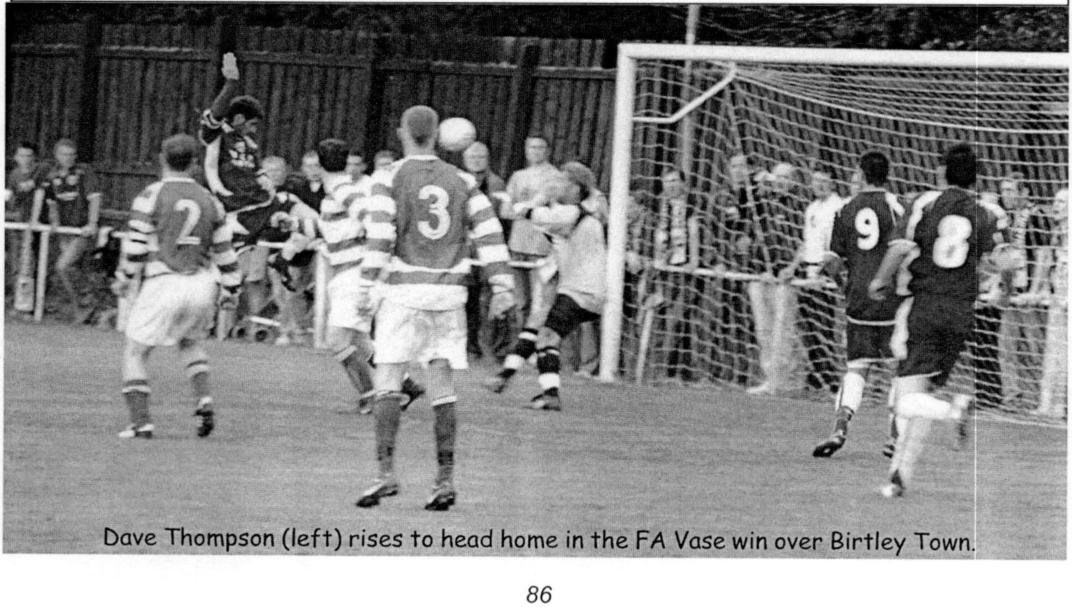

Dave Thompson (left) rises to head home in the FA Vase win over Birtley Town.

Ellis' second goal at Teversal that confirmed promotion....

.....Fans and players celebrate.

A group of Boro fans gather beneath the Angel of the North, before the FA Vase tie against Birtley Town.

The final icing on the cake....

A draw at home to Leeds Carnegie ensures the championship. Skipper Graham Botham lifts the trpohy, and once again there is more for the supporters to cheer!

Season 2008-09 New club, Town, stroll to Teeside League second division title.

Scarborough Town FC Officials

President- John Birley
Vice-presidents- Tony Stockdale, Rod Robinson
Chairman- Hugh Bellamy
Vice-chairman- Nigel Wood
Director of Football- Mitch Cook
Secretary- Sean Hunter
Treasurer- Dave Metcalf
Committee- Derek Megginson, Stuart Canvin, Steve Colley, Gavin Barker, Karola Powell

Scarborough Town had been elected to membership of the Teesside League Second Division, to become the first Scarborough club to play in the league since Eastfield left to return to local league football in 1991. The club was an extension of the highly acclaimed School of Excellence, which had become affiliated to the George Pindar Community Sports College after the demise of Scarborough FC in June 2007. The club began the season playing home matches at the McCains Sports & Social Club in Cayton, but soon moved to the Pindar School site, where they had plans to develop an enclosed stadium, boasting floodlights and a seated stand.

The club began their debut season with a squad of talented, young local players, the vast majority of whom had progressed through the School of Excellence ranks, and many of those who started the campaign had played for the Under-19's team in the Northern Youth Alliance, under coach Bob MacDonald last season. It was a young team, although experienced former Scarborough FC midfielder Marcus Jones had a brief spell as player-coach early in the season. Some local football followers expressed concern about a second club being formed after the old club's demise, but club president John Birley, who had previously held a similar position with Scarborough FC for almost 20 years said, *"We don't want to be in competition with Scarborough Athletic at all, but just want to have a senior team playing here in Scarborough. There are some people who may not want to go out of town to watch their local team, and this gives them the option to do that."*

At a Scarborough Athletic FC fans forum at the Conservative Club in July, Scarborough Town chairman Hugh Bellamy was a guest speaker, and gave further assurances that the new club had not been set up to compete with Athleic. He stated, *"We have formed Scarborough Town as a next step up for the Under-19's players, and we will be working with them to allow them to move on to the highest level they possibly can. We are a nursery club and are not trying to rival Scarborough Athletic."* The club chose red and white stripes as their colours, and raffle tickets, match programmes and a bucket collection would be fund-raising methods used at home matches, with no admission charge to spectators.

After two very encouraging displays in pre-season matches, including a 3-1 defeat of Northern Counties East League club Hall Road Rangers, Town began their Teesside League campaign in emphatic style, with a 5-0 away success over Teesside Athletic Reserves, with Robbie Hawkes hitting a hat trick and Jamie Patterson scoring twice. Josh Greening, younger brother of West Brom star Jonathan, then netted in a 1-1 draw at Great Ayton United, and Greening then hit the winner in a 3-2 victory at Acklam Steelworks. A 2-2 draw at Redcar Rugby Club extended the unbeaten start. On 30 August the team played its first ever home fixture, when they ran out convincing 3-0 winners against Grangetown YCC watched by 223 spectators.

The team quickly became known for its entertaining brand of passing football, with emphasis on pace and skill, which some

Teesside second division sides couldnt cope with. South Bank St Peters were beaten 3-0 in the first round of the MacMillan Bowl (League Cup), and Whinney Banks YCC were thrashed 9-0 in the league, with Neil Thomas notching a hat trick. Town rose to the top of the table and also won two games in the Alex Burness Plate (Second Division Cup), including 10-0 against Great Ayton United, before the competition was abandoned when bad weather caused a fixture pile-up. Pacey winger Darren Clough netted twice in a 3-1 away win over South Bank St Peters, and Joel Ramm converted two spot kicks in a 5-1 home success over Billingham Kader. First division side Grangetown Boys Club ended the unbeaten record with a 2-1 North Riding Senior Cup win, but Town bounced back with some more big wins, including 7-2 against Guisborough Quoit in the MacMillan Bowl and 9-1 against Billingham Town Reserves in the league (with hat tricks for Neil Thomas and Darren Clough).

On 6 December fellow title challengers South Bank St Peters were brushed aside 4-0, and a 2-0 defeat of Great Ayton United in the next match took Town's record to 11 wins and 2 draws from 13 league games. A rare defeat came at the hands of top flight Nunthorpe Athletic in the MacMillan Bowl quarter-finals, but four straight league wins, including 5-1 against Coulby Newham and 3-0 against Acklam Steelworks left Town seven points clear at the top of the table and looking firm favourites to land the championship at their first attempt. Unfortunately the league was badly hit by the withdrawals of three teams from the second division during the season, as Billingham Kader, Billingham Town Reserves and Coble Ennis Square all pulled out, and their records were deleted.

Town failed to score in a match for the first time, when they were held to a goalless draw by Norton & Stockton Reserves on 21 March, but a week later they thrashed Grangetown YCC 7-0, with Wayne Brooksby and Joe Danby both scoring twice.

Two late goals secured a 3-1 home success over Teesside Athletic Reserves on 18 April, and a 2-0 away win against Whinney Banks YCC, with goals from Neil Thomas and Josh Greening all but secured the title for Town, as they were three points ahead of nearest rivals South Bank St Peters, with both sides having one match left to play; Town also had a hugely superior goal-difference. Town head coach Mitch Cook comented, *"We have all-but won the league now and the players have done superbly this season. They are all young, Scarborough lads who have gone into this league and given 100% every game. They have worked hard and gained their just reward, I am very proud of them all."*

The final match of the season, at home to Redcar Rugby Club turned into a real celebration, as Town romped to a record breaking 12-0 win as they outclassed their opponents with some breathtaking football. Neil Thomas struck a hat trick, but the most spectacular goal was a stunning 40-yard strike from Nathan Cook. After the match, Town skipper Georgie Rose received the championship trophy from Scarborough mayor, Councillor Eileen Vickers, while 19-year-old winger Wayne Brooksby was presented with the Scarborough Evening News Player of the Year trophy by sports editor, Charles Place. Two players, keeper Rob Clark and defender Dean Craig played in every match, and midfielder Jamie Patterson missed just one game during the season. Winger Darren Clough became the first Town player to join a higher club when he signed for NCEL club Pickering Town towards the end of the season.

Town became the first club to complete a Teesside League season with an unbeaten record for 26 years, since Nunthorpe Athletic in season 1982-83, and the team was clearly too good for that standard of football.

It had been a phenomenally successful campaign for the newly formed club, and as the season neared its climax, plans were announced for major ground improvements at the Pindar site, including the erection of floodlights, and an application was made for the club to join the Wearside League for the 2009-2010 campaign.

As well as the Teesside second division title success, the Under-19's side, under coach Bob MacDonald also enjoyed a terrific season, capturing the league and cup double in the Northern Youth Alliance. They finished six points clear of Pickering Town at the top of the East Division table, their best result being a 10-3 trouncing of Pontefract Collieries, with goals by Joe Danby 3, Adi Hammond 2, Josh Greening 2, Darren Clough 2 and Nathan Cook.

In the League Cup, wins over Hall Road Rangers 7-0, Selby Town 3-1, Bradford Park Avenue 5-2 and Farsley Celtic 7-1, secured the team a place in the final against Yorkshire Amateur at Liversedge FC on 26 April, when Darren Clough 2 and Nathan Cook (penalty) were on target in a 3-2 victory.

NorthernUnder-19'sAlliance(EastDivision)

	P	W	D	L	F	A	Pts
Scarborough	12	10	2	0	57	17	32
PickeringTown	12	8	2	2	30	13	26
SelbyTown	12	6	1	5	26	21	19
WhitbyTown	12	5	1	6	19	18	16
GlasshoughtonWel.	12	3	4	5	15	17	12
GooleAFC	12	1	4	7	12	22	6
PontefractCollieries	12	1	2	9	10	51	5

(Glasshoughton & Goole both deducted 1point)

Teesside League Division 2, Saturday, 30 August 2008
SCARBOROUGH TOWN 3 GRANGETOWN YCC 0

Having started their debut campaign with a run of four away matches which yielded two wins and two draws, Town turned on the style in their historic first ever home fixture at a sun-soaked McCains Sports Field. Ahead of the game, coach Mitch Cook said, "The lads can't wait to play in Scarborough after our first four games were all away. They are nearly all local boys and I am sure there will be plenty of friends and family down to watch. The pitches at McCains are probably the best in the area, and I am positive we will take advantage of that, because we like to get the ball down and play good football." Despite playing their fifth league match in the space of 18 days, the young Town team played some sparkling football against a Grangetown side that had won two and lost two of their opening matches.

After an even first ten minutes, Town began to get on top and Neil Thomas had a shot tipped over the bar by Grangetown keeper Steve Williams. Thomas had the ball in the net on 35 minutes, but was ruled offside, and shortly before the interval Robbie Hawkes twice came close, having one shot saved, and then shooting narrowly wide. The second half saw Town well in control, Dean Craig had a shot saved and Tom Hickin headed wide from a Mark Barber throw. They finally took the lead on 57 minutes when Matt Perry slammed home a cross from Robbie Hawkes. Substitute Darren Clough used his pace to double the lead soon after, and both Nathan Cook and Georgie Rose went close, before Rose completed the scoring in the last minute after being set-up by Josh Greening, to give the scoreline a more realistic look, after a thoroughly commanding display from the Town players.

Scarborough Town Rob Clark, Jamie Patterson (Nathan Cook 75), Dean Craig, Matt Perry, Tom Hickin, Georgie Rose, Joel Ramm, Mark Barber, Neil Thomas, Wayne Brooksby, Robbie Hawkes (Darren Clough 55), (Josh Greening 65)
Grangetown YCC Steve Williams, Scott Bell, Adam Dixon (Stu Hodgson 75), Carl Bailey, Steve Sherrington (Sean Porritt 50), Russ Buckley, Mark Jones, Dean Carney, Sam Noteyoung, Alex Davies, Kenny Portas (Paul Ritchie 50)

Referee Keith Kellerman (Middlesbrough) *Attendance 223*

Teesside League Division 2, Saturday, 28 February 2009
SCARBOROUGH TOWN 3 ACKLAM STEELWORKS 0

Town were still unbeaten after 15 league matches, 13 of which had been won, and they held a seven point lead over nearest challengers South Bank St Peters at the top of the table. Visitors Acklam Steelworks were midtable, but in the meeting at Middlesbrough earlier in the season, Town had needed a last minute strike from Josh Greening to snatch a narrow 3-2 win. Like Town, Acklam were also newcomers to the Teesside League this season, having joined from the Stokesley League, although they had previously been long standing Teesside League members between 1953-2003, winning the title on seven occasions. Town had former Scarborough FC junior and Blyth Spartans defender Liam Gildea making his debut, while Joel Ramm returned to the side after being unavailable for the 3-1 win at Billingham Kader last week.

After early half-chances for both sides, Town started to dictate play with Dean Craig making some probing runs down the left wing. Georgie Rose and Dean Craig came close to opening the scoring, and Mark Barber had a shot blocked just before the interval, while some of the Acklam tackling was fierce, and they had 4 players booked in the first half. Acklam keeper Robert Green saved well to deny Mark Barber early in the second period, but the pressure finally paid off on the hour, when Wayne Brooksby was brought down in the area, and Josh Greening scored from the spot. On 76 minutes Joel Ramm crossed from the bye-line for Darren Clough to score the second goal, and the win was wrapped up five minutes from time when Joel Ramm fired home in a crowded goalmouth. Town could have added to the score as both Darren Clough and Mark Barber were foiled by the in-form keeper late on.

Scarborough Town Rob Clark, Joel Ramm, Matt Perry, Liam Gildea, Dean Craig, Jamie Patterson (Robbie Hawkes 75), Georgie Rose (Nathan Cook 70), Mark Barber, Wayne Brooksby, Neil Thomas (Darren Clough 57), Josh Greening
Acklam Steelworks Robert Green, Kenny Gibson, Andrew Richardson, Gary South (Ian Boyle 55), Adam Abdi, Jonathan Sharkey (Matt Brown 55), Richard Cook, Steven Trainer, Lee Bowes, Paul Blake (Ben Wheatley 70), Brett Meekings

Referee Kevin Blackburn (Stockton) *Attendance 80*

Scarborough Town skipper, Georgie Rose, on the ball (left), and Carl Cook (right)

Scarborough Council buys the stadium

When Scarborough Football Club was liquidated in June 2007, administrators Begbie Traynor were left with the club's only asset, the stadium and its contents. Their only concern was to raise as much money as possible to pay back the creditors, and the future of senior football in Scarborough was totally irrelevant to them. An auction of some of the contents of the stadium raised a little money, but they then turned their attentions to trying to sell the stadium, which would not be easy as the Council had still not lifted the restrictive covenant on the site, limiting its use to sporting purposes only.

Begbie Traynor applied to the Lands Tribunal to have the covenant discharged in order that they could market the site for building or possible retail development, however, this was refused, as the Council had a clause in the covenant, giving them first refusal on buying back the site. On 5 September 2007 the liquidators offered Scarborough Council the stadium at a "fair market price" which would be determined by an independent arbitrator. On 26 September, the leader of Scarborough Council, Councillor Tom Fox agreed that the Council would exercise their legal right to buy back the site, and the matter was referred for arbitration to determine a "fair market price". The Council had obtained their own independent valuation of the site, which concluded that there was a 'hope value', based on the hope that the land would ultimately be developed for an alternative use. However, the Council already owned land adjacent to the football stadium, and they had the legal right to retain the restrictive covenant on the land if they so wished.

The ground had been blighted by vandalism ever since Boro's demise, and in October an arson attack caused severe damage to the main stand. Begbie Traynor were finding it increasingly difficult to secure the site, and they were probably relieved when both they, and the Council filed their submissions to the arbitrator, who would decide the price that the Council would have to pay for the stadium. Fortunately, the arbitrator accepted the Council's submissions, and put a value on the stadium of £1.335 million, while Begbies Traynor had hoped for a much higher valuation.

The Council were happy to accept that figure, and on 19 December 2008, the former McCain Stadium became the property of Scarborough Borough Council, who set aside the sum of £25,000 to improve security at the stadium, including the installation of CCTV to deter vandals from entering the site.

Hopes were raised that the ground would be returned to use as a football stadium, but a survey of the damage found the situation to be much worse than had at first been thought. All the electrical wires had been removed, plumbing had been smashed, crash barriers had been removed and a minimum of £250,000 would be needed just to repair the basic infrastructure. Council officers estimated that the cost of returning the stadium to an acceptable standard would be around £1 million, and a report concluded, "Whatever solution is found for football in the Borough, has to provide a sustainable future for the game. Even with the expenditure already identified to bring the ground up to standard, repairs and maintenance costs at the stadium, with its single remit for football, would place an unsustainable burden on the football club. A solution to provide a sustainable future for football in the town, will need to be provided on an alternative site to the current ground, and will need to be a solution that provides sufficient revenue from wide scale usage, to bring costs to manageable levels."

The Council identified a possible site for a new sporting complex, which would include a football stadium, at Weoponess Valley, which is a large Council owned site close to the centre of town.

As this book was going to print, this was still the Council's preferred option, but progress has been painfully slow for Boro fans, desperately yearning for senior football to return to the town. The new Scarborough Town club, which won the Teesside League second division championship in their debut season, are in the process of trying to develop their home ground at the Pindar Community Sports College at Eastfield, and that has also been identified as the site of a possible new football stadium, where the two senior clubs in town could possibly share facilities until a new venue is developed by the Council.

Scarborough FC - post war officials

Chairman

Aug 45 - May 47	H. Storry
May 47 - Jan 48	Walter Smith
Jan 48 - May 48	C. A. Marriner
May 48 - May 49	F. Monkman
May 49 - Jun 49	S. G. McWhan
Jun 49 - Aug 54	A. S. Merriweather
Aug 54 - Aug 55	W.Gibson
Aug 55 - May 57	S. A. Bell
May 57 - Apr 59	C. A. Marriner
Apr 59 - Feb 62	T. H. Stephenson
Feb 62 - Jan 67	Les Skelton
Jan 67 - Nov 72	T. H. Stephenson
Nov 72 - Dec 73	John Barnes
Dec 73 - Jun 74	Bob Whelpton
Jun 74 - Sep 75	Don Robinson
Sep 75 - Feb 77	John Fawcett
Feb 77 - Jun 83	Don Robinson
Jun 83 - Mar 86	Tony Burnard
Mar 86 - Jan 87	Barry Adamson
Jan 87 - Aug 87	Terry Wood
Aug 87 - Jun 88	Peter Gargett
Jun 88 - Jan 94	Geoffrey Richmond
Jan 94 - Mar 94	Dave Simpson
Mar 94 - May 98	John Russell
May 98 - Sep 98	Ken Ferrie
Sep 98 - Dec 98	Anton Johnson
Dec 98 - Aug 00	John Russell
Aug 00 - May 01	Trevor Milton
May 01 - Nov 01	Darrell Littlewood
Nov 01 - May 06	Malcolm Reynolds
May 06 - May 07	Ian Scobbie

Secretary

Aug 45 - Jun 47	B.W. Chapman
Jun 47 - Mar 48	Harold Taylor
Apr 48 - Jul 66	Herbert Temple
Jul 66 - Jun 67	Peter Richardson
Jun 67 - May 70	Herbert Temple
May 70 - Dec 72	Edith McKelvie
Dec 72 - Jun 73	Jack Moses
Jul 73 - Dec 74	Jim Crawford
Dec 74 - Feb 81	Maureen Crawford
Feb 81 - Oct 82	Jim Crawford
Oct 82 - May 86	Walter Hunter
Jun 86 - Jan 88	Jim Crawford
Jan 88 - Oct 89	Mike Dooley
Oct 89 - Mar 90	Andrew Jenkinson
Mar 90 - Dec 91	Eric Hall
Jan 92 - May 92	Jim Crawford
May 92 - Apr 93	Ken Shepherd
Apr 93 - Feb 94	Shaun Harvey
Mar 94 - Oct 95	Eric Hall
Oct 95 - Sep 98	Gillian Russell
Sep 98 - Dec 98	Clive Purdy
Dec 98 - Dec 99	Gillian Russell
Dec 99 - Aug 00	John Birley
Aug 00 - May 02	Jade Sprintall
May 02 - Jan 03	Kevin Philliskirk
Jan 03 - Apr 03	Stuart Dawes
Apr 03 - Feb 06	Stephen Graham
Feb 06 - May 07	Derek Megginson

Managers

Jun 46 - Jun 47	George Hall
Jun 47 - Mar 48	Harold Taylor
Mar 48May 48	Selection committee
May 48 - Aug 50	Frank Taylor
Aug 50 - Feb 53	A. C. Bell (Director)
Feb 53 - Jan 54	Reg Halton
Jan 54 - Apr 57	C. J. Robson (Director)
May 57 - Nov 58	George Higgins
Nov 58 - Feb 59	Selection committee
Feb 59 - Feb 61	Andy Smailes
Feb 61 - Jun 64	Eddy Brown
Jul 64 - Dec 65	Albert Franks
Dec 65 - Jun 66	Stewart Myers
Jun 66 - Mar 68	Selection committee
Mar 68 - Jan 69	Graham Shaw
Jan 69 - Jun 69	Selection committee
Jun 69 - Oct 73	Colin Appleton
Oct 73 - Dec 73	Gerry Donoghue (caretaker)
Dec 73 - May 74	Ken Boyes (caretaker)
Jun 74 - Jun 75	Ken Houghton
Jun 75 - Jan 81	Colin Appleton
Jan 81 - Apr 82	Jimmy McAnearney
Apr 82 - May 82	Harry Dunn (caretaker)
Jun 82 - Nov 84	John Cottam
Nov 84 - May 86	Harry Dunn
May 86 - Dec 88	Neil Warnock
Jan 89 - Nov 89	Colin Morris
Nov 89 - Mar 93	Ray McHale
Apr 93 - Oct 93	Phil Chambers
Oct 93 - Jul 94	Steve Wicks
Aug 94 - Dec 94	Billy Ayre
Dec 94 - Mar 96	Ray McHale
Mar 96 - May 96	Mitch Cook
Jun 96 - Jan 99	Mick Wadsworth
Feb 99 - Jul 00	Colin Addison
Jul 00 - Sep 01	Neil Thompson
Sep 01 - Nov 01	Ian Kerr
Nov 01 - May 04	Russell Slade
Jun 04 - Oct 05	Nicky Henry
Oct 05 - May 06	Neil Redfearn
Jun 06 - May 07	Mark Patterson

Scarborough FC - home attendances

1926 - 2009

A survey of average HOME attendances (league matches only) for every season since the club turned professional in 1926. It should be noted however, that attendances figures for some matches have not been traced, and the figures for some seasons are therefore based on the crowd figures that are available.

Yorkshire League

1926-27	3008

Midland League

1927-28	3222
1928-29	2762
1929-30	2717
1930-31	1516
1931-32	1532
1932-33	1702
1933-34	1538
1934-35	1193
1935-36	1838
1936-37	1461
1937-38	2076
1938-39	1733
1966-47	3212
1947-48	2833
1948-49	3159
1949-50	3872
1950-51	2598
1951-52	3341
1952-53	2406
1953-54	2547
1954-55	1882
1955-56	2134
1956-57	2200
1957-58	2689
1958-59	2509
1959-60	1628

Northern Counties League

1960-61	1626
1961-62	1492

North Eastern League

1962-63	1781

Midland League

1963-64	2154
1964-65	1735
1965-66	1558
1966-67	1489
1967-68	1715

Northern Premier League

1968-69	1848
1969-70	2369
1970-71	2342
1971-72	1709
1972-73	1642
1973-74	1179
1974-75	1225
1975-76	1400
1976-77	1499
1977-78	2023
1978-79	1601

Alliance Premier League

1979-80	2224
1980-81	1663
1981-82	1845
1982-83	1081
1983-84	922

Gola League

1984-85	782
1985-86	666

GM Vauxhall Conference

1986-87	1564

Barclays Football League Div 4

1987-88	3003
1988-89	2962
1989-90	2325
1990-91	1597
1991-92	1667

Barclays Football League Div 3

1992-93	1929

Endsleigh Football League Div 3

1993-94	1681
1994-95	1771
1995-96	1714

Nationwide Football League Div 3

1996-97	2455
1997-98	2489
1998-99	2211

Nationwide Conference

1999-00	1612
2000-01	1114
2001-02	1194
2002-03	1381
2003-04	1334
2004-05	1791
2005-06	1606

Conference North

2006-07	912

SCARBOROUGH ATHLETIC FC

Northern Counties East League Div 1

2007-08	487
2008-09	493

SCARBOROUGH TOWN FC

Teesside League Div 2

2008-09	136

The club record average was 3872 in season 1949-50, when a total of 89,070 fans watched the 23 home games in the Midland League. The record low was 666 in season 1985-86, when a total of 13,994 watched the 21 home games.

Seasonal Statistics

1998/99

24th in Football League Division Three

No	Month	Day	Opponent	Score	Scorers	Att	Elliott	Jackson	P Atkinson	Worrall	Lydiate	Marinkov	Bullimore	Hoyland	Campbell	Brodie	Milbourne	Carr	Russell	Tate	Radigan	Williams	Kay	Robinson	McNaughton	Dablesteen	Weaver	Greenacre	Rennison	Mountfield	Naisbett	Hodges	Roberts	Goodlad	G Atkinson	Parks	McAuley	Porter	Jones	Saville	Rainford	Todd	Renshaw	Morris
1	Aug	8	SOUTHEND UNITED	1-2	Brodie	2298	1	2	3	4	5	6	7	8	9	10	11			12																								
2		15	Exeter City	0-1		2703	1	2	3	4	5	6	7	8	9	10	12		13		14	11																						
3		22	MANSFIELD TOWN	2-3	Williams, Brodie	1972	1	3		4	5	6	7	8	14	10	12				13	9	2	11																				
4		29	Leyton Orient	3-0	Brodie, Robinson, Russell	3845	1	3	12	4	5	6	7	8		10	13		14			9	2	11																				
5		31	BRIGHTON & HOVE ALBION	1-2	Bullimore	2528	1	3		4	5	6	7	8		10	12		13			9	2	11																				
6	Sep	5	Cambridge United	3-2	Lydiate, Marinkov, Williams	2385	1	3	14	4	5	6	7	8		10	12		13			9	2	11																				
7		9	SHREWSBURY TOWN	2-0	Robinson, Brodie	1910	1		3	4	5	6	7	8	14	10	13		12			9	2	11																				
8		12	Swansea City	0-2		3360	1		3	4	5	6	7	8	12	10			13			9	2	11																				
9		19	BRENTFORD	3-1	Brodie 2, Marinkov (pen)	2028	1		3	12	5	6	7	8	13	10			14		4	9	2	11																				
10		26	Plymouth Argyle	0-0		5216	1	8	3		5	6	7			10		13	14	12	4		2	11	9																			
11	Oct	3	CHESTER CITY	2-4	Marinkov, Tate	2028	1	3		12	5	6	7	8		10			13	14	4	9	2	11																				
12		9	Carlisle United	0-1		3502	1	3		4	5	6	7	8		10	12			13		9	2	11																				
13		17	HULL CITY	1-2	Hoyland	2762	1	3		4	5	6	7	8		10	11		2		13	9		12	14																			
14		21	BARNET	0-0		1056	1	3		12	5	6	7	8		10	13				4	9	2	11	14																			
15		31	TORQUAY UNITED	1-1	Robinson	1365	1		3	4	5	6	12	8	7	10	13					9	2	11																				
16	Nov	7	Rotherham United	0-4		3954	1		3	4	5	6	7	8	12	10			13			9	2	11	14																			
17		10	Cardiff City	0-1		4432	1		3	4	5	6	7	8	12	10			14			9	2	11	13																			
18		17	Rochdale	1-0	Russell	1536	1		3	4	5		7	8		9			6			11	2	12	10																			
19		21	HARTLEPOOL UNITED	1-2	Hoyland	1715	1		3	4	5		7	8		9			6			11	2	12	10																			
20		28	Darlington	0-3		2660	1	12	3	4	5		7	8	13	9		14	6				2		10	11																		
21	Dec	12	HALIFAX TOWN	1-0	Brodie	2251		2	3		5	6	7	8	12	9			13					4	14	11	1	10																
22		19	Peterborough United	1-3	Dablesteen	4444		2	3	7	5	6		8					9		13			4	12	11	1	10															14	
23		26	Mansfield Town	2-3	Greenacre, McNaughton	3495		2	3	7				8		9	12		4					13	6	11	1	10	5															
24		28	SCUNTHORPE UNITED	1-4	Rennison	2300		2	3	7	4		12	8		9	13						6	14	11	1	10	5															
25	Jan	9	Southend United	0-1		3453		2	3	7		6	11			9			12	13			8		5		1	10		4											14			
26		16	EXETER CITY	1-0	Marinkov (pen)	2002			3		12	6	11	5		9			2	7			8		13		1	10		4														
27		23	Brighton & Hove Albion	0-1		3499			3		7	6	11	5		9			2	12			8		13			10		4	1										14			
28		30	Scunthorpe United	1-5	Greenacre, McNaughton	3779		3			5		7	6		9	13		2	12			8					10		4	1	11												
29	Feb	6	CAMBRIDGE UNITED	1-5	Tate	1650		3			4		7	5		8			12	9			2		6			10					11	1								13		
30		13	Shrewsbury Town	1-3	Brodie	2378		2	3				10	4		8	13	14	12						5			9	6	7			11	1										
31		20	SWANSEA CITY	2-1	Tate, Roberts	1512			3				8	7		10	13		2	9	12				6				5				11	1				4						
32		27	Brentford	1-1	Tate	4783			13				8	7		10			2	9					5			12	6				11		3	1		4						
33	Mar	9	Chester City	3-1	Tate 2, Russell	1954							8	7		10			2	9			12		5			13	6				11		3	1		4						
34		13	ROTHERHAM UNITED	0-4		3326								7		10			8	9			2	12	6				5				11		3	1		4		13				
35		20	Torquay United	1-0	Brodie	1891							8	7		10			2	9					5				6	12			11		3	1		4						
36		28	ROCHDALE	1-0	Brodie	2206							8	7		10			2	9					5				6				11		3	1	12	4		13				
37	Apr	3	Hull City	1-1	Hoyland	13949			8	12				7				2		9				13					6				11		3	1	5	4	10	14				
38		5	CARLISLE UNITED	3-0	Tate 3	3604			8	12				7				2		9				13					6				11		3	1	5	4	10	14				
39		10	Barnet	0-1		1689			13					7		10		2	12	9					6								11		3	1	5	4	8	14				
40		14	DARLINGTON	0-2		2125				12				7		10		2		9				13	6								11		3	1	5	4	8	14				
41		17	Hartlepool United	0-3		5098				4			8	7		10		2	12	9				13	6								11		3	1	5			14				
42		21	LEYTON ORIENT	1-3	Tate	1410							8	7		10			2	9				13	6								11		3	1	5	4	12					
43		24	CARDIFF CITY	1-2	Roberts	1834				4				7		10			2	9				12	6				5				11		3	1			8					
44	May	1	Halifax Town	2-1	G Atkinson,Brodie	3308				4				7		10		12	2	9				13	6				5				11		3	1			8					
45		5	PLYMOUTH ARGYLE	3-0	Tate 2, Brodie	2398				4				7		10			2	9					6				5				11		3	1		12	8	13				
46		8	PETERBOROUGH UNITED	1-1	Roberts	4769				4				7		10		13	2	9					6				5				11		3	1		14	8	12				
						Apps	20	19	23	25	26	22	33	44	3	43	2	5	20	18	4	17	23	17	22	5	6	10	15	5	2	1	18	3	15	15	6	11	8	0	0	0	0	0
						Subs		1	4	6	1		2		8		14	5	17	7	5		1	12	9			2		1							1	2	1	9	2	1	1	
						Goals					1	4	1	3		12			3	12		2		3	1	1		2	1				3		1									

F.A. Cup

No	Month	Day	Opponent	Score	Scorers	Att	Elliott	Jackson	P Atkinson	Worrall	Lydiate	Marinkov	Bullimore	Hoyland	Campbell	Brodie	Milbourne	Carr	Russell	Tate	Radigan	Williams	Kay	Robinson	McNaughton	Dablesteen	Weaver	Greenacre	Rennison	Mountfield	Naisbett	Hodges	Roberts	Goodlad	G Atkinson	Parks	McAuley	Porter	Jones	Saville	Rainford	Todd	Renshaw	Morris
1	Nov	14	ROCHDALE	1-1	Williams	1860	1		3	4	5	6	7	8	13	10			12			9	2	11																				
1r		24	Rochdale	0-2		1850	1		3	4	5		7	8		9			6			11	2		10																			12

League Cup (Worthington's Cup)

No	Month	Day	Opponent	Score	Scorers	Att	Elliott	Jackson	P Atkinson	Worrall	Lydiate	Marinkov	Bullimore	Hoyland	Campbell	Brodie	Milbourne	Carr	Russell	Tate	Radigan	Williams	Kay	Robinson	McNaughton	Dablesteen	Weaver	Greenacre	Rennison	Mountfield	Naisbett	Hodges	Roberts	Goodlad	G Atkinson	Parks	McAuley	Porter	Jones	Saville	Rainford	Todd	Renshaw	Morris
1H	Aug	12	BARNSLEY	0-1		3064	1	2	3	13	5	6	7	8	9	10	11			14	12	4																						
1A		18	Barnsley	0-3		7978	1	2	3	4	5	6		8	9	10	13		12		14	7		11																				

Auto Windscreens Shield

No	Month	Day	Opponent	Score	Scorers	Att	Elliott	Jackson	P Atkinson	Worrall	Lydiate	Marinkov	Bullimore	Hoyland	Campbell	Brodie	Milbourne	Carr	Russell	Tate	Radigan	Williams	Kay	Robinson	McNaughton	Dablesteen	Weaver	Greenacre	Rennison	Mountfield	Naisbett	Hodges	Roberts	Goodlad	G Atkinson	Parks	McAuley	Porter	Jones	Saville	Rainford	Todd	Renshaw	Morris
1	Jan	19	Wigan Athletic	0-3		1693			3		7		11	8			12		2	10					5			9	6		1										4			

Friendlies / Minor Cups

	Jul	14	Whitby Town	0-3		500
		18	Barnsley (at York)	1-0	Williams	355
		19	Airdrie (at York)	4-4*	Robinson,Bullimore(pen),Williams,Brodie	260
SF		24	YORK CITY(NRSC)	2-2**	Tinkler(og), Campbell	1023
		27	MANCHESTER CITY	1-4	Bullimore	722
		30	BURY	1-2	Brodie	481
	Aug	3	NEWCASTLE UTD RES	2-1	Arnison(og), Brodie	1735
	Mar	31	FC TROMSO	1-1	Robinson	306

*won 5-4 on penalties in four-team tournament

NRSC = North Riding Senior Cup. ** lost 3-4 on penalties

Scarborough FC: 1998-99

Back(L to R) Campbell, Lydiate, Hoyland, Marinkov, McNaughton, Tate, Bazelya
Middle(L to R) Worrall, Kay, Williams, Buxton, Elliott, Martin, Milbourne, Bullimore, Robinson
Front(L to R) Murray(physio), Brodie, Jackson, Carr, Wadsworth(manager), Ferrie(chairman), McHale(asst manager), Kerr(youth coach), Bass, Marples, Middlemass

Boro's Football League Record:
1987 - 1999

OPPONENTS	HOME						AWAY					
	P	W	D	L	F	A	P	W	D	L	F	A
Aldershot	2	2	0	0	3	0	2	0	2	0	3	3
Barnet	7	1	4	2	5	9	7	1	1	5	7	15
Blackpool	2	0	0	2	1	3	2	0	1	1	2	4
Bolton Wanderers	1	1	0	0	4	0	1	0	0	1	1	3
Brentford	1	1	0	0	3	1	1	0	1	0	1	1
Brighton & Hove Albion	3	1	1	1	4	4	3	0	1	2	3	5
Burnley	5	4	0	1	9	4	5	2	1	2	4	6
Bury	4	1	0	3	3	7	4	3	0	1	6	1
Cambridge United	7	4	2	1	8	7	7	2	1	4	12	18
Cardiff City	8	2	3	3	10	11	8	0	3	5	4	10
Carlisle United	10	3	4	3	15	14	10	1	2	7	7	21
Chester City	5	1	2	2	6	6	5	1	1	3	5	12
Chesterfield	6	2	2	2	9	9	6	3	1	2	7	4
Colchester United	9	1	5	3	7	9	9	4	2	3	12	9
Crewe Alexandra	5	4	0	1	8	4	5	1	3	1	8	8
Darlington	10	5	1	4	17	14	10	4	1	5	13	15
Doncaster Rovers	10	6	2	2	19	9	10	4	1	5	17	15
Exeter City	8	4	1	3	14	11	8	0	2	6	7	16
Fulham	3	1	1	1	5	5	3	1	0	2	2	6
Gillingham	7	2	3	2	6	7	7	0	2	5	5	14
Grimsby Town	2	1	0	1	5	4	2	0	0	2	1	5
Halifax Town	7	5	1	1	16	6	7	5	1	1	14	9
Hartlepool United	9	3	3	3	16	13	9	0	2	7	6	21
Hereford United	10	4	3	3	13	11	10	2	5	3	14	17
Hull City	3	2	0	1	6	5	3	1	1	1	3	4
Leyton Orient	6	4	1	1	10	6	6	3	0	3	9	9
Lincoln City	9	2	5	2	10	8	9	2	3	4	7	13
Macclesfield Town	1	1	0	0	2	1	1	0	0	1	1	3
Maidstone United	3	1	0	2	2	3	3	1	0	2	3	6
Mansfield Town	7	1	4	2	9	12	7	1	0	6	10	18
Newport County	1	1	0	0	3	1	1	1	0	0	4	0
Northampton Town	7	4	3	0	12	7	7	3	0	4	12	10
Notts County	1	0	0	1	1	2	1	0	0	1	0	1
Peterborough United	6	3	2	1	10	8	6	2	2	2	7	7
Plymouth Argyle	2	1	1	0	5	2	2	0	1	1	1	5
Preston North End	3	0	1	2	5	7	3	0	1	2	4	6
Rochdale	12	6	5	1	20	16	12	2	5	5	13	20
Rotherham United	4	1	0	3	2	9	4	1	2	1	3	5
Scunthorpe United	12	5	3	4	17	15	12	6	3	3	19	18
Shrewsbury Town	4	1	1	2	4	5	4	1	0	3	2	7
Southend United	2	0	1	1	2	3	2	0	0	2	0	2
Stockport County	4	1	2	1	4	4	4	0	3	1	7	8
Swansea City	4	3	0	1	7	4	4	1	1	2	2	6
Torquay United	11	6	3	2	20	11	11	4	1	6	9	12
Tranmere Rovers	2	1	1	0	2	0	2	0	1	1	1	2
Walsall	5	3	0	2	9	6	5	0	2	3	3	8
Wigan Athletic	4	2	1	1	7	3	4	1	1	2	4	11
Wolverhampton Wands	1	0	1	0	2	2	1	0	1	0	0	0
Wrexham	6	3	1	2	11	10	6	3	0	3	6	8
Wycombe Wanderers	1	1	0	0	3	1	1	0	0	1	0	4
York City	5	2	2	1	8	7	5	1	1	3	3	8

Not included above is the 2-0 home defeat by Aldershot on 14 September 1991, which was deleted from the records when Aldershot subsequently went into liquidation and resigned from the League. Boro played 51 different clubs in twelve seasons as members of the Football League.

1999-2000

4th in Football Conference

No.	Month	Day	Opponent	Score	Scorers	Att	Martin	Betts	Tyrrell	Sinnott	Middlemass	Jones	McAlindon	Bass	Brodie	McGinty	Roberts	Milbourne	McNaughton	Rennison	Gildea	Woods	Carr	Stoker	Harriott	Russell	Quinn	S Morris	A Morris	Tate	Ellender	McNiven	Ingram	Williams	Thompson	Bogan	Walker	Alkhatib	Brunton
1	Aug	8	YEOVIL TOWN	5-0	Brodie, Brown(og), McAlindon 2, Roberts(pen)	2005	1	2	3	4	5	6	7	8	9	10	11	12			13																		
2		17	Southport	2-2	Roberts (pen), Brodie	1632	1	2	3	4	5	6	7	8	9	10	11																						
3		21	Forest Green Rovers	1-0	Betts	863	1	2	3	4	5	6	7	8	9	10	11	12		13																			
4		24	HEDNESFORD TOWN	1-1	Brodie	2198	1	2	3	4	5	6	7	8	9	10	11	12																					
5		28	STEVENAGE BOROUGH	1-3	Love (og)	2291	1	2	3	4	5	6	7	8	9	10	11		12	13	14																		
6		30	Morecambe	1-0	Betts	2301	1	2	3	4		6		8	9	10	11	7	12	5	14							13											
7	Sep	4	KINGSTONIAN	0-1		1671	1	2	3	4		6	7	8		10	11	9		5			14		13			12											
8		11	Kidderminster Harriers	0-2		1784		2	3	4		6	7	8	9	10	12			5		1		11	13														
9		14	Northwich Victoria	0-2		1036		2		4	10	6	7		9		11			5		1		8	3														
10		18	NUNEATON BOROUGH	1-1	Stoker	1662		2		4	5	6		7	9		11			13		1		8	3		12		10										
11		25	HAYES	4-1	A Morris, Brodie, Roberts, Quinn	1295		2		4	5	6		7	9		11			12		1		8	3		14		10								13		
12	Oct	2	Hereford United	4-4	A Morris, Harriott, Stoker, Brodie	1886		2			5	6	13	7	9		11		12	4		1		8	3				10										
13		9	Dover Athletic	1-1	Roberts (pen)	945	1	2	3			6	13	7	9		11			5				8	4		12		10										
14		23	RUSHDEN & DIAMONDS	0-1		1702		2	12	4			14		9		13			5		1	11	8	6	3	7		10										
15	Nov	6	Stevenage Borough	1-0	Russell	1743		3		4	12	6	10		9		11			7		1		8	5	2													
16		13	TELFORD UNITED	2-0	Jones, McAlindon	1317		3		4		6	10	13	9					7		1		8	5	2			12							11			
17		20	KETTERING TOWN	0-0		1348		3		4		6	10		9		11			7		1		8	5	2			13							12			
18	Dec	4	Welling United	1-2	Brodie	540		3				6		10	9		12			7		1		8	5	2		13	11		4								
19		11	KIDDERMINSTER HARRIERS	0-0		1125		3				6		10	9					14	7	1		8	4	2		12	13		5			11					
20		18	HEREFORD UNITED	3-0	Stoker, Brodie, Bass	1242		3				6		7	9		14				12	1		8	4	2		13		10	5			11					
21		27	Doncaster Rovers	1-0	Tate	4706						6		7	9		11					1		8	4	2				10	5			3					
22	Jan	3	DONCASTER ROVERS	0-0		3510		3		6					9		7					1		8	4	2		12		10	5			11					
23		8	Hednesford Town	3-0	Tate, Stoker, Brodie	1057		3		6		12		13	9		7					1		8	4	2		14		10	5			11					
24		22	NORTHWICH VICTORIA	3-0	Betts(pen), Brodie, Roberts	1506		2		6		7			10		11					1		8	4					9	5			3					
25		29	Telford United	0-1		1041		2		6		7			10		11					1		8	4					9	5			3				12	
26	Feb	12	Kettering Town	0-0		1270		3		6		7										1		8	4	2				9	5	10		11				12	
27		19	SUTTON UNITED	3-0	Tate 2, McNiven	1395		3		6		7					12					1		8	4	2		11		9	5	10							
28		22	Altrincham	1-2	Hodson (og)	761		3		6		7								13		1		8	4	2				9	5	10		11				12	
29		29	SOUTHPORT	3-0	Rennison, Tate, S Morris	1002		3				7		6						4		1		8		2		11		9	5	10							13
30	Mar	4	DOVER ATHLETIC	1-2	McNiven	1376		3				6						12	13	4		1		8		2		11		9	5	10		7					
31		11	Nuneaton Borough	1-1	Tate	1351		3				6			10		11			4		1		8		2		12		9	5			7					
32		18	WOKING	3-2	Tate, Brodie, Betts (pen)	1345		3	13			6			10					4		1		8		2		12		9	5		11	7					
33		25	Yeovil Town	2-1	Betts, Tate	2031		3							10				6	4		1		8		2		7		9			11		5				
34	Apr	1	WELLING UNITED	0-0		1310		3				6			10		13			4		1		8	14	2		7		9	5		11					12	
35		8	Kingstonian	0-2		952		2				6			10		11		14	4	13	1		8				12			5		7	3	9				
36		11	Hayes	1-0	Roberts	506		2							10		11		13	4		1		8				12		9	5		7	3	6				
37		15	FOREST GREEN ROVERS	5-0	Hedges(og), Roberts, Tate, Brodie, Thompson	1636		2							10		11			4	13	1		8				12		9	5		7	3	6				
38		20	Sutton United	2-1	Rennison, Brodie	463		2							10		11			4		1		8				12		9	5		7	3	6				
39		26	ALTRINCHAM	1-0	S Morris	1273						7			10		11			4		1		8				12		9	5		2	3	6				
40		29	Rushden & Diamonds	0-0		2641						7			10		11			4	13	1		8				12		9	5		2	3	6				
41	May	1	MORECAMBE	0-2		1505						7			10		11			4	13	1		8	12			14		9	5		2	3	6				
42		6	Woking	2-0	Brodie, McNaughton	2214						7			10		11		14	4		1		8	12			13		9	5		2	3	6				
						Apps	8	37	9	22	9	35	11	17	36	8	28	2	1	25	1	34	1	35	20	19	1	5	6	22	24	5	11	20	9	1	0	0	0
						Subs			2		1	1	3	2			6	4	7	6	8		1		5		3	17	3							1	1	4	1
						Goals		5				1	3	2	13		6		1	2				4	1	1	1	2	2	9		2			1				

F.A. Cup

Rd	Month	Day	Opponent	Score	Scorers	Att	Martin	Betts	Tyrrell	Sinnott	Middlemass	Jones	McAlindon	Bass	Brodie	McGinty	Roberts	Milbourne	McNaughton	Rennison	Gildea	Woods	Carr	Stoker	Harriott	Russell	Quinn	S Morris	A Morris	Tate	Ellender	McNiven	Ingram	Williams	Thompson	Bogan	Walker	Alkhatib	Brunton
4Q	Oct	16	TAMWORTH	0-1		1374		2	3		12	6	13	7	9		11			4		1		8	5		14		10										

F.A. Trophy

Rd	Month	Day	Opponent	Score	Scorers	Att	Martin	Betts	Tyrrell	Sinnott	Middlemass	Jones	McAlindon	Bass	Brodie	McGinty	Roberts	Milbourne	McNaughton	Rennison	Gildea	Woods	Carr	Stoker	Harriott	Russell	Quinn	S Morris	A Morris	Tate	Ellender	McNiven	Ingram	Williams	Thompson	Bogan	Walker	Alkhatib	Brunton
2	Nov	27	Ilkeston Town	4-2	Betts 2(1pen), Jones, A Morris	842		2		3		6	10	7	9					4		1			5	8		12	11										
3	Jan	15	Stocksbridge Park Steels	0-0		634		2		4		12			10		7					1		8	5	3				9	6			11					
3r		18	STOCKSBRIDGE PARK STEELS	5-0	Betts 3(1 pen), Brodie 2	960		2		4		7	13		10		11				12	1		8	5			14		9	6			3					
4	Feb	5	Burnham	1-1	O'Sullivan (og)	469		2		6		7		12	10							1		8	4	11				9	5			3					
4r		8	BURNHAM	6-0	Williams, Tate, Russell, Roberts, Jones, Stoker	877		3		6		7		14	10		13					1		8	4	2				9	5			11				12	
5		26	Bishop Auckland	1-2	Jones	747		3	13	6		7		10			11			4		1		8		2		14		9	5	12							

MacMillan Trophy

Rd	Month	Day	Opponent	Score	Scorers	Att	Martin	Betts	Tyrrell	Sinnott	Middlemass	Jones	McAlindon	Bass	Brodie	McGinty	Roberts	Milbourne	McNaughton	Rennison	Gildea	Woods	Carr	Stoker	Harriott	Russell	Quinn	S Morris	A Morris	Tate	Ellender	McNiven	Ingram	Williams	Thompson	Bogan	Walker	Alkhatib	Brunton
2	Nov	9	Southport	2-1	Betts (pen), Brodie	339		3		4		6	10	12	9				7			1		8	5	2										11			
3	Feb	1	DONCASTER ROVERS	1-2	Roberts	1188		2		6		7			10		11					1		8	4					9	5			3				12	

Friendlies / Minor Cups

SF	Jul	15	YORK CITY (NRSC)	0-0*		1220
		17	HUDDERSFIELD TOWN	0-0		1505
		21	BRADFORD CITY	0-2		1210
		24	AIRDRIE**	0-2		522
		25	DARLINGTON**	1-2	Milbourne	646
		27	Gateshead	0-3		246
		29	Bedlington Terriers	2-4	McNaughton, McAlindon	201
		31	HULL CITY	0-1		1100
	Aug	5	DARLINGTON	1-0	McAlindon	812
		7	Grantham	1-0	Brodie	217
		11	York City	3-2	Roberts 2, Rennison	229
		25	HULL CITY XI	1-0	Rennison	***
	Oct	29	MIDDLESBROUGH RES	3-3	Brodie, Milbourne, OG	536
	Dec	9	MANCHESTER UTD RES	1-2	Brodie	3193
	Jan	12	NEWCASTLE UTD RES	2-3	Betts (pen), Grant	675

* North Riding Senior Cup. Lost 3-5 on penalties

** Minster Carpets Cup, four-team tournament *** played "behind closed doors"

Scarborough FC: 1999-2000

Back(L to R) Gildea, Rennison, Milbourne, McNaughton, Brodie, McAlindon, Harriott
Middle(L to R) Tremble, Brunton, Jones, Carr, Woods, Martin, Roberts, Tyrell, Sinnott, Betts
Front(L to R) Grant, Quinn, Morris, Sullivan(physio), Addison(manager), McHale(asst manager), Kerr(youth coach), Bass, Marples, Middlemass

2000-01

10th in Football Conference

							Woods	Russell	Betts	Ingram	Ellender	Rennison	Williams	Stoker	Jones	Brodie	Pounder	Tate	Thompson	Morris	Brunton	Fauré	Savic	Gildea	Shuttleworth	Diallo	Priestley	Atkinson	Blunt	Burt	Stamp	Dawson	Reed	Lyth	Keegan	Jordan	Windross	Robinson	Di Lella	Jewell	Piercewright	Toone
1	Aug	15	Stevenage Borough	1-1	Brodie	2032	1	2	3	4	5	6	7	8	9	10	11																				12					
2		22	MORECAMBE	2-2	Betts, Ellender	1536	1	2	3	4	5	6	7	8	9	10	11			12																						
3		26	KINGSTONIAN	1-0	Williams	1275	1	2	3	4	5	6	7	8	9	10	11	12																								
4		28	Leigh RMI	0-2		903	1	2	3	4	5	6	7	8	11	10	12	9		13																						
5	Sep	2	DAGENHAM & REDBRIDGE	0-2		1202	1	12	3	4	5	6	7	8	9	10	11	13	2																							
6		5	Southport	1-3	Tate	1269	1		2	4	5		7	8	6	10	11	9		12	3																					
7		9	Hayes	1-0	Brodie	562	1	2	11	4	5		7	8	6	10		9			3																					
8		12	RUSHDEN & DIAMONDS	0-3		1107	1	2	11	4	5	12	7	8	6	10	13	9			3																					
9		16	NORTHWICH VICTORIA	4-0	Brodie 2, Pounder 2	845	1	2	8	4	5		7	12		10	11	9		14	3	6		13																		
10		23	Dover Athletic	2-0	Williams 2	933	1	2	8	4	5	13	7		9	10	11			12	3	6		14																		
11		27	Forest Green Rovers	3-2	Williams, Betts, Brodie	542	1	2	8	4	5		7	12	9	10	11				3	6																				
12		30	WOKING	3-2	Williams, Rennison, West (og)	1156	1	2	8	4	5	9	7	12	6	10	11				3																					
13	Oct	3	CHESTER CITY	0-2		1193	1	2	8	4	5	6	7	13	11	10	14	12			3		9																			
14		6	Telford United	0-1		395	1	2	8	4	5		7	12	6		11	10			3		9			13																
15		14	NUNEATON BOROUGH	0-0		1089	1	2	7	4		5		8	11			9	6	12					3	10																
16		21	Kettering Town	1-1	Brodie	1159	1	2	8	4	5	11	7	13	14	10	12	9	6						3																	
17	Nov	4	HEREFORD UNITED	2-4	Diallo, Pounder	891	1		2	4	5		12	8	7	10	11				3	6		13		9																
18		11	Boston United	2-2	Diallo, Brodie	1752	1		2		5	4	7	8		10	11		3			6				9																
19		18	STEVENAGE BOROUGH	2-2	Betts (pen), Pounder	789	1		2		5	4	7	8		10	11		3			6				9											12					
20		25	YEOVIL TOWN	2-2	Betts (pen), Diallo	972			2	6	5	4	7	8		10	11		3							9	1															12
21	Dec	2	Hednesford Town	1-0	Ellender	753			2	6	5	4	7	8		10	11		3					12		9	1															
22		16	Morecambe	4-4	Brodie 3, Diallo	2023		2		6	5	4	7	8		10	11		3	13	12					9	1															
23		26	DONCASTER ROVERS	3-1	Thompson, Ingram, Diallo	2381		2		6	5	4	7			10	11		3		8					9	1															
24	Jan	2	Doncaster Rovers	2-0	Ellender, Pounder	3024		2		6	5		7	4		10	11		3	12	8						1										9					
25		6	LEIGH RMI	1-1	Rennison	1087				6	5	4	7	8		10	11		2	12	3	14				9	1										13					
26		27	SOUTHPORT	1-1	Diallo	1125	1	2			5	4	7	8		10	11		6	12	3	13				9		14														
27	Feb	10	HAYES	2-0	Stoker, Pounder	814	1			6		4	7	8			11				3	10						2		12		13		5				9	14			
28		17	Rushden & Diamonds	0-1		3553	1			6		4	7	8			11			12	3							2		13				5				9	10			
29		24	DOVER ATHLETIC	2-0	Ellender, Pounder	1082	1				5	4	7	8			11			12	3	13						2		10				6				9				
30	Mar	3	Northwich Victoria	0-3		942	1				5	4		8		13	11			12	3	7						2						6				9	10			
31		6	Dagenham & Redbridge	0-1		788	1				5	4		8		10	11		6	7	3	13						2				14						12	9			
32		17	Woking	1-1	Diallo	1625	1				5	4		8		10	12			13	3					9		2	7	11				6								
33		25	FOREST GREEN ROVERS	1-0	Diallo	838	1				5	4		8			11			13	3	6				9		2	7	10						12						
34	Apr	3	Kingstonian	2-2	Ellender, Jordan	694	1				5	4		8					6		3					9		2	7	12	10					11					13	
35		7	KETTERING TOWN	0-1		1082	1				5	4		8			12		6		3					9			7	10		2				11					13	
36		10	TELFORD UNITED	1-1	Pounder	723	1				5	4	13	12			11			14	3	6				9		2	7	10						8						
37		14	Nuneaton Borough	2-1	Williams 2	1247	1				5	4	10	8			11				3	6				12		2	7	9												
38		16	BOSTON UNITED	2-2	Burt, Pounder	1279	1				5	4	10	8			11				3	6						2	7	9			12			13					14	
39		21	Hereford United	1-1	Ellender	1304	1				5		10	8			11		6		3					12		2	7	9			4			13						
40		28	HEDNESFORD TOWN	0-0		943	1					4	10	8		13	11		6		3					12		2		9		14	5			7						
41	May	1	Chester City	2-3	Jordan, Burt	805	1					4	11			10	9				3					14		2	8	12		13			5	7					6	
42		5	Yeovil Town	1-0	Thompson (pen)	2823	1					3				11	10		4		6					14		2	7	9		12			5		13			8		
						Apps	36	18	21	25	36	32	32	31	15	28	33	8	18	1	30	12	2	0	2	15	6	15	10	10	1	1	2	5	2	5	1	4	3	1	1	0
						Subs		1				2	2	7	1	2	6	3		16	1	4		4		6		1		4		5	1			3	4	1	1		3	1
						Goals			4	1	6	2	7	1		10	9	1	2							8				2						2						

F.A. Cup

							Woods	Russell	Betts	Ingram	Ellender	Rennison	Williams	Stoker	Jones	Brodie	Pounder	Tate	Thompson	Morris	Brunton	Fauré	Savic	Gildea	Shuttleworth	Diallo	Priestley	Atkinson	Blunt	Burt	Stamp	Dawson	Reed	Lyth	Keegan	Jordan	Windross	Robinson	Di Lella	Jewell	Piercewright	Toone
4Q	Oct	28	LEIGH RMI	3-4	Rennison, Betts (pen), Diallo	858	1	13	9	2	5	4	7	8		10	11	9	6						3	12																

F.A. Trophy

							Woods	Russell	Betts	Ingram	Ellender	Rennison	Williams	Stoker	Jones	Brodie	Pounder	Tate	Thompson	Morris	Brunton	Fauré	Savic	Gildea	Shuttleworth	Diallo	Priestley	Atkinson	Blunt	Burt	Stamp	Dawson	Reed	Lyth	Keegan	Jordan	Windross	Robinson	Di Lella	Jewell	Piercewright	Toone
3	Jan	13	Runcorn	4-0	Russell, Ingram, Stoker, Pounder	420	1	2		6	5	4	7	8			10		2	12	3	11		14		9									13							
4	Feb	3	BURTON ALBION	0-1		1462	1			6	5	4		8			11		6	10	3	7				9		2									12					

LDV Trophy

							Woods	Russell	Betts	Ingram	Ellender	Rennison	Williams	Stoker	Jones	Brodie	Pounder	Tate	Thompson	Morris	Brunton	Fauré	Savic	Gildea	Shuttleworth	Diallo	Priestley	Atkinson	Blunt	Burt	Stamp	Dawson	Reed	Lyth	Keegan	Jordan	Windross	Robinson	Di Lella	Jewell	Piercewright	Toone
1	Dec	6	Stoke City	1-3	Brunton	2336			2	6	5	4	7	8		10	11		3		12					9	1								14					13		

Nationwide Variety Cup

							Woods	Russell	Betts	Ingram	Ellender	Rennison	Williams	Stoker	Jones	Brodie	Pounder	Tate	Thompson	Morris	Brunton	Fauré	Savic	Gildea	Shuttleworth	Diallo	Priestley	Atkinson	Blunt	Burt	Stamp	Dawson	Reed	Lyth	Keegan	Jordan	Windross	Robinson	Di Lella	Jewell	Piercewright	Toone
2	Oct	9	Nuneaton Borough	0-2		614	1		2		5	4	7	8	11		12	10	6	12			9	11	3	13																

Friendlies / Minor Cups

SF	Jul	21	MIDDLESBROUGH RES (NRSC)	1-1*	Gavin(og)	1200
		28	MANCHESTER UTD RES	3-2	Brodie, Williams, Savic	3650
		30	Tipperary South XI	5-0	Brunton,McNaughton2,Toone,Morris	400
	Aug	1	Waterford Town	2-2	Windross, Fauré	204
		2	Cork City	0-1		311
		5	NEWCASTLE UTD RES**	2-0	Pounder 2	833
		6	DARLINGTON**	0-7		358
		8	SUNDERLAND RES	0-3		410
F		9	YORK CITY (NRSC)	0-1		300
	Sep	12	Newcastle Utd Res	2-2	Shuttleworth, Tate	196
	Dec	12	Leeds Utd Res	3-1	Rennison, Brodie, Ingram	***
	Mar	21	SHEFFIELD UTD	2-3	Pounder, Beavers	250

* Semi-final of 1999-2000 season. Won 5-4 on penalties

** Minster Carpets Cup, four-team tournament

*** played "behind closed doors"

Scarborough FC: 2000-01

Back(L to R) Ingram, Tremble, Morris, Tate, Williams, McNaughton, Woods, Newton, Rennison, Jones, Ellender, Faure, Thompson, Russell
Front(L to R) Betts, Brodie, Stoker, Sullivan(physio), Kerr(youth coach), Addison(manager), McHale(asst manager), Cook(community officer), Hodgson(kit man), Grant, Brunton, Gildea

2001-02

12th in Football Conference

No	Month	Day	Opponent	Score	Scorers	Att	Woods	Short	Fitzsimmons	Rennison	Fauré	Ingram	Blunt	Fickling	Stamp	Burt	Pounder	Brodie	Stoker	Atkinson	Turley	Barnwell-Edinbo	Wilford	Swales	Keegan	Elliott	Jones	Windross	Patterson	Jordan	Dryden	Rose	Shepherd	Shields	Hotte	Connell	Newton	Smith	Sugden	Mann	Baker	Wright	Salt	Burley	Bennett	Sherwood	Hogg	Jewell	O'Riordan	Crawford	Tracey	Brunton	Torpey
1	Aug	18	FOREST GREEN ROVERS	1-1	Stamp	1104	1	2	3	4	5	6	7	8	9	10	11	12	13																																						
2		21	Northwich Victoria	1-1	Pounder	760	1	2	3	4	5	6	7	8	9		11	10	12		14																									13							
3		25	Barnet	1-1	Brodie	1276	1		3	4	5	6	7	8	9			10	11	2	13																									12							
4		27	MARGATE	0-1		886	1	2	3	4		6	7	5	9	12	11	10	8																											13							
5	Sep	1	Woking	2-1	Stamp 2	1244	1	2	3	4		6	7	5	9	11		10	8			12																															
6		4	STALYBRIDGE CELTIC	1-1	Brodie	837	1	2	3	4		6	7	5	9	11		10	8	13		12																															
7		8	HAYES	1-2	Burt	896	1		3	12	4	6	8	5	9	14		10	13	2		11	7																														
8		10	Stevenage Borough	0-2		1794	1		3	4	5	6	7				12	10	8	13		9	2																							11							
9		15	Yeovil Town	2-2	Brodie, Wilford	2390	1		3	4	5	6	7			13	11	10	8	2	12		9																														
10		18	MORECAMBE	0-2		617	1		3	4	5	6	7			13	11	10	8	2	12		9																														
11		22	NUNEATON BOROUGH	1-2	Stamp	890	1		3	4	5	6	7		9		11	10		2	12		8																														
12		29	Dagenham & Redbridge	2-4	Stamp, Stoker	1482	1		12	4	5	6	7		9			10	8	2			11	14	3																							13					
13	Oct	2	CHESTER CITY	2-1	Stamp, Rennison	783	1			4	5	6	7		9		11	10		2			8		3			13																			14	12					
14		6	Boston United	2-2	Blunt, Windross	1700	1		3	4			7				11	10		5				2	6	8		9																									
15		9	Southport	0-1		701	1		3	4			7				11	10		5			12	2	6	8		9																				14					
16		13	DOVER ATHLETIC	1-1	Windross	873	1		3		6		7				11	10	12	2			4	13		8	5	9																									
17		20	Hereford United	0-6		1346	1		3		4		7		9		11		10	2				13	6	8	5																						12				
18	Nov	3	LEIGH RMI	2-5	Brodie, Elliott	859			3	4			7		9		11	10		6			5	2		8		13									1													12			
19		10	Telford United	0-3		853	1			4	5		7				3	10		2				13		8	11	9																	6			12					
20		24	FARNBOROUGH TOWN	1-0	Windross	930				5	4		7				11										6	9	8	3				10				1			2					12		13					
21	Dec	1	Forest Green Rovers	2-2	Pounder, Dryden	751				5			7		9		11									14	6	12	8	2	3			10				1			4					13							
22		15	NORTHWICH VICTORIA	1-2	Pounder	986				5					10		11		2							14	6	13	8	12	3		7	9				1			4												
23		26	Doncaster Rovers	3-4	Rennison, Miller(og), Blunt	3279				6	12		7				11		4									13	8	2	3	9	5	10				1			14												
24		29	BARNET	3-0	Shepherd, Shields, Rose	1050	1			5			7		12		11		4										8	2	3	9	6	10																			
25	Jan	15	DONCASTER ROVERS	1-0	Blunt	1791	1			5			7		12		11		6										8	3		9	4	10	2	13					14												
26		19	WOKING	1-0	Rose	1238	1			5			7		9		11		4										8			12	6	10	2	13					14			3									
27		26	Margate	1-1	Shepherd (pen)	637	1			5			7		9		13		4										8			10	6	11	2						12			3									
28	Feb	16	Dover Athletic	2-0	Shields, Stamp	1005	1				5				9		13		4											2		12		10	3				8		6		7	11									
29	Mar	2	Morecambe	0-2		1015	1			5			7		12		11		4										8	2			6		3				9	10													
30		5	Chester City	0-0		1475	1			5			7		9		11		4										8	2		12	6		3				10														
31		9	STEVENAGE BOROUGH	1-1	Blunt	1121	1			5			7		9		14		4										8	2		12	6		3				10	11											13		
32		12	Stalybridge Celtic	3-2	Murphy(og), Blunt, Stamp (pen)	627	1			5			7		9		11		4										8	2		10	6		12						3												
33		16	Hayes	2-1	Rose 2	681	1			5	12		7		9		11		4											2		10			3				13		6		8										
34		23	YEOVIL TOWN	0-0		1300	1			5			7		9		11		4											2		10			3				12		6		8										
35		30	HEREFORD UNITED	3-2	Baker (pen), Blunt, Sugden	1493	1			5			7				12		4										13	2		10			3				9		6	11	8										
36	Apr	1	Leigh RMI	1-1	Rose	541	1			5	12		7				11		4										13	2		10			3				9		6		8									14	
37		6	TELFORD UNITED	3-1	Rennison, Stamp, Sugden	1439	1			5			7		9		12												8	2		10			3				13		6	11	4										
38		10	SOUTHPORT	2-0	Rose, Jordan	1240	1			5			7		9														8	2		10			3	12			13		6	11	4										
39		13	Farnborough Town	2-4	Connell, Stamp	843	1			5	6		7		9		12										13		8	2					3	11			10				4										
40		16	BOSTON UNITED	2-0	Pounder, Stamp	2229	1			5			7		9		11												8	2					3	12			10		6		4										
41		20	DAGENHAM & REDBRIDGE	0-0		2349	1			5			7		9		11												8	2					3	12			10		6		4										
42		27	Nuneaton Borough	2-1	Stamp, Connell	1475	1			5			7		9		11													2		10			3	12					6	8	4										
						Apps	37	5	16	38	16	13	40	7	28	3	29	17	24	13	0	2	9	3	5	6	6	5	17	20	4	12	10	9	17	1	1	4	9	2	14	4	11	3	1	1	0	0	0	0	0	0	0
						Subs			1	1	3				3	4	7	1	4	2	5	2	1	4		2	1	5	2	1		4			1	6			4		4					5	1	5	1	1	1	1	
						Goals				3			6		12	1	4	4	1				1			1		3		1	1	6	2	2		2			2		1												

F.A. Cup

Rd	Month	Day	Opponent	Score	Scorers	Att	Woods	Short	Fitzsimmons	Rennison	Fauré	Ingram	Blunt	Fickling	Stamp	Burt	Pounder	Brodie	Stoker	Atkinson	Turley	Barnwell-Edinbo	Wilford	Swales	Keegan	Elliott	Jones	Windross	Patterson	Jordan	Dryden	Rose	Shepherd	Shields	Hotte	Connell	Newton	Smith	Sugden	Mann	Baker	Wright	Salt	Burley	Bennett	Sherwood	Hogg	Jewell	O'Riordan	Crawford	Tracey	Brunton	Torpey
4Q	Oct	27	Whitby Town	1-3	Stamp	1862	1		13	4	5		7		9		3	10	2					12	8	6	11																						14				

F.A. Trophy

Rd	Month	Day	Opponent	Score	Scorers	Att	Woods	Short	Fitzsimmons	Rennison	Fauré	Ingram	Blunt	Fickling	Stamp	Burt	Pounder	Brodie	Stoker	Atkinson	Turley	Barnwell-Edinbo	Wilford	Swales	Keegan	Elliott	Jones	Windross	Patterson	Jordan	Dryden	Rose	Shepherd	Shields	Hotte	Connell	Newton	Smith	Sugden	Mann	Baker	Wright	Salt	Burley	Bennett	Sherwood	Hogg	Jewell	O'Riordan	Crawford	Tracey	Brunton	Torpey
2	Jan	12	Hednesford	2-0	Connell, Stamp	953	1			5	3		7		13		11		4						12					2		9	6			10					8												
3	Feb	2	Barnet	0-0		1140	1			5			7		13		11		4										8			9	6	10		12					2			3									
3r		5	BARNET	2-2*	Shields, Rennison	928	1			5			7		9		2		4										8			12	6	10	14	11					3			13									
4		23	MORECAMBE	1-1	Shepherd	1511	1						7		9		2		4											13		11	6		3	12			10		5			8									
4r		26	Morecambe	0-3		801	1			13			7		9		11		4											6			5		3	12			10		2			8									

LDV Trophy

Rd	Month	Day	Opponent	Score	Scorers	Att	Woods	Short	Fitzsimmons	Rennison	Fauré	Ingram	Blunt	Fickling	Stamp	Burt	Pounder	Brodie	Stoker	Atkinson	Turley	Barnwell-Edinbo	Wilford	Swales	Keegan	Elliott	Jones	Windross	Patterson	Jordan	Dryden	Rose	Shepherd	Shields	Hotte	Connell	Newton	Smith	Sugden	Mann	Baker	Wright	Salt	Burley	Bennett	Sherwood	Hogg	Jewell	O'Riordan	Crawford	Tracey	Brunton	Torpey
1	Oct	16	Leigh RMI	1-2**	Pounder	300	1		4		3		7				11		8	12		5			6	2	10																										9

* aet, won 5-3 on penalties, ** aet, lost on "golden goal"

Friendlies / Minor Cups

	Month	Day	Opponent	Score	Scorers	Att
	Jul	17	Bridlington Town	0-2		197
		20	Hull City	0-4		3909
SF		25	MIDDLESBROUGH (NRSC)	0-3	***	2042
		28	ROTHERHAM UNITED	0-1		558
	Aug	3	YORK CITY	3-3	Pounder, Fitzsimmons, Burt	658
		11	DERBY COUNTY	1-2	Ingram (pen)	520
		14	North Ferriby United	1-1	Turley	122

***North Riding Senior Cup of 2000-01 season.

Scarborough FC: 2001-02

Back(L to R) Cook(community officer), Brunton, Keegan, Ellender, Faure, Newton, Woods, Stamp, Rennison, Atkinson, Pounder, Tarmey(physio)
Front(L to R) Brodie, Jewell, Stoker, McHale(asst manager), Thompson(manager), Kerr (youth coach), Burt, Ingram, Blunt

2002-03

7th in Football Conference

#	Month	Day	Opponent	Score	Scorers	Att	Woods	Rennison	Baker	Dryden	Shepherd	Henry	Stoker	Brassart	Rose	Scott	Campbell	Pounder	Hotte	Ormerod	Jordan	Blunt	Fatokun	Patterson	Sillah	Cryan	Holdsworthy	Mallon	Dempsey	Price	Cohen	Taylor	Kerr	Ridler	Gilroy	Hall	Bradshaw	Raw	Walker	Henderson	Crawford	Connell
1	Aug	17	Burton Albion	1-1	Rose	1821	1	2	3	4	5	6	7	8	9	10	11	12	13	14																						
2		20	SOUTHPORT	2-2	Shepherd, Scott	1346	1	2	3	4	5	7	6	8	11	10		12		9	13																					
3		24	DAGENHAM & REDBRIDGE	0-1		1192	1	2	3		5	7	6		11	10	13	8	4	9		12																				
4		26	Chester City	0-0		2292	1	2		3	5	7	6		11	10	12	9	4	8																						
5		31	WOKING	1-1	Scott	1192	1	2		3	5		6	7	11	10	12	9	4	8																						
6	Sep	3	Halifax Town	1-2	Shepherd (pen)	1557	1	2		3	5		6	7	11	10	12	9	4	8			13																			
7		7	KETTERING TOWN	4-1	Shepherd(pen),Fatokun 2, Dryden	1078	1	5		10	4		14	7	13	11	6		3	12	2		8	9																		
8		14	Farnborough Town	1-1	Fatokun	629	1	4		9	3	10	8	6	12	11		13	2	5			7	14																		
9		16	Telford United	2-0	Brown (og), Pounder	756	1	2		3	5	8	13	7	12	10		11	4				9	6																		
10		21	BARNET	1-1	Scott	1266	1	2		3	5	6	13	7	11	9		10	4			12		8																		
11		24	LEIGH RMI	2-0	Fatokun, Sillah	950	1	2			3	7	12	8		10	13	11	4	14	5		9		6																	
12		28	Hereford United	1-0	Pounder	2171	1	3		4	2		6	12	14	10	13	9	5		8		11		7																	
13	Oct	5	Gravesend & Northfleet	2-5	Scott 2	1259	1			3	5		7	9	14	10	11	8	4	13	6		12		2																	
14		8	MORECAMBE	1-0	Fatokun	1179	1			2	3		6	7	11	10	12	8	4	5			9																		13	
15		13	NORTHWICH VICTORIA	4-1	Campbell2, Scott, Pounder	1156	1			14	3		8	7	11	10	12	5	2	6	13		9			4																
16		19	Forest Green Rovers	0-0		751	1			3	6		5	7			11	9	4	8	12	13	10			2																
17	Nov	2	MARGATE	3-2	Ormerod, Pounder, Raw	1131					2	6	7		9	10		8	4	5		12					3											11	1			
18		9	Nuneaton Borough	1-1	Scott	1253				3		6	7	8		10	9	13	2	5		12					4											11	1			
19		23	GRAVESEND & NORTHFLEET	3-2	Mallon, Campbell, Scott	1205	1			4	3		6		13	9	10	8		5	12	7					2	11														
20		30	Stevenage Borough	1-1	Campbell2, Scott, Pounder	1629	1				3		6	13		9	10	12	4	7	8	5	14				2	11														
21	Dec	7	YEOVIL TOWN	2-1	O'Brien (og), Fatokun	1470	1				3		6			10		13	4	8	7	5	12				2	9														
22		14	Kettering Town	3-1	Scott, Holdsworth, Ormerod	1372	1			14	3			6	10	9		12	4	8	7	5	13				2	11														
23		21	FARNBOROUGH TOWN	1-0	Bunce (og)	1403	1				3		6	12	14	9	10	13	4	8	7	5					2	11														
24		26	DONCASTER ROVERS	2-5	Shepherd (pen), Henry	3435	1				3	13	6	7		9	10	12	4	8		5					2	11														
25		28	Southport	1-1	Brassart	1049	1			2	3	5	6	7	14	9	10	11	4	8		12						13														
26	Jan	4	BURTON ALBION	4-1	Shepherd(pen), Fatokun, Blunt 2	1428	1				3		6	7	10	9	13	8	4	5		12	11				2															
27		18	Dagenham & Redbridge	0-1		1566	1			3		8	7	9	10			5	2			6	11				4											12				
28		25	CHESTER CITY	0-1		1938				3	5	7	6	8	11	13	10	12	4	9		14					2												1			
29	Feb	8	Woking	1-2	Rose	1631	1			4	3		6	7	10	9	13	8		5							2		14									11	12			
30		15	HALIFAX TOWN	0-1		1835	1			4	2		7			9	13	11	5	8			12				3		6								10					
31		22	Barnet	0-3		1056					2		8					9	5	6					12		4		3		10	11				7			1			
32	Mar	1	TELFORD UNITED	1-4	Sillah	1224	1				3		7					8	4	13			12		6		2		5		9	10					11					14
33		8	Leigh RMI	2-0	Cohen, Taylor	525	1				3		7	5				11	4						6		2		12		9	10	8									
34		15	HEREFORD UNITED	2-1	Pounder, Taylor	1179	1				3		6	7				9							4				2	5	10	11	8									12
35		22	STEVENAGE BOROUGH	1-2	Shepherd (pen)	1193	1				3			7				9		6			12		4				2	5	11	10	8									
36		28	Yeovil Town	0-1		7008	1				3			7				6	12				13		4				2		11	10	8	5	9							
37	Apr	1	Doncaster Rovers	1-0	Sillah	4155	1						7					6					10		4				2	3	11	12	8	5	9							
38		5	Northwich Victoria	2-0	Pounder 2	503	1		13				7	14				6		12			10		4				2	3		11	8	5	9							
39		12	FOREST GREEN ROVERS	3-0	Pounder 2, Taylor	1146	1				12		7	8				6	14				10		4				2	3		11		5	9							13
40		19	Morecambe	1-3	Fatokun	1937	1				2		7					6					10		4					3		11	8	5	9							12
41		21	NUNEATON BOROUGH	4-1	Sillah,Gilroy(pen),Love(og),Taylor	1451	1						7					6					10		4				2	3		11	8	5	9							12
42		26	Margate	1-3	Cohen	525	1						7	6					13				10		4				2	3	12	11	8	5	9							
					Apps		38	12	3	20	35	13	35	27	15	27	11	30	29	24	8	7	16	3	14	2	16	6	11	8	7	11	9	7	7	1	2	3	4	0	0	0
					Subs				1	2	1	1	4	4	8	1	11	10	4	6	4	8	9	1	1			1	2		1	1						1	1		1	5
					Goals					1	6	1		1	2	9	4	9		2		2	8		4		1	1			2	4			1			1				

F.A. Cup

Rd	Month	Day	Opponent	Score	Scorers	Att	Woods	Rennison	Baker	Dryden	Shepherd	Henry	Stoker	Brassart	Rose	Scott	Campbell	Pounder	Hotte	Ormerod	Jordan	Blunt	Fatokun	Patterson	Sillah	Cryan	Holdsworthy	Mallon	Dempsey	Price	Cohen	Taylor	Kerr	Ridler	Gilroy	Hall	Bradshaw	Raw	Walker	Henderson	Crawford	Connell
4Q	Oct	26	Arnold Town	2-0	Scott 2	910				3	4	6	7		13	11	9	5	2	8		12	14															10	1			
1	Nov	16	CAMBRIDGE UNITED	0-0		2084	1				2	6	7			9	11	8	4	5		13	12		14		3											10				
1r		26	Cambridge United	1-2*	Jordan	3373	1				4		6		14	10	9	8	2	5	7	13	12				3											11				

F.A. Trophy

Rd	Month	Day	Opponent	Score	Scorers	Att	Woods	Rennison	Baker	Dryden	Shepherd	Henry	Stoker	Brassart	Rose	Scott	Campbell	Pounder	Hotte	Ormerod	Jordan	Blunt	Fatokun	Patterson	Sillah	Cryan	Holdsworthy	Mallon	Dempsey	Price	Cohen	Taylor	Kerr	Ridler	Gilroy	Hall	Bradshaw	Raw	Walker	Henderson	Crawford	Connell
3	Jan	11	Stalybridge Celtic	3-0	Bowman (og),Raw, Sillah	613				3	4	7	8	9	10			5	2	6			11		13													12	1	14		
4	Feb	11	DOVER THLETIC	1-1	Pounder	965	1			4	3		6	7	10	9	12	8	2	5									13									11				
4r		17	Dover Athletic	1-2	Dempsey	801	1			4	2		7	8		9	10	11	5	12							3		6											13		

LDV Trophy

Rd	Month	Day	Opponent	Score	Scorers	Att	Woods	Rennison	Baker	Dryden	Shepherd	Henry	Stoker	Brassart	Rose	Scott	Campbell	Pounder	Hotte	Ormerod	Jordan	Blunt	Fatokun	Patterson	Sillah	Cryan	Holdsworthy	Mallon	Dempsey	Price	Cohen	Taylor	Kerr	Ridler	Gilroy	Hall	Bradshaw	Raw	Walker	Henderson	Crawford	Connell
1	Oct	22	Doncaster Rovers	1-2**	Scott	1206	1				3	12	6	7		9	10	8	4	5		13	11			2												14				

*after extra time **lost on "golden goal" in extra time

Friendlies / Minor Cups

Rd	Month	Day	Opponent	Score	Scorers	Att
	Jul	23	HULL CITY	1-3	Robinson	1377
		27	WHITBY TOWN	2-1	Pounder, Stoker	377
		31	SHEFFIELD UNITED	0-0		506
	Aug	3	HARTLEPOOL UNITED	1-2	Scott	500
		8	MIDDLESBROUGH RES	2-3	Shepherd, Rennison	614
1	Jan	21	Marske United (NRSC)	3-0	Brassart, Rose 2	250
SF	Feb	25	WHITBY TOWN (NRSC)	3-2	Pounder, Cohen 2	551

Scarborough FC: 2002-03

Back(L to R) Hodgson(kit man), Farley(physio), Ormerod, Baker, Tracey, Rennison, Woods, Walker, Scott, Campbell, Dryden, Henderson, Cook(school of excellence), Kerr(youth manager)
Front(L to R) Shepherd, Wright, Pounder, Connell, Rose, Slade(manager), Patterson(asst manager), Stoker, Brassart, Blunt, Jordan, Hotte.

2003-04

7th in Football Conference

No.	Month	Day	Opponent	Score	Scorers	Att	Sollitt	Capper	Hotte	Redmile	Price	Gilroy	Kerr	Gill	Williams	Quayle	Rose	Senior	Sherlock	Raw	Baker	Burt	Kelly	Walker	Downey	Henry	Donaldson	Nesovic	Dudgeon	Blackman	Marcelle	McSweeney	Graydon	Batchelor	Lyth	Cryan	Sestanovich	Leadbetter	O'Neill	Robinson	Whitman	Brownrigg	Ketchanke	Nicholson	Hackworth	Davidson
1	Aug	9	FARNBOROUGH TOWN	2-1	Rose, Gilroy (pen)	1419	1	2	3	4	5	6	7	8	9	10	11	12																														
2		12	Northwich Victoria	1-1	Gill	854	1	2	3	4	5	6	7	8		10	11	12	13							9																				
3		16	Woking	1-2	Henry	1902	1	2	3	4	5	6	7	8		10		11		12						9																				
4		23	BURTON ALBION	1-2	Quayle	1445	1	2	3	4	5	6	7	8	9	10	13	12	14								11																			
5		25	Accrington Stanley	0-1		2017	1	2	3	4	5		7	8		10	11	9	12	6																										
6		31	TELFORD UNITED	1-1	Quayle	1113	1	2	3	4	5			8		10	11	12		6	7	9																								
7	Sep	6	GRAVESEND & NORTHFLEET	2-0	Quayle (pen), Senior	1249			3	4				8		10	11	13	14	6	5		9	1	2	7		12																		
8		13	Hereford United	1-2	Quayle	4850			3	4	5			8		10		13	14		6		9	1	2	7	11		12																	
9		20	FOREST GREEN ROVERS	2-2	Quayle 2 (1pen)	1120		2	3	4	12		14	8		10		13			6		9	1		7				11					5											
10		23	Tamworth	0-0		1004		2	3		12		6	8		10		13		14	5		9	1		7				11					4											
11		27	Exeter City	0-0		2776			3	4	12		6	14		10		13		8	5		9	1		7				11					2											
12	Oct	4	SHREWSBURY TOWN	1-1	Quayle	1608		7	3	4	5		6	8		10		12					9	1						11	13	14			2											
13		7	MORECAMBE	1-0	Price	1619			3	4	7		6	13		10		12		8	5		9	1							11				2											
14		11	Stevenage	2-2	Hotte, Senior	1786		7	3	4			6			10		13		8	5		9	1						12	11	14			2											
15		18	MARGATE	0-1		1263		8		3	5		6	14				7			4		9	1						10	11	12	13		2											
16	Nov	1	CHESTER CITY	2-2	Quayle, Marcelle	1441		4		3			6			10	11	12			5		9	1							8					2	7									
17		11	Leigh RMI	4-1	Rose,Quayle2(1pen),Senior	375		4		3			6	12	14	10	11	13			5		9	1							8					2	7									
18		15	ALDERSHOT TOWN	1-0	Redmile	1624		4	13	3			6	8	12	10		14			5			1		9					11					2	7									
19		22	Dagenham & Redbridge	0-1		1107			4	3			6	8	7		10	13			5		9	1							11			14	12	2										
20		25	BARNET	2-2	Redmile, Kelly	1208			4	3		14	6	8	7		10	12					9	1							11				5	2										
21		29	Gravesend & Northfleet	1-1	Cryan	747			4		3	14	6	8	13	11	10	12			5		9	1							7					2										
22	Dec	13	Farnborough Town	2-1	Sestanovich, Quayle	620			4	3	14		6	8	12	11					13		9	1							10				5	2	7									
23		20	NORTHWICH VICTORIA	1-0	Sestanovich	1264			4				6	8	12	11		13			3		9	1							10				5	2	7									
24		26	Halifax Town	0-1		2136			4	3			6	8	12	11		13					9	1							10				5	2	7					14					
25	Jan	17	WOKING	2-2	Williams, Quayle(pen)	2503		13	4						6	11		12			3		9	1							8				5	2	7					10					
26	Feb	3	HEREFORD UITED	3-3	Marcelle, Downey, Redmile	1459	13	2	4	3			6	7	8		14	12					9	1	5						11											10					
27		7	Forest Green Rovers	0-4		846		2					6			11	12	14	8				9	1	5						7				4					3		10					
28		21	Shrewsbury Town	1-4	Senior	3333			3		2		6	7		11		10					9	1	5										12						4	8					
29	Mar	6	Morecambe	1-2	Quayle	1623			3							11	6	10	13		2		9	1	5						7										4	12					8
30		13	LEIGH RMI	4-1	Hackworth,Nicholson,Rose,Harrison(og)	1093			3				7	12		11	6	13			2		9	1											5									4	8	10	
31		16	TAMWORTH	0-1		1059			3				7	12		11	6	13			2		9	1							14				5									4	8	10	
32		20	Aldershot Town	2-1	Ketchanke, Senior	2442			3				7	5			6	12					9	1							11												2	4	8	10	
33		23	EXETER CITY	2-3	Kelly (pen), Hackworth	1200			3				7	12		11	6	13					9	1							5				14								2	4	8	10	
34		25	HALIFAX TOWN	1-0	Senior	1220			3				7			11	6	13					9	1	12						5				2								14	4	8	10	
35		27	DAGENHAM & REDBRIDGE	0-0		1302		2	3				7	6		11	12	10					9	1	4						5				13										8		
36	Apr	3	Barnet	0-0		1560		13	3			12	7	6		11	9	10						1	4						5				2										8		
37		6	STEVENAGE BOROUGH	2-2	Marcelle, Rose	1018			3				7	6		11	9	12		13				1	4						5				2										8	10	
38		10	Burton Albion	0-2		1370			3			12	7	6		11	9	14		13				1	4						5				2										8	10	
39		12	ACCRINGTON STANLEY	2-1	Hackworth, Gilroy	1523		2	3			12	7	6		11	9	13						1	4						5														8	10	
40		14	Telford United	1-2	Marcelle	1654	1		3			12	7			11	9	13		6					4						5				14										8	10	2
41		17	Chester Ciity	0-1		5987			3			11	7	6			9	13					5	1	4						12				2										8	10	
42		24	Margate	2-0	Gilroy, Quayle	401	13		3			12	7	6		14	9						5	1	4						11				2										8	10	
						Apps	7	18	37	22	12	5	36	28	6	35	23	7	1	7	19	1	30	35	14	8	2	0	0	5	26	0	0	0	21	10	7	0	1	2	4	2	5	13	11	2
						Subs	2	2	1		4	7	1	7	6	1	4	33	6	4	1				1			1	1	1	3	3	1	1	5						2	1				
						Goals			1	3	1	3		1	1	14	4	6					2		1	1					4					1	2						1	1	3	

F.A. Cup

Rd	Month	Day	Opponent	Score	Scorers	Att	Sollitt	Capper	Hotte	Redmile	Price	Gilroy	Kerr	Gill	Williams	Quayle	Rose	Senior	Sherlock	Raw	Baker	Burt	Kelly	Walker	Downey	Henry	Donaldson	Nesovic	Dudgeon	Blackman	Marcelle	McSweeney	Graydon	Batchelor	Lyth	Cryan	Sestanovich	Leadbetter	O'Neill	Robinson	Whitman	Brownrigg	Ketchanke	Nicholson	Hackworth	Davidson
4Q	Oct	25	HINCKLEY UNITED	3-1	Lyth, Kerr 2	1206	12	4		3			6	8		10	14	7			5		9	1							11		13		2											
1	Nov	8	DONCASTER ROVERS	1-0	Rose	3497		4		3			6			10	11				5		9	1							8				12	2	7									
2	Dec	7	Port Vale	1-0	Sestanovich	4651			4	3			6	8		11	12						9	1							10				5	2	7									
3	Jan	3	Southend United	1-1	Kerr	6902			4				6	8	12	11					3		9	1							10				5	2	7					13					
3r		14	SOUTHEND UNITED	1-0	Quayle	4859			4				6			11					3		9	1							8				5	2	7					10					
4		24	CHELSEA	0-1		5941		13	4				6			11		12			3		9	1							8				5	2	7					10					

F.A. Trophy

Rd	Month	Day	Opponent	Score	Scorers	Att	Sollitt	Capper	Hotte	Redmile	Price	Gilroy	Kerr	Gill	Williams	Quayle	Rose	Senior	Sherlock	Raw	Baker	Burt	Kelly	Walker	Downey	Henry	Donaldson	Nesovic	Dudgeon	Blackman	Marcelle	McSweeney	Graydon	Batchelor	Lyth	Cryan	Sestanovich	Leadbetter	O'Neill	Robinson	Whitman	Brownrigg	Ketchanke	Nicholson	Hackworth	Davidson
3	Jan	10	STAFFORD RANGERS	1-2	Senior	1120	1	3			5				7			10		12			9		4								6	8		2		13			11					

LDV Trophy

Rd	Month	Day	Opponent	Score	Scorers	Att	Sollitt	Capper	Hotte	Redmile	Price	Gilroy	Kerr	Gill	Williams	Quayle	Rose	Senior	Sherlock	Raw	Baker	Burt	Kelly	Walker	Downey	Henry	Donaldson	Nesovic	Dudgeon	Blackman	Marcelle	McSweeney	Graydon	Batchelor	Lyth	Cryan	Sestanovich	Leadbetter	O'Neill	Robinson	Whitman	Brownrigg	Ketchanke	Nicholson	Hackworth	Davidson
1	Oct	14	PORT VALE	2-1	Senior, Kelly	1003			3		5		6	8				7			4		9	1						10	11	13	14		2											
2	Nov	4	HALIFAX TOWN	0-1		899		4	3				6	12		10	11	13			5		9	1							8			14		2	7									

Friendlies / Minor Cups

Rd	Month	Day	Opponent	Score	Scorers	Att
	Jul	16	Selby Town	6-4	Cohen,Pounder2,Gilroy2(1p),Henderson	202
		19	Bridlington Town	1-3	Rose	323
F		23	MIDDLESBROUGH (NRSC)*	1-2	Kerr (pen)	552
		26	York City	0-2		1152
		30	HULL CITY	4-2	Senior, Gilroy, Quayle 2	587
	Aug	2	MANSFIELD TOWN	0-1		635
		5	SHEFFIELD UTD RES	2-3	Quayle, Jean	628
1	Feb	11	Guisborough Town (NRSC)	1-0	Kelly	254
SF	Mar	9	YORK CITY RES (NRSC)	2-0	Quayle (pen), Rose	539

* Final of 2002-03 North Riding Senior Cup

Scarborough FC: 2003-04

Back(L to R) Rose, Gilroy, Rennison, Gareth Downey, Walker, Dudgeon, Glenn Downey, Quayle
Front(L to R) Lyth, Williams, Raw, Pounder, Henry(player-coach), Slade(manager),
Hodgson(kit man), Price, Hotte, Kerr, Baker.

2004-05

13th in Nationwide Conference

No.	Month	Day	Opponent	Score	Scorers	Att.	Walker	Lyth	Cryan	Hotte	Nicholson	Thompson	Redfearn	Kerr	Gilroy	Hackworth	Gill	Senior	Burton	Foot	Baker	Foster	Pounder	Townson	Horrigan	Keen	Coulson	Grant	Reeves	Bishop	Jones	Beadle	Heinemann	Warwick
1	Aug	14	WOKING	2-0	Hackworth, Redfearn (pen)	1602	1	2	3	4	5	6	7	8	9	10	11	12	13															
2		17	Halifax Town	1-2	Redfearn	1887	1	2	3	4	5	6	7	8	9	10	11	14	13	12														
3		21	Farnborough Town	1-0	Redfearn	633	1	2	3	4	5	6	7	8	9	10	11	13	14	12														
4		28	MORECAMBE	1-1	Senior	1742	1	2	3	4	5	6	7	8	9	10	11	12	13															
5		30	Burton Albion	3-2	Redfearn, Austin (og), Gill	1306	1	14	3	4	5	6	7	8		10	11	12	9		2		13											
6	Sep	4	CANVEY ISLAND	1-1	Burton	1732	1		3	4	5	6	7	8	12	10	11	13	9		2													
7		11	EXETER CITY	1-1	Redfearn	1715	1		3	4	5	6	7	8	13	10	11	12	9		2		14											
8		18	Hereford United	0-1		2874	1		3	4	5	6	7	8	12	10	14	11			2	13	9											
9		21	Carlisle United	1-2	Redfearn	5111	1	2	3		5	6	7	8	9	10	13	11		12		4												
10		25	BARNET	1-1	Thompson	1542	1		3	2	5	6	7	8	9	10		11				4												
11	Oct	2	Forest Green Rovers	1-0	Gilroy	686			6	3	5	7	8		9		13	12	10	4	2	14		11		1								
12		5	NORTHWICH VICTORIA	3-0	Redfearn (pen), Senior 2	1598			3		5	7	8	6	9	14		13	10	4	2		12	11		1								
13		9	ALDERSHOT TOWN	2-2	Senior 2	1662			6	3	5	7	8	9		10		12	14	4	2			11	13	1								
14		16	Tamworth	0-1		1027	1		4	3	5	7	8	9		10		12	13		2		6	11										
15		23	ACCRINGTON STANLEY	4-0	Hackworth,Redfearn,Nicholson,Senior	1704	1	2	6	3	5	7	8	9		10		11		4			13				12							
16	Nov	6	Dagenham & Redbridge	3-0	Senior, Redfearn, Cryan	1186	1		6	3	5	7	8	9			10	11		4	2	12	14				13							
17		20	STEVENAGE BOROUGH	3-3	Senior 2, Nicholson	1689	1	13	6		5	7	8	9		12	10	11		4	2	3												
18		27	Crawley Town	1-2	Burton	1804	1		6		5	7	8	9	12	13	10	11	14	4	2	3												
19	Dec	4	GRAVESEND & NORTHFLEET	1-0	Hackworth	1634	1	13	3		5	7	8	9	6	12	10	11		4	2													
20		7	Leigh RMI	1-1	Gill	325	1	13	3	12	5	7	8	9	6	14	10	11		4	2													
21		11	HEREFORD UNITED	0-0		1608	1		8	3	5	7	12	9	6	10	14	11	13	4	2													
22		18	Exeter City	1-3	Redfearn	4529	1		8	3	5	7	9		6	10		11	12	4	2													
23		26	YORK CITY	5-1	Thompson,Redfearn2(1p),Hackworth,Lyth	4586	1	12	8	3	5	7	9		6	10	13	11	14	4	2													
24		28	Barnet	0-1		2504	1		8	3	5	7	9	12	6	10		11		4	2													
25	Jan	2	York City	2-0	Senior, Hackworth	4469	1		8	3	5	7	9	12	6	10		11		4	2													
26		8	FOREST GREEN ROVERS	0-0		1420	1	14	8	3	5	7	9	12	6	10		11		4	2							13						
27		22	Northwich Victoria	0-1		638	1	14	8	3	5	7	9	10	6	11		12		4	2		13											
28		29	CARLISLE UNITED	1-1	Hotte	2828	1		4	3	5	7	9	8	6	13		11			2		12						10					
29	Feb	5	Accrington Stanley	1-2	Hackworth	1315	1	12	4	3	5	7	9	8	6	13		11			2								10					
30		12	DAGENHAM & REDBRIDGE	2-0	Cryan 2	1358	1		6	3	5	7	9	8		11		12		4	2								10					
31		19	Stevenage Borough	0-1		1728	1	14	6	3	5	7	9	8		11	10	13		4	2		12											
32		26	CRAWLEY TOWN	2-2	Hackworth, Pounder	1451	1		6	3	5	7		8		11	10	12		4	2		9											
33	Mar	5	Gravesend & Northfleet	0-4		1178	1	14	6	3	5	7				11		13		4	2		9						10	8	12			
34		12	LEIGH RMI	3-0	Senior, Cryan, Hotte	1219	1	12	6	3	5	7		8		11	13	10			2		9				14			4				
35		15	TAMWORTH	2-2	Hackworth, Coulson	1158	1	13	6	3	5	7	12	8		11		10			2		9				14			4				
36		19	HALIFAX TOWN	3-1	Bishop, Senior, Reeves (pen)	2109	1	12	6	3	5	7	4	8				10			2		9				13		11	10				
37		23	Woking	1-1	Coulson	2587	1	12	6		5	7	10	8				13		3	2		9				14		11	4				
38		26	BURTON ALBION	1-1	Redfearn	1675	1	2	6		5	7	9	8				10		3							12		11	4	13			
39	Apr	2	Morecambe	1-2	Redfearn (pen)	1632	1	2	6	3	5	7	10	8		13		12					9				14		11	4				
40		9	FARNBOROUGH TOWN	4-0	Reeves 3, Kerr	1451	1	2	6	3	5	7	9	8		12		10									13		11	4		14		
41		16	Canvey Island	0-1		610	1	2	6	3	5	7	12	8		9		10					13				14		11	4				
42		23	Aldershot Town	0-2		4437	1	13	6	3	5	7	11	8		9		10		2			12				14			4				
						Apps	39	10	42	34	42	42	36	35	19	28	14	24	5	23	30	4	9	4	0	3	0	0	10	10	0	0	0	0
						Subs		15		1			3	3	4	9	6	18	10	3		3	10		1		11	1			2	1		
						Goals		1	4	2	2	2	14	1	1	8	2	12	2				1				2		4	1				

F.A. Cup

Rd	Month	Day	Opponent	Score	Scorers	Att.	Walker	Lyth	Cryan	Hotte	Nicholson	Thompson	Redfearn	Kerr	Gilroy	Hackworth	Gill	Senior	Burton	Foot	Baker	Foster	Pounder	Townson	Horrigan	Keen	Coulson	Grant	Reeves	Bishop	Jones	Beadle	Heinemann	Warwick
4Q	Oct	30	Lancaster City	1-1	Hotte	800	1	2	6	3	5	7	8	9		10		11		4		13					12							
r	Nov	2	LANCASTER CITY	0-1		1073	1	2	6	3	5	7	8	9		10		11		4		13					12							

F.A. Trophy

Rd	Month	Day	Opponent	Score	Scorers	Att.	Walker	Lyth	Cryan	Hotte	Nicholson	Thompson	Redfearn	Kerr	Gilroy	Hackworth	Gill	Senior	Burton	Foot	Baker	Foster	Pounder	Townson	Horrigan	Keen	Coulson	Grant	Reeves	Bishop	Jones	Beadle	Heinemann	Warwick
3	Jan	15	Barrow	1-2	Senior	1076	1		8	3	5	7	9	6	12	10		11		4	2		13											

LDV Trophy

Rd	Month	Day	Opponent	Score	Scorers	Att.	Walker	Lyth	Cryan	Hotte	Nicholson	Thompson	Redfearn	Kerr	Gilroy	Hackworth	Gill	Senior	Burton	Foot	Baker	Foster	Pounder	Townson	Horrigan	Keen	Coulson	Grant	Reeves	Bishop	Jones	Beadle	Heinemann	Warwick
1	Sep	28	Rochdale	1-4	Gilroy	837	1	12	3	2	5	6		8	9	10	14	11	13			4	7											

Conference Challenge Cup

Rd	Month	Day	Opponent	Score	Scorers	Att.	Walker	Lyth	Cryan	Hotte	Nicholson	Thompson	Redfearn	Kerr	Gilroy	Hackworth	Gill	Senior	Burton	Foot	Baker	Foster	Pounder	Townson	Horrigan	Keen	Coulson	Grant	Reeves	Bishop	Jones	Beadle	Heinemann	Warwick
1	Jan	25	Morecambe	1-2	Hackworth (pen)	406		3	4					6	11	10		13			2		8			1	9			7			5	12

Friendlies / Minor Cups

	Jul	17	LEEDS UNITED RES	1-1	Gilroy	1228
		20	GRIMSBY TOWN	2-0	Hackworth, Senior	633
F		24	MIDDLESBROUGH (NRSC)*	1-0	Gill	836
		27	Grantham Town	1-3	Senior	150
		31	SHEFFIELD UTD RES	1-1	Redfearn	722
	Aug	7	Whitby Town	2-1	Thompson 2	310
	Nov	12	Leeds United Res	2-1	Gill, Foster	**
1	Jan	10	DORMANS (NRSC)	5-1	Kerr,Coulson,Burton2,Beadle	293
SF	Apr	6	MIDDLESBROUGH (NRSC)	1-4	Hackworth	220

* the game on Jul 24 was the Final of of 2003-04 North Riding Senior Cup

** this game was "behind closed doors"

Scarborough FC: 2004-05

Back(L to R) Barnes, Beadle, Hackworth, Glenn Downey, Cryan, Gareth Downey, Walker, Ossai, Burton, Gill, Baker, Gilroy, Heinemann, Coulson
Front(L to R) Blackburn, Senior, Lyth, Kerr, Woodmansey(physio), Redfearn(asst manager), Henry(manager), Cook(youth director), Hodgson(kit man), Hotte, Pounder, Thompson, Blott.

2005/06

22nd in Football Conference

							Walker	S Baker	Elebert	Weaver	Nicholson	Lyth	Bishop	Hackworth	Clark	Wake	Quayle	Palmer	Redfearn	Eccles	Coulson	Harper	Foot	Speight	Blott	Beadle	Cook	Rix	Hughes	Parton	McClare	Atkinson	Fowler	Dunbavin	Jarvis	McNiven	Ingram	Pounder	Kell	T Baker	Bertos	Blunt	Yates
1	Aug	13	Hereford United	0-4		3173	1	2	3	4	5	6	7	8	9	10	11	12	13	14																							
2		16	MORECAMBE	0-1		1750	1	2	3	4	5	6	7		9	14	11	10	8	13	12																						
3		20	KIDDERMINSTER HARRIERS	1-1	Foot	1401	1	2	3	4	5	6		8	9		11	10		12	14	7	13																				
4		27	Dagenham & Redbridge	2-0	Speight, Wake	1074	1	2	3		5	13		8	9	14	11			10	6	7	4	12																			
5		29	ACCRINGTON STANLEY	2-2	Quayle, Spewight	1541	1	2	3		5	12		8	9		11	14		10	6	7	4	13																			
6	Sep	3	Burton Albion	1-2	Wake	1336	1	2	3		5	14	6	8	9	10	11		13			7	4	12																			
7		10	GRAVESEND & NORTHFLEET	3-1	Nicholson, Wake. og	1207	1	2	3		5	12	6	8	9	10	11		13		14		4	7																			
8		17	Canvey Island	0-1		744	1	2	3	4	5	14	6	8	9		11		7		13			10	12																		
9		20	Altrincham	1-1	Coulson	862	1	2	3		5	13	6	8	9				7	11	12		4	10	14																		
10		24	FOREST GREEN ROVERS	1-0	Redfearn (pen)	1341	1	2	3		5	13	6	8	10				7	9	12		4	11																			
11		27	SOUTHPORT	0-1		1290	1	2	3		5	13	6	8	10				7	12	9		4	11																			
12	Oct	1	Woking	0-4		1840	1	2	12		5	3	6	8	11				7		10		4			9	13																
13		8	CRAWLEY TOWN	1-2	Coulson	1257	1	2			8	3	6		10		11				9		4			7	5																
14		15	Grays Athletic	0-5		1515	1			2	13	3	6	14	10	12	11				9		4			7	5	8															
15		29	ALDERSHOT TOWN	2-2	Quayle, Coulson	1618	1	2		4	5	3	6	10	9	13	11				12						8		7														
16	Nov	12	Tamworth	1-0	Quayle	1165	1	2		4	5	3		10	9		11				12						8		7				6										
17		19	STEVENAGE BOROUGH	1-1	Nicholson	1552	1	2		4	5	3	12	10	9		11				13						8		7				6										
18		26	HALIFAX TOWN	2-0	Fowler, Clark (pen)	1843	1			4	5	3	2	10	9		11										8		7	12	13		6										
19	Dec	3	Cambridge United	1-2	Hackworth	2809	1	4			5	3	2	10	9		11				14						8		7	12		13	6										
20		10	EXETER CITY	0-1		1428		4		2	5	3	7	10	9		13										8		14	11			6	1	12								
21		26	York City	1-3	Wake	4921		4			5	3	7	10		11			14		13						8		2		9	12	6	1									
22		30	Halifax Town	0-1		1682	1	4		2		3	7	10		11					12						8		13	14	9	5	6										
23	Jan	2	YORK CITY	2-2	Wake, Hughes	4057	1	4		2		3	7	10		11	14				13		12				8		9			5	6										
24		7	HEREFORD UNITED	0-1		1582	1	4			6	3	7	10		11	13				12								9		8	5					2						
25		14	Southport	2-0	Fowler, McNiven	1035	1	4			6	3	7	10									2						9				5			11		8					12
26		21	Kidderminster Harriers	1-2	McNiven	1740	1	4			6		7	10		12													9			3	5			11	2	8					
27		24	Morecambe	3-0	Fowler, Hughes, McNiven	1478	1	4			6		7	10		12													9			3	5			11	2	8					
28		28	DAGENHAM & REDBRIDGE	0-1		1505	1	4			6	12	7	10			13						14						9			3	5			11	2	8					
29	Feb	4	ALTRINCHAM	1-2	McNiven	1405	1				6	4		10							12		13						9			3	5			11	2	14	7	8			
30		11	Forest Green Rovers	1-5	McNiven	732	1				6			10					8		13		4								12	3	5			11	2	14	7		9		
31		18	WOKING	1-1	Coulson	1278		12		4	6	7									10								9		8	3	5	1		11	2						
32		25	Gravesend & Northfleet	0-0		930					6	7		12					4		10								9		8	3		1		11	2	5					
33	Mar	11	Crawley Town	0-2		1181					6	7		13					4		10		14						9		8	3	12	1		11	2	5					
34		21	CANVEY ISLAND	1-2	Coulson	1153		5		4	6			10							12								9			3	8	1		11	2					7	
35		25	Aldershot Town	1-0	Coulson	2245		2		4	6			10					5		11					12			9		13	3	8	1		14						7	
36	Apr	8	Stevenage Borough	0-2		1861		5		2	6			11					4		10								9			3	7	1		13	12					8	
37		11	TAMWORTH	0-0		1648		5		2	6			11					4		12								9		13	3	7	1		10	8						
38		15	BURTON ALBION	3-0	Redfearn(pen),Hackworth, Coulson	1808		5		2	6			11					4		12								9		13	3	7	1		10	8						
39		17	Accrington Stanley	0-1		3320		5		2	6			11					4							12			9		13	3	7	1		10	8					14	
40		19	GRAYS ATHLETIC	2-7	Weaver, McNiven	1560				2				11					4		13		5			14					12	3	7	1		10	8	6				9	
41		22	CAMBRIDGE UNITED	1-2	Redfearn	1831		8		2	6			11					4		12		5		13	9					14	3	7	1		10							
42		29	Exeter City	1-1	Hackworth	3382		8		2	6			11					4		13		14			9	5				12	3	7	1		10							
						Apps	28	34	11	22	38	21	23	36	20	7	15	2	17	4	11	4	14	5	0	5	12	1	22	1	6	20	24	14	0	16	14	7	2	1	1	4	0
						Subs		1	1		1	9	1	3		6	4	2	4	4	22		6	3	3	3	1		2	3	9	2	1		1	2	1	2				1	1
						Goals				1	2			3	1	5	3		3		7		1	2					2				3			6							

F.A. Cup

4Q	Oct	22	Harrogate Town	0-1		1591	1	2			5	3	6	12	10	9	11		7		14		4		13			8																

F.A. Trophy

1	Dec	17	Kidderminster Harriers	0-4		957		4		2	5	3	7	10	14		11										12		9		13		6	1	8								

Friendlies / Minor Cups

	Jul	19	BARNSLEY	0-2		611
		23	CHESTERFIELD	1-1	Wake	670
		26	Bridlington Town	3-0	Udenkwour 2, Eccles	331
		30	SCUNTHORPE UNITED	2-4	Quayle, Clark	455
	Aug	3	SHEFFIELD UNITED	2-3	Wake, Nicholson	856
		6	SUNDERLAND RES	4-0	Hughes, Quayle 2, Coulson	678
	Nov	5	HARTLEPOOL UNITED	0-0		*
1	Jan	4	MIDDLESBROUGH (NRSC)	5-1	Eccles 2, Quayle 2, Coulson	301
SF	Mar	20	YORK CITY (NRSC)	0-3		108

* This game was held "behind closed doors"

Scarborough FC: 2005-06

(L to R) Perry, Wake, Nicholson, Quayle, Jackson, Hackworth, Palmer, Pecora, Walker, Bishop, Foot, Weaver, Beadle, Elebert, Baker
Front(L to R) Lyth, Eccles, Clark, Hodgson(kit man), Redfearn(asst manager), Henry(manager), Mitch Cook(youth director), Woodmansey(physio), Carl Cook, Blott, Coulson, Hughes.

2006-07

20th in Football Conference North

							Aspden	Lyth	Cook	Cartwright	Hotte	Ingram	Bilunt	Vermiglio	Hackworth	Whittington	Thornton	Thompson	Brisco	Beadle	Davies	Blott	Dalton	Wilberforce	Amos	Patterson
1	Aug	12	Worksop Town	0-0		610	1	2	3	4	5	6	7	8	9	10	11	12								
2		15	GAINSBOROUGH TRINITY	0-0		1095	1	2	3	4	5	6	7	8	9	10	11	12								
3		19	VAUXHALL MOTORS	0-1		789	1	2	3	7	5	6	11	8	10	13		9	4	12						
4		22	Stalybridge Celtic	2-2	Whittington, Thompson	401	1	2	11	7	5			8		9		11	4	6	3					
5		26	Nuneaton Borough	1-1	Hackworth	873	1	2	11	7	5			8	12	9		10	4	6	3					
6		28	MOOR GREEN	3-0	Thornton,Thompson (pen), Blott	770	1	2	3	7	5			8	9	13	11	10	4	6	12	14				
7	Sep	2	Redditch United	1-1	Thompson	472	1	2	11	7	5			8	9	13	12	10	4	6	3	14				
8		9	WORKINGTON	0-1		902	1	2	7	4	5			8	9	11	13	10		6	3	12				
9		12	FARSLEY CELTIC	0-0		640	1	2	3	7	5			8	9	10	11			4	6					
10		16	Kettering Town	1-3	Whittington	1235	1	2	3	7	5			8	9	10	11			4	6		12			
11		23	LANCASTER CITY	1-2	Thompson (pen)	986	1	4	3	7	5			8	9		11	12		2	6	10				
12	Oct	7	HUCKNALL TOWN	1-2	Blott	833	1		3	4	2	6		8	9		11	10		5		7				
13		21	Leigh RMI	1-1	Hackworth	215				4	5	6		8	9	7	11	10		2	3		12	1		
14	Nov	4	Droylsden	3-1	Cartwright, Robinson(og), Thompson (pen)	967		2		4	3	6		8	10	7	11	9		5		12	13	1		
15		11	HARROGATE TOWN	1-1	Thompson (pen)	1031		2		4	5	6		8	9	11		10			3	7	12	1		
16		14	BARROW	1-1	Thompson (pen)	679		2		4	5	6		8		11		10		9	3	7		1		
17		18	Worcester City	2-3	Vermiglio, Whittington	1053		2		4	5	6		8		11		10		9	3	7	12	1		
18	Dec	2	HINCKLEY UNITED	3-0	Thompson, Whittington, Cartwright	796		2		4	3	6		8	9	7	11	10		5	13	14	12	1		
19		9	Hyde United	1-1	Dalton	388		2			5	6		8	9		11	10		4	3	12	7	1		
20		12	REDDITCH UNITED	3-2	Hackworth, Thompson, Dalton	759		2		12	5	6		8	9		11	10		4	3	13	7	1		
21		26	Blyth Spartans	0-2		903		2		4	3	6		8	9		11	10		5		12	7	1		
22		30	Farsley Celtic	2-0	Vermiglio, Thornton	604		2		4	5	6		8	9		11	10		13	3	12	7	1		
23	Jan	1	BLYTH SPARTANS	0-1		1239		2		4	5	6		8	9		11	10		13	3	12	7	1		
24		6	Workington	1-0	Hackworth	577		2		4	5	6			9		11	10		8	3	7	12	1		
25		20	ALFRETON TOWN	0-1		977		2		4	5	6			9		11	10		8	3	12	7	1		
26		27	Lancaster City	5-1	Beadle2,Hackworth,Thornton,OG	317		2	12	4	5	6			9		11	10		8	3	7	13	1	14	
27		30	KETTERING TOWN	1-1	Blott	915		2	12	4	5	6			9		11	10		8	3	7		1		
28	Feb	3	Harrogate Town	1-0	Thompson	1058		2	3	4	5	6			9		11	10		8		7	12	1		
29		10	WORCESTER CITY	1-0	Hackworth	756		2	3	4	5	6			9		11	10		8		7	12	1		
30		17	Hinckley United	1-1	Thompson	568		2	8	4	5	6					11	10			3	9	7	1		12
31		24	HYDE UNITED	1-2	Cartwright	748		2		4	5	6		8	9		11			10	3	12	7	1		
32	Mar	3	Barrow	1-1	Dalton	852		2		4	5	6		8	9	12	11	10		7	3	14	13	1		
33		10	DROYLSDEN	1-0	Thompson (pen)	836		2	3	4	5	6		8	9		12	10		13		7	11	1		
34		17	Vauxhall Motors	1-1	Thompson	301		2	13	4	5	6		8	9		11	10		14	3	12	7	1		
35		20	Alfreton Town	1-1	Cook	236		2	11	4	3	6		8	9			10		5		7		1		
36		23	WORKSOP TOWN	2-1	Blott, Cartwright	1089		2	11	4	3	6		8	9		13	10		5	14	7	12	1		
37		31	Gainsborough Trinity	1-3	Beadle	671		2	11	4	5	6			9		12	10		8	3	7		1		
38	Apr	7	NUNEATON BOROUGH	1-3	Blott	1077		2	11	4	3	6		8	9		12	10		5		7	13	1		
39		9	Moor Green	2-1	Hackworth, Blott	250		2	3	4	5	6		8	9		11	10		13		12	7	1		
40		14	STALYBRIDGE CELTIC	0-1		1043		7	3	4	5	6		8	9		11	10		2		13	12	1		
41		21	LEIGH RMI	1-1	Beadle	1196		12	3	4	5	6		8	9		11	10		2		7	13	1		
42		28	Hucknall Town	1-0	Hackworth	646		2	11	4	5	6		8	7			10			3	9	12	1	13	
						Apps	12	39	24	40	42	34	3	34	37	13	28	36	5	31	25	18	11	30		
						Subs		1	3	1					1	4	6	3		6	3	16	16		2	1
						Goals			1	3				2	9	4	3	13		4		6	3			

F.A. Cup

2Q	Sep	30	LANCASTER CITY	1-1	Blott	667			11	4	2	6			8	9		10		5	3	12	7	1		
r	Oct	4	Lancaster City	2-1	Thompson, Blott	248			3	4	2	6		8	9		11	10		5		12	7	1		
3Q		14	Ossett Albion	1-1	Vermiglio	582			3	4	2	6		8	7	13		10		5	12	9	11	1		
r		17	OSSETT ALBION	2-0	Thompson, Vermiglio	802				4	2	6		8	9	7	11	10		5	3	12		1		
4Q		28	Stafford Rangers	0-3		1034		12		4	2	6		8	9	7	11	10		5	3	13		1		

F.A. Trophy

3Q	Nov	25	Burscough	2-1	Vermiglio, Whittington	409		2		4	3	6		8		9	11	10		5			7	1		
1	Dec	16	Rushden & Diamonds	2-3	Hackworth, Dalton	1152		2		4	3	6		8	9		11	10		5		12	7	1		

Friendlies, Minor Cups

	Jul	15	LEEDS UTD RES	2-1	Thornton, Own Goal	471
		19	Northallerton Town	4-2	Whittington 3, Thornton	136
		22	ROSSINGTON MAIN	3-1	Whittington 3	289
		25	Retford United	2-1	Whittington, McStay (pen)	121
		29	Bradford Park Avenue	1-1	Hackworth (pen)	156
	Aug	1	Bridlington Town	3-0	Whittington 2, Thornton	102
		2	SHEFFIELD UTD RES	1-0	Whittington	399
		5	WHITBY TOWN	1-0	Farthing (og)	415
1	Feb	19	YORK CITY (NRSC 1)	2-1	Anderson, Dalton	168
SF	Mar	29	MIDDLESBROUGH (NRSC)	0-3		185

Scarborough FC: 2006 - 07

Back(L to R) Hackworth, Perry, Byron, Vermiglio, Aspden, Beadle, Thornton, Dalton, Cook
Front(L to R) Lyth, Blunt, Hotte, Woodmansey(physio), Ingram, Patterson(manager), Blott, Whittington, Cartwright.

Scarborough FC: Friendlies / minor cups

(This is an overall summary and is a repeat from the details given for each individual season)

1998-99

July	14	Whitby Town	A	0-3		500
	18	Barnsley (York Tournament)	(York)	1-0	Williams	355
	19	Airdrie (York Tournament)	(York)	4-4	Robinson, Bullimore(pen), Williams, Brodie	
			(Won 5-4on pens)			260
	24	York City (NR Senior Cup S/F)	H	2-2	Tinkler (og),Campbell	1023
			(Lost 3-4 on pens)			
	27	Manchester City	H	1-4	Bullimore	722
	30	Bury	H	1-2	Brodie	481
Aug	3	Newcastle United Reserves	H	2-1	Arnison (og), Brodie	1735
Mar	31	FC Tromso (Norway)	H	1-1	Robinson	306

1999-2000

July	15	York City (NR Senior Cup S/F))	H	0-0	*(Lost 3-5 on pens)*	1220
	17	Huddersfield Town	H	0-0		1505
	21	Bradford City	H	0-2		1210
	24	Airdrie (Minster Carpets Cup)	H	0-2		522
	25	Darlington (Minster Carpets Cup)	H	1-2	Milbourne	646
	27	Gateshead	A	0-3		246
	29	Bedlington Terriers	A	2-4	McNaughton, McAlindon	201
	31	Hull City	H	0-1		1100
Aug	5	Darlington	H	1-0	McAlindon	812
	7	Grantham	A	1-0	Brodie	217
	11	York City XI	A	3-2	Roberts 2, Rennison	229
	25	Hull City XI	H	1-0	Rennison	Private
Oct	29	Middlesbrough Res	H	3-3	Kilgannon(og), McAlindon, Brodie	536
Dec	9	Manchester United Res	H	1-2	Brodie	3193
Jan	12	Newcastle United Res	H	2-3	Betts(pen), Grant	675

2000-01

July	21	Middlesbrough Res(NRS Cup S/F)	H	1-1	Gavin(og)	1200
			(Won 5-4 on pens)			
	28	Manchester United Res	H	3-2	Brodie, Williams, Savic	3650
	30	Tipperary Southern Dist League XI	A	5-0	Brunton,McNaughton 2,Toone,Morris	400
Aug	1	Waterford Town	A	2-2	Windross, Faure	204
	2	Cork City	A	0-1		311
	5	Newcastle Utd Res(Minster Carpets)	H	2-0	Pounder 2	833
	6	Darlington (Minster Carpets Cup)	H	0-7		358
	8	Sunderland Reserves	H	0-3		410
	9	York City (NR Senior Cup Final)	H	0-1		300
Sept	12	Newcastle Utd Res	A	2-2	Shuttleworth, Tate	196
Dec	12	Leeds United Reserves	A	3-1	Rennison, Brodie, Ingram	Private
Mar	21	Sheffield United	H	2-3	Pounder, Beavers(trialist)	250

2001-02

July	17	Bridlington Town	A	0-2		197
	20	Hull City	A	0-4		3909
	25	Middlesbrough(NR Sen Cup S/F)	H	0-3		2042
	28	Rotherham United	H	0-1		558
Aug	3	York City	H	3-3	Pounder, Fitzsimmons, Burt	658
	11	Derby County	H	1-2	Ingram(pen)	520

2002-03

July	23	Hull City	H	1-3	Robinson	1377
	27	Whitby Town	H	2-1	Pounder, Stoker	377
	31	Sheffield United	H	0-0		506
Aug	3	Hartlepool United	H	1-2	Scott	500
	8	Middlesbrough Reserves	H	2-3	Shepherd, Rennison	614
Jan	21	Marske United(NR Sen Cup R1)	A	3-0	Brassart, Rose	2250
Feb	25	Whitby Town(NR Sen Cup S/F)	H	3-2	Pounder, Cohen 2	551

2003-04

July	16	Selby Town	A	6-4	Cohen, Pounder 2, Gilroy 2(1pen), Henderson	202
	19	Bridlington Town	A	1-3	Rose	323
	23	Middlesbro Res(NRSC 03 Final)	H	1-2	Kerr(pen)	552
	26	York City	A	0-2		1152
	30	Hull City	H	4-2	Senior, Gilroy, Quayle 2	587
Aug	2	Mansfield Town	H	0-1		635
	5	Sheffield United Reserves	H	2-3	Quayle, Jean(trialist)	628
Feb	11	Guisborough Town(NRSC R1)	A	1-0	Kelly	254
Mar	9	York City Res(NRS Cup S/F)	H	2-0	Quayle, Rose	539

2004-05

July	17	Leeds United Reserves	H	1-1	Gilroy	1228
	20	Grimsby Town	H	2-0	Hackworth, Senior	633
	24	Middlesbro Res(NRSC 04 Final)	H	1-0	Gill	836
	27	Grantham Town	A	1-3	Senior	150
	31	Sheffield United Reserves	H	1-1	Redfearn	722
Aug	7	Whitby Town	A	2-1	Thompson 2	310
Nov	12	Leeds United Reserves	A	2-1	Gill, Foster	Private
Jan	10	Dormans (NR Senior Cup R1)	H	5-1	Kerr, Coulson, Burton 2, Beadle	293
Apr	6	Middlesbrough Res(NRSC S/F)	A	1-4	Hackworth	220

2005-06

July	19	Barnsley	H	0-2		611
	23	Chesterfield	H	1-1	Wake	670
	26	Bridlington Town	A	3-0	Udenkwour(trialist) 2, Eccles	331
	30	Scunthorpe United	H	2-4	Quayle, Clark	455
Aug	3	Sheffield United	H	2-3	Wake, Nicholson	856
	6	Sunderland Reserves	H	4-0	Hughes, Quayle 2, Coulson	678
Nov	5	Hartlepool United	H	0-0		Private
Jan	4	Middlesbrough Res(NRSC R1)	H	5-1	Eccles 2, Quayle 2, Coulson	301
Mar	20	York City Res(NR Sen Cup S/F)	A	0-3		108

2006 -07

July	15	Leeds United Reserves	H	2-1	Thornton, Own Goal	471
	19	Northallerton Town	A	4-2	Whittington 3, Thornton	136
	22	Rossington Main	H	3-1	Whittington 3	289
	25	Retford United	A	2-1	Whittington, McStay(pen)	121
	29	Bradford Park Avenue	A	1-1	Hackworth(pen)	156
Aug	1	Bridlington Town	A	3-0	Whittington 2, Thornton	102
	2	Sheffield United Reserves	H	1-0	Whittington	399
	5	Whitby Town	H	1-0	Farthing(og)	415
Feb	19	York City Res(NRS Cup R1)	H	2-1	Anderson, Dalton	168
Mar	29	Middlesbro Res(NRS Cup S/F)	H	0-3		185

Scarborough FC: FA Youth Cup

1998-99					(Att.)
Round 1	Rochdale	A	0-2		100
1999-2000					
1 Qual	Altrincham	A	4-2	Toone, Swales, Ferguson 2	70
2 Qual	Morecambe	A	2-1	O'Riordan, Atkinson	156
3 Qual	Burscough	H	2-2	Windross, Pounder	94
Replay	Burscough	A	2-3	Pounder, Jewell	79
2000-01					
1 Qual	Farsley Celtic	H	1-0	O'Riordan	96
2 Qual	Oldham Town	H	5-2	Milner, Windross 2, Swales(pen), Wadsworth	42
3 Qual	Doncaster Rovers	H	1-3	Ashley Lyth	90
2001-02					
1 Qual	Glossop North End	H	5-0	L.Gildea 2, Temperton, Raw, Own Goal	58
2 Qual	Hallam	A	2-1	Naylor, Temperton	85
3 Qual	Doncaster Rovers	A	2-0	Wadsworth, Crawford	148
Round 1	Burscough	H	1-2	Temperton	65
2002-03					
1 Qual	Whitley Bay	H	6-2	Wilkinson, Raw 2, McCoubrey, Temperton, Batchelor	16
2 Qual	Chadderton	H	4-0	L.Gildea, Wilkinson, Raw	52
3 Qual	Burscough	H	2-3	Temperton, D.Cook	48
2003-04					
				(Did not compete)	
2004-05					
1 Qual	Guiseley	H	5-2	Barnes, Blott 2, Coulson, Batchelor	110
2 Qual	Retford United	A	1-0	Adam Lyth	56
3 Qual	Whitley Bay	H	1-2	Goundry	86
2005-06					
1 Qual	Ryton	A	3-4	Anderson 2, Adam Lyth	45
2006-07					
1 Qual	Silsden	A	2-3	Anderson (2pens)	55

The Scarborough team in Boro's last ever FA Youth Cup match, against Silsden on 25 September 2006, was: Liam Watson, Callum Scott, Jack Perry, Dominic Amos, Adie Hammond (Andy Allcock), Nathan Billany, Craig Marsay, Wayne Brooksby (Callum Reid), Ged Dalton, Danny Anderson, Adam Daley.

SCARBOROUGH FC
PLAYER STATS 1998-99

	Apps	Goals
Graeme ATKINSON	15	1
Paddy ATKINSON	29 (4)	-
Steve BRODIE	48	12
Wayne BULLIMORE	38 (2)	1
Neil CAMPBELL	5 (10)	1
Graeme CARR	5 (5)	-
Thomas DABLESTEEN	5	1
Tony ELLIOTT	25	-
Mark GOODLAD	3	-
Chris GREENACRE	11 (2)	2
Glyn HODGES	1	-
Jamie HOYLAND	50	3
Richard JACKSON	22 (1)	-
Nathan JONES	8 (1)	-
John KAY	25 (1)	-
Jason LYDIATE	32 (1)	1
Sean McAULEY	6 (1)	-
Mike McNAUGHTON	24 (9)	1
Alex MARINKOV	26	4 (2pens)
Ian MILBOURNE	3 (17)	-
Stewart MORRIS	0 (1)	-
Derek MOUNTFIELD	5 (1)	-
Phil NAISBETT	3	-
Tony PARKS	15	-
Gary PORTER	11 (2)	-
Neil RADIGAN	4 (7)	-
David RAINFORD	1 (2)	-
Shaun RENNISON	16	1
Ian RENSHAW	0 (1)	-
Darren ROBERTS	18	3
Liam ROBINSON	19 (12)	3
Matthew RUSSELL	22 (19)	-
Andy SAVILLE	0 (9)	-
Chris TATE	20 (8)	12
Andrew TODD	0 (1)	-
Luke WEAVER	6	-
Gareth WILLIAMS	22	3
Ben WORRALL	29 (7)	-

SCARBOROUGH FC
PLAYER STATS 1999-2000

	Apps	Goals
Mounir ALKHATIB	0 (6)	-
Paul BAKER	1	-
David BASS	21 (4)	2
Simon BETTS	47	11 (5pens)
Darren BOGAN	2 (1)	-
Steve BRODIE	44 (1)	16
Danny BRUNTON	0 (1)	-
Graeme CARR	1 (1)	-
Paul ELLENDER	30	-
Alex GILDEA	1 (9)	-
Marvin HARRIOTT	29 (5)	1
Denny INGRAM	11	-
Scott JACKSON	0 (1)	-
Marcus JONES	44 (2)	4
Kevin MARTIN	9	-
Gareth McALINDON	13 (5)	3
Brian McGINTY	8	-
Mike McNAUGHTON	2 (7)	1
David McNIVEN	5 (1)	2
Simon MARPLES	1	-
Scott MIDDLEMASS	10 (2)	-
Ian MILBOURNE	3 (4)	-
Andy MORRIS	8 (3)	3
Stewart MORRIS	5 (20)	2
Andrew QUINN	1 (5)	1
Shaun RENNISON	28 (6)	2
Darren ROBERTS	34 (7)	8 (3pens)
Matthew RUSSELL	25	2
Lee SINNOTT	31	-
Gareth STOKER	43	5
Chris TATE	28	10
Neil THOMPSON	9	1
Mark TYRELL	10 (3)	-
Johnny WALKER	0 (1)	-
Gareth WILLIAMS	25	1
Andy WOODS	43	-

SCARBOROUGH FC
PLAYER STATS 2000-01

	Apps	Goals
Paul ATKINSON	16 (1)	-
Simon BETTS	265	(3pens)
Jason BLUNT	10	-
Steve BRODIE	32 (2)	10
Danny BRUNTON	33 (2)	1
Jamie BURT	10 (4)	2
Andrew DAWSON	1 (5)	-
Cherif DIALLO	18 (8)	9
Gustavo DI LELLA	3 (1)	-
Paul ELLENDER	43	6
Romain FAURE	14 (5)	-
Alex GILDEA	1 (6)	-
Denny INGRAM	31	2
Adam JEWELL	1 (1)	-
Marcus JONES	17 (1)	-
Scott JORDAN	5 (3)	2
John KEEGAN	2 (2)	-
Ashley LYTH	5	-
Stewart MORRIS	3 (19)	-
Brad PIERCEWRIGHT	1 (3)	-
David POUNDER	38 (7)	10
Phil PRIESTLEY	7	-
Martin REED	2 (1)	-
Shaun RENNISON	38 (2)	3
Gerard ROBINSON	4 (1)	-
Matthew RUSSELL	21 (1)	1
Sinisa SAVIC	3 (1)	-
Barry SHUTTLEWORTH	4	-
Darryn STAMP	1	-
Gareth STOKER	38 (7)	2
Chris TATE	11 (3)	1
Neil THOMPSON	23	2(1pen)
Leigh TOONE	0 (1)	-
Gareth WILLIAMS	38 (2)	7
Andy WINDROSS	1 (6)	-
Andy WOODS	42	-

SCARBOROUGH FC
PLAYER STATS 2001-02

	Apps	Goals
Paul ATKINSON	14 (3)	-
Steve BAKER	19 (4)	1(pen)
Justin BARNWELL -EDINBORO	3 (2)	-
Gary BENNETT	1	-
Jason BLUNT	48	6
Steve BRODIE	19 (1)	4
Danny BRUNTON	0 (2)	-
Adam BURLEY	6 (1)	-
Jamie BURT	3 (4)	1
Ben CHAPMAN	1	-
Darren CONNELL	3 (9)	3
Richard CRAWFORD	0 (1)	-
Richard DRYDEN	4	1
Paul ELLENDER	1	-
Stuart ELLIOTT	8 (2)	1
Romain FAURE	19 (3)	-
Ashley FICKLING	7	-
Peter FITZSIMMONS	17 (2)	-
David HENDERSON	0 (2)	-
Tim HOGG	0 (1)	-
Mark HOTTE	19 (2)	-
Denny INGRAM	14	-
Adam JEWELL	0 (5)	-
Marcus JONES	8 (1)	-
Scott JORDAN	22 (2)	1
John KEEGAN	7 (2)	-
Neil MANN	2	-
Mick MORRELL	1	-
Paul NEWTON	1 (1)	-
Martin O'RIORDAN	0 (2)	-
Mark PATTERSON	19 (2)	-
David POUNDER	37 (7)	4
Shaun RENNISON	43 (2)	4
Karl ROSE	15 (5)	6
Phil SALT	11	-
Paul SHEPHERD	15	3(2pens)
Ben SHERWOOD	1 (5)	-
Dene SHIELDS	11	3
Christian SHORT	5	-
Mark SMITH	4	-
Darryn STAMP	32 (5)	14(1pen)
Gareth STOKER	32 (4)	1
Ryan SUGDEN	11 (4)	2
Mark SWALES	3 (5)	-
Steve TORPEY	1	-
Richard TRACEY	0 (1)	-
James TURLEY	0 (5)	-
Aaron WILFORD	9 (1)	1
Andy WINDROSS	5 (5)	3
Andy WOODS	45	-
Andy WRIGHT	4	-

SCARBOROUGH FC
PLAYER STATS 2002-03

	Apps	Goals
Steve BAKER	3 (1)	-
Jason BLUNT	8 (12)	2
Gary BRADSHAW	3	-
Olivier BRASSART	32 (4)	2
Neil CAMPBELL	18 (12)	4
Gary COHEN	8 (1)	4
Darren CONNELL	0 (5)	-
Richard CRAWFORD	0 (1)	-
Colin CRYAN	3	-
Paul DEMPSEY	13 (3)	1
Glen DOWNEY	1	-
Richard DRYDEN	25 (2)	1
Bimbo FATOKUN	18 (13)	8
Keith GILROY	7	1(pen)
Danny HALL	1	-
David HENDERSON	0 (3)	-
Nick HENRY	17 (2)	1
Graeme HODGSON	0 (1)	-
David HOLDSWORTH	19	1
Mark HOTTE	38 (4)	-
Scott JORDAN	9 (4)	1
Scott KERR	9	-
Ryan MALLON	6 (1)	1
Anthony ORMEROD	31 (7)	2
Mark PATTERSON	3 (1)	-
David POUNDER	39 (10)	11
Michael PRICE	8	-
Tom RAW	7 (3)	2
Shaun RENNISON	12	-
David RIDLER	7	-
Karl ROSE	18 (10)	4
Keith SCOTT	33 (1)	12
Paul SHEPHERD	44 (1)	6(4pens)
Mohammed SILLAH	11 (1)	4
Gareth STOKER	43 (5)	-
Cleveland TAYLOR	11 (1)	4
Leigh WALKER	8 (1)	-
Jack WILKINSON	0 (1)	-
Andy WOODS	43	-

SCARBOROUGH FC
PLAYER STATS 2003-04

	Apps	Goals
Steve BAKER	27 (1)	-
Chris BATCHELOR	2 (2)	-
Lloyd BLACKMAN	6 (1)	-
Andy BROWNRIGG	2 (1)	-
Jamie BURT	1	-
Stephen CAPPER	22 (3)	-
Gary COHEN	1	-
Colin CRYAN	17	1
Yomi DADA	1	-
Iain DAVIDSON	2	-
Clayton DONALDSON	2	-
Glen DOWNEY	17 (1)	1
James DUDGEON	1 (1)	-
Wayne GILL	32 (8)	1
Keith GILROY	5 (7)	3(1pen)
Keith GRAYDON	1 (3)	-
Tony HACKWORTH	11	3
David HENDERSON	0 (1)	-
Nick HENRY	9	1
Mark HOTTE	45 (1)	1
Jimmy KELLY	41	4(1pen)
Scott KERR	45 (1)	4(1pen)
Bertrand KETCHANKE	6	1
Steve LEADBETTER	1 (2)	-
Jason LEE	1	-
Ashley LYTH	28 (6)	1
Clint MARCELLE	35 (3)	4
Leon McSWEENEY	0 (4)	-
Alex NESOVIC	0 (1)	-
Kevin NICHOLSON	13	1
Paul O'NEILL	2	-
Michael PRICE	15 (4)	1
Mark QUAYLE	44 (1)	16(5pens)
Tom RAW	8 (5)	-
Matthew REDMILE	25	3
Mark ROBINSON	3	-
Karl ROSE	25 (7)	6
Chris SENIOR	11 (35)	8
Ashley SESTANOVICH	13	3
Jamie SHERLOCK	2 (7)	-
SMITH	0(1)	-
Adam SOLLITT	9 (3)	-
THORNTON	1	-
Leigh WALKER	45	-
Tris WHITMAN	8 (4)	-
Jacques WILLIAMS	8 (7)	1
Anthony YALE	1	-

SCARBOROUGH FC
PLAYER STATS 2004-05

	Apps	Goals
Steve BAKER	33	-
Steve BARRATT	1	-
Chris BATCHELOR	1 (1)	-
Jimmy BEADLE	2 (1)	1
Neil BISHOP	11	1
Jonathan BLACKBURN	0 (1)	-
Ryan BLOTT	0 (1)	-
Steve BURTON	6 (11)	4
Carl COOK	2	-
Michael COULSON	3 (13)	3
Colin CRYAN	48	4
Paul FOOT	26 (3)	-
Luke FOSTER	5 (5)	-
Matthew FRIEND	0 (1)	-
Robert GILL	15 (7)	3
Keith GILROY	22 (5)	1
Gareth GRANT	1 (1)	-
Tony HACKWORTH	35 (9)	10(1pen)
HASKINS	1	-
Danny HAYSTEAD	1	-
Nick HEINEMAN	2	-
Darren HORRIGAN	0 (1)	-
Mark HOTTE	39 (1)	3
Griff JONES	1 (2)	-
Peter KEEN	5	-
Scott KERR	42 (3)	2
Adam LYTH	0 (1)	-
Ashley LYTH	16 (16)	1
Kevin NICHOLSON	46	2
David POUNDER	13 (12)	1
Neil REDFEARN	40 (3)	14(3pens)
David REEVES	10	4(1pen)
Chris SENIOR	28 (20)	13
Tyrone THOMPSON	47	2
Kevin TOWNSON	4	-
Leigh WALKER	44	-
Mike WARWICK	0 (1)	-
Callum WOOD	1 (1)	-

SCARBOROUGH FC
PLAYER STATS 2005-06

	Apps	Goals
Rob ATKINSON	20 (2)	-
Steve BAKER	36 (1)	-
Tom BAKER	1	-
Jimmy BEADLE	5 (3)	-
Leo BERTOS	1	-
Neil BISHOP	25 (1)	-
Ryan BLOTT	0 (4)	-
Jason BLUNT	4 (1)	-
Ian CLARK	21 (1)	1(pen)
Carl COOK	12 (2)	-
Michael COULSON	11 (23)	7
Ian DUNBAVIN	15	-
Mark ECCLES	4 (4)	-
David ELEBERT	11 (1)	-
Paul FOOT	15 (6)	1
Lee FOWLER	25 (1)	3
Tony HACKWORTH	37 (4)	3
Adrian HARPER	4	-
Chris HUGHES	23 (2)	2Denny
INGRAM	14 (1)	-
Dan JARVIS	1 (1)	-
Richard KELL	2	-
Ashley LYTH	23 (9)	-
Sean McCLARE	6 (10)	-
David McNIVEN	16 (2)	6
Kevin NICHOLSON	40 (1)	2
Jermaine PALMER	2 (2)	-
Andy PARTON	1 (3)	-
David POUNDER	7 (2)	-
Mark QUAYLE	17 (4)	-
Neil REDFEARN	18 (4)	3(2pens)
Ben RIX	2	-
Jake SPEIGHT	5 (3)	2
Brian WAKE	8 (6)	5
Leigh WALKER	29	-
Simon WEAVER	23	1
Steve YATES	0 (1)	-

SCARBOROUGH FC
PLAYER STATS 2006-07

	Apps	Goals
Dominic AMOS	0 (2)	-
Curtis ASPDEN	12	-
Jimmy BEADLE	38 (5)	4
Ryan BLOTT	19 (21)	8
Jason BLUNT	3	-
Neil BRISCO	5	-
Lee CARTWRIGHT	47 (1)	4
Carl COOK	27 (3)	1
Ged DALTON	16 (16)	4
Sean DAVIES	28 (4)	-
Tony HACKWORTH	43 (1)	9
Mark HOTTE	49	-
Denny INGRAM	40	-
Ashley LYTH	41 (2)	-
Mark PATTERSON	0 (1)	-
Chris THOMPSON	43 (3)	15 (6 pens)
Darren THORNTON	33 (6)	2
Jamie VERMIGLIO	40	5
Lee WHITTINGTON	17 (5)	5
Mark WILBERFORCE	37	-

Scarborough F.C.'s last Christmas with Santa!

2007-08

Scarborough Athletic

5th in Northern Counties East League Division One

							Bramley	Hyam	D Phillips	Davies	Kennett	Widdowson	Griffin	Thompson	Hogg	Lightowler	Smethurst	Reveley	S Phillips	Chadburn	Ferrey	Evans	Cappleman	Ellwood	Pinder	Exley	Kemp	Powley	Wood	Botham	Milner	Waltham	Bowsley	Hepples	Hartley	Blott	Medcalf	Wilberforce	Morton	Barker	Tate	Neill	Wood
1	Aug	11	Teversal	1-2	Thompson	427	1	2	3	4	5	6	7	8	9	10	11	12	13	14																								
2		18	Leeds Met Carn	4-1	Kennett 2, Lightowler, Hogg	278	1	2	3	4	5	6	7	11	10	9		14			8	12	13																				
3		25	BARTON TOWN OB	2-6	Hogg, S Philliips (pen)	591	1		3	4	5	8	7	6	10		11	9	12				13	2	14																			
4	Sep	15	AFC Emley	3-2	Hepples, Hogg, Kemp	331	1	2			5		7		9				6	13		3			11	10	13					4		8				12					
5		22	WORSBOROUGH BRIDGE	4-0	Griffin, S Phillips 2 (1p), OG	441	1	2				13	7	12	9			14	8			3				10	5					4		6				11					
6		29	Hall Road Rangers	0-2		407	1	2				6	7	11	10			13	8			3			14	9	4					5						12					
7	Oct	6	TADCASTER ALBION	2-2	Pinder, Barker	486	1	4				2	7	8	9			13	10			3			11								5		6				12		14			
8		20	Bottesford Town	1-3	S Phillips (pen)	196	1	2				8		7	9				6			3			14				4	11		5		13		10					12		
9		27	YORKSHIRE AMATEUR	3-0	S Phillips 2 (1 pen), Blott	406	1					8	7		10				5			14			13		3		2	11		4	12	6		9							
10	Nov	3	Gedling Town	2-1	S Phillips 2	180	1					7	10		9				5			12					3		2	11		4	8	6							14		13	
11		10	Rossington Main	5-1	S Phillips,Griffin, Pinder, 2 OGs	224	1					7	10		9				5			3			13		2			11		4	8	6			12					14	
12		17	ROSSINGTON MAIN	4-0	Blott 2, Medcalf, S Phillips (pen)	493	1					8	7		10				5			13					3		2	11		4		6		9	12			14			
13		24	LEEDS MET CARN	0-2		420	1					8	7						5								3		2	11		4	12	6		9	10	13			14		
14	Dec	1	Staveley MW	3-0	Blott 2, Bowsley	292	1			13		2	7	11						5						14		3					4	8	6		9	10	12					
15		29	PONTEFRACT COLL	1-0	Hogg	604				12		2	7	13	14				5								3	1		11		4	8	6		9	10						
16	Jan	5	Barton Town OB	3-3	Medcalf, Kemp, Blott	320	1						7	11	12				8						14		4		2	3			5	6		9	10	13					
17		12	Worsborough Bridge	3-0	Blott, S Phillips, Hogg	211	1					13	7	6	12				8								3		2	5		4	14			9	10		11				
18		27	AFC EMLEY	2-2	Hogg, Phillips	538	1			12		2	7	8	9				5			14					3			6		4	13				10		11				
19	Feb	2	Dinnington Town	2-4	Morton, Hogg	276	1	13				2		7	12						3					5			6		4	8			9	10		11			14	
20		9	RAINWORTH MW	1-3	Blott	457	1					14	13	7	9				8								5		2	6	3	4				12	10		11				
21		12	HALL ROAD RANGERS	3-1	Morton, Hogg 2	376	1			13		5	7		9				8								3		2	6	14	4				10	12		11				
22		16	Rainworth MW	3-1	Blott, Medcalf 2	218	1					5	14	7	9				8			2					3			6	13	4				10	12		11				
23	Mar	1	BOTTESFORD TOWN	1-1	Botham	412				2		5	9	6	14				13								4	1	8	12	3			7			10		11				
24		8	Yorkshire Amateur	5-0	Hepples, Griffin 2, S Phillips, Thompson	220	1			2		5	7	6	9				8			14					4			11	3			12			10						13
25		11	Tadcaster Albion	1-0	S Phillips (pen)	240	1			13		5	9	7	12				8			3					4		2	11				6		14	10						
26		15	GEDLING TOWN	4-1	Griffin, Blott 2, S Phillips	446	1					5	7		14				8								3		2	6	13	4		12		9	10		11				
27		24	BORROWASH VICTORIA	8-0	Phillips,Griffin,Widdowson,Hepples,Hogg,Blott3(1p)	559	1			13		5	7		14				8								4		2	11	3			6		9	10		12				
28		29	TEVERSAL	2-2	Blott, S Phillips (pen)	493	1			14		5	7		10				8								4		2	6	3			13	12	9			11				
29	Apr	6	DINNINGTON TOIWN	1-1	Medcalf	539	1			13		5	7	6	14				8								4		2	3					12	9	10		11				
30		12	Pontefract Coll	2-1	S Phillips, Blott	280	1			2		5	7	6	14				8											3		4		13	11	9	10		12				
31		19	Borrowash Victoria	2-2	Hepples, Blott	252	1			2		5	10	8	12	13						3						14		11		4		6	7	9							
32		26	STAVELEY MW	2-1	Botham, Blott	496				2		5	7	8	13	14											3	1		11		4		6	13	9	10						
					Apps		29	7	3	8	4	27	28	20	18	2	2	1	25	0	1	10	0	1	2	3	24	3	15	23	5	22	6	16	2	18	16	1	10	0	0	0	0
					Subs			1		8		3	2	2	14	2		5	3	2		6	2		7		1	1		1	3		4	4	3	2	4	6	2	3	2	3	1
					Goals							2	1	6	2	10	1				18						2		2			2			1	4		18	5		2	1			

Wilkinson Sword Trophy

							Bramley	Hyam	D Phillips	Davies	Kennett	Widdowson	Griffin	Thompson	Hogg	Lightowler	Smethurst	Reveley	S Phillips	Chadburn	Ferrey	Evans	Cappleman	Ellwood	Pinder	Exley	Kemp	Powley	Wood	Botham	Milner	Waltham	Bowsley	Hepples	Hartley	Blott	Medcalf	Wilberforce	Morton	Barker	Tate	Neill	Wood
	Aug	21	RAINWORTH MW	0-1*		401				4	5	8	7		10	9	13	12	6		11	3	14	2				1																

* after extra time

NCEL Cup

							Bramley	Hyam	D Phillips	Davies	Kennett	Widdowson	Griffin	Thompson	Hogg	Lightowler	Smethurst	Reveley	S Phillips	Chadburn	Ferrey	Evans	Cappleman	Ellwood	Pinder	Exley	Kemp	Powley	Wood	Botham	Milner	Waltham	Bowsley	Hepples	Hartley	Blott	Medcalf	Wilberforce	Morton	Barker	Tate	Neill	Wood
	Aug	25	PONTEFRACT COLL	1-1**	Exley	343		2		4	5	6		7	9		13		8			3	12		11	10	14	1																

** after extra time - lost 1-3 on penalties

North Riding Senior Cup

							Bramley	Hyam	D Phillips	Davies	Kennett	Widdowson	Griffin	Thompson	Hogg	Lightowler	Smethurst	Reveley	S Phillips	Chadburn	Ferrey	Evans	Cappleman	Ellwood	Pinder	Exley	Kemp	Powley	Wood	Botham	Milner	Waltham	Bowsley	Hepples	Hartley	Blott	Medcalf	Wilberforce	Morton	Barker	Tate	Neill	Wood
P1	Oct	13	Kirkbymoorside	2-0	Hogg 2	317	1	2		5		8		11	9			14	7			3			13	12						4		6							10			
P2	Nov	14	Fishburn Park	4-0	S Phillips (pen), Griffin, Hogg, Blott	356	1					8	7		9				5			3			11							4	6	12		10				13		14	2
1	Jan	9	Thornaby	2-0	Hogg, Blott	124	1			12			7	11	6				5								2			3		4	8			9	10						
SF	Feb	26	YORK CITY RES.	0-2		505	1	14		2		5	7	6	12				8								4				3			13		9	10		11				

Friendlies

Jul	15	Edgehill	0-0		316
	18	Northallerton Town	2-2	Chadburn, S Phillips	202
	25	Bridlington Town	4-2	Wilberforce,Lightowler,Thompson,Cappleman	455
	28	Hutton Cranswick	2-2	Hogg, McCoubrey	249
Aug	2	Goole AFC	0-3		200
	4	SUTTON TOWN	6-1	Lightowler2,Thompson,Bell,Reveley2	200
	7	Pocklington Town	2-2	Gill, Griffin	150
Oct	24	WINTERTON RANGERS	0-1		100

Scarborough Athletic FC: 2007-08

Back(L to R) Exley(coach), Darren France(asst manager), Hepples, Hogg, Scott Phillips, Bramley, Evans, Kemp, Brian France(manager), Neaves(physio)
Front(L to R) Neill, Medcalf, Wood, Griffin, Blott, Waltham, Barker, Widdowson, Botham, Pinder

2008-09

1st in Northern Counties East League Division One

Scarborough Athletic

							Bramley	Wood	Kemp	Hartas	Widdowson	Ellis	Griffin	Thompson	Blott	Medcalf	Morton	Hepples	Guthrie	Danforth	Phillips	Botham	Hartley	Hogg	Hoyle	Waltham	A Reid	Farthing	T Reid	Gray	Spencer	Routledge
1	Aug	9	ASKERN VILLA	2-2	Thompson 2	454	1	2	3	4	5	6	7	8	9	10	11	12	13													
2		12	Rainworth MW	0-1		215	1	2	3	5		6	7	8	9	10	11	12		4	13											
3		23	GRIMSBY BOROUGH	5-0	Hogg 2, Phillips 2 (1 pen), Blott	440	1	2	3	4	13		11	6	9			12			8	5	7	10	14							
4		25	Brighouse Town	4-1	Philllips 2 (pens), Hogg, Blott	341	1	2	3	4	14		11	6	9	13					8	12	7	10		5						
5		30	AFC EMLEY	4-0	Botham 3, Waltham	450	1		3	2			11	6	9	12					8	5	7	10	13	4					14	
6	Sep	9	HEMSWORTH MW	2-2	Botham, Phillips (pen)	389	1		3	2		8	7	11	9	10					6	5	14	12	13	4						
7		13	Staveley MW	4-0	Phillips, Blott, Hogg 2	165	1		3	4		12	14	11	9	13					8	6	7	10	2	5						
8		16	Glasshoughton W	2-0	Blott, Phillips (pen)	231	1		3	4		12	14	11	9	13					8	6	7	10	2	5						
9		27	Bottesford Town	3-1	Phillips 2, Thompson	204			3	4		8		7	10	9		13			6	11	12		2	5	1			14		
10	Oct	11	Rossington Main	4-1	Hartas, Blott 3	198			5	4		6	13		9	12		11	14		8	3	7		2		1			10		
11		14	TADCASTER ALBION	7-0	Phillips(p),Hartas,Blott(p),Hepples,Medcalf2,Hartley	442		14	5	4		11	13		9	12		6			8	3	7		2		1			10		
12		18	STAVELEY MW	2-2	Barnes(og), Blott	522			5	4		13	11	14	9	10		6			8	3	7		2		1			12		
13		25	Worsbrough Bridge	3-0	Blott, Ellis, Gray	195			5	4		13	14	6	9	10	11				8	3	7		2		1			12		
14	Nov	1	TEVERSAL	6-0	Ellis2,Phillips,Blott,Hartley,Gray	544			5	4		6	12	11	9	10		14			8	3	7		2		1			13		
15		8	Yorkshire Amateur	6-1	Blott 5, Phillips (pen)	220			3	2		5	14	6	9	10		13			8	11	7			4	1			12		
16		29	AFC Emley	6-1	Botham, Blott2,Gray,Phillips(p),Griffin(p)	461		2	3	4			12	11	9			13			8	6	7	14		5	1			10		
17	Dec	9	APPLEBY FRODINGHAM	6-1	Blott,Griffin,Gray,Medcalf,Hepple,Hogg	301			3	4			11		9	12		6	13		8		7	14	2	5	1			10		
18		16	PONTEFRACT COLLIERIES	2-0	Blott, Medcalf	334		13		4			11		9	14		6			8	3	7	12	2	5	1			10		
19		20	BARTON TOWN OB	6-1	Blott3, Griffin,Kemp,Hogg	560		7	3	4		6	11		9	10			13		8	14		12	2	5	1					
20		27	Askern Villa	3-0	Blott 2, Phillips (pen)	380		14	3	4		6	11		9	10					8	12	7	13	2	5	1					
21	Jan	3	RAINWORTH MW	1-0	Hogg	573		12	4			6	11		9	10					8	3	7	13	2	5	1			14		
22		24	Tadcaster Albion	4-0	Gray 2, Blott 2	340			3	2		6		11	9	12		8			14			13		4	1	5	7	10		
23		31	GLASSHOUGHTON W	5-3	Blott 3 (1pen), Philips, Griffin	521			3	2		8	7		9	14		6			12	11		13		5	1	4		10		
24	Feb	14	BOTTESFORD TOWN	6-0	Ellis,Hartas,Blott,Gray2,Medcalf	477			3	4		6	7		9	12		14			8	11		10	2	5	1			13		
25		21	Leeds Carnegie	2-1	Gray, Hogg	332				4		6	7	14	9	12		11			8	3		13	2	5	1			10		
26		28	ROSSINGTON MAIN	1-0	Thompson	545	1		3	4		6		7	13	10		14			8	11		9	2	5				12		
27	Mar	7	Hemsworth MW	3-1	Gray, Blott, Medcalf	424			3	4		6	12	11	9	13		14			8			7	2	5	1			10		
28		11	Grimsby Borough	2-2	Kemp,Griffin	166		14	3	5		6	7	11	9	10		2			8	12		13		4	1					
29		14	WORSBROUGH BRIDGE	5-0	Botham,Waltham,Darby(og),Routledge2	488			3	5		6	7	12	9			13			8	11		10	2	4	1					14
30		17	BARTON TOWN OB	1-2	Hartas	332			3	4		6	7	13	9						8	11	14	10	2	5	1					12
31		21	Teversal	2-1	Ellis 2	320				4		6	10	11	9			13	14		8	3	7		2	5	1					12
32		24	BRIGHOUSE TOWN	3-0	Ellis, Gray, Hartas	533			14	4		6	12	7	9			8			13	3		11	2	5	1			10		
33		28	YORKSHIRE AMATEUR	6-0	Hoyle(p),Blott2,Phillips,Routledge,Kemp	503			3	4		6	13	7	9			8			12	11			2	5	1			10		14
34	Apr	4	Pontefract Collieries	1-0	Griffin	223		13	2	4		12	7	11				6			8	3		9		5	1			10		14
35		18	LEEDS CARNEGIE	0-0		791			2	4		14	7	11	9			6			8	3		13	12	5	1			10		
36		25	Appleby Frodingham	2-0	Gray, Hogg	272		5		4		6	7	13	9	10		12			8	3		11	2		1			14		
						Apps	9	7	31	35	1	24	22	22	34	14	3	12	0	1	30	27	17	13	23	27	27	2	1	13	0	0
						Subs		6	1		2	6	11	5	1	13		14	5		5	4	3	12	4					9	1	5
						Goals			3	5		7	6	4	34	6		2			16	6	2	10	1	2				12		3

F A Vase

							Bramley	Wood	Kemp	Hartas	Widdowson	Ellis	Griffin	Thompson	Blott	Medcalf	Morton	Hepples	Guthrie	Danforth	Phillips	Botham	Hartley	Hogg	Hoyle	Waltham	A Reid	Farthing	T Reid	Gray	Spencer	Routledge
2Q	Sep	20	Birtley Town	3-2	Thompson, Ellis, Phillips	240			3	4		12		11	10	9		13			8	6	7		2	5	1			14		
1	Oct	4	Esh Winning	2-1	Blemmings(og), Gray	241			3	4		6		7	9	10		13			8	11	12		2	5	1			14		
2	Nov	16	SUNDERLAND NISSAN	3-2*	Thompson, Gray, Hartley	664			3	2		5		7	9	10		6			8	11	13	12		4	1			14		
3	Dec	6	BLACKSTONES	6-1	Blott 3, Gray 3	461			3	4			11		9			6	13		8		7	12	2	5	1			10		
4	Jan	17	Bideford	0-1		570			3	5		6	7			9		13			8	11		10	2		1	4		12		

* after extra time

Wilkinson Sword Trophy

							Bramley	Wood	Kemp	Hartas	Widdowson	Ellis	Griffin	Thompson	Blott	Medcalf	Morton	Hepples	Guthrie	Danforth	Phillips	Botham	Hartley	Hogg	Hoyle	Waltham	A Reid	Farthing	T Reid	Gray	Spencer	Routledge
1	Sep	2	Askern Villa	2-1	Blott, Medcalf	190	1		3	2		13	11	6	9	12					8	5	7	10	14	4						
2	Oct	21	Yorkshire Amateur	0-2		138			3	2		6	14	7	12	9		5			8	11	13			4	1			10		

NCEL Cup

							Bramley	Wood	Kemp	Hartas	Widdowson	Ellis	Griffin	Thompson	Blott	Medcalf	Morton	Hepples	Guthrie	Danforth	Phillips	Botham	Hartley	Hogg	Hoyle	Waltham	A Reid	Farthing	T Reid	Gray	Spencer	Routledge
1	Aug	19	LEEDS CARNEGIE	2-1	Kemp, Blott	274	1	2	3	5	14		7	11	9	10		6		4	8	12		13								
2	Nov	11	Askern Villa	1-2*	Ellis	76			3	2		6	12	11	9	10		14			8	5	7			4	1			13		

* after extra time

President's Cup

							Bramley	Wood	Kemp	Hartas	Widdowson	Ellis	Griffin	Thompson	Blott	Medcalf	Morton	Hepples	Guthrie	Danforth	Phillips	Botham	Hartley	Hogg	Hoyle	Waltham	A Reid	Farthing	T Reid	Gray	Spencer	Routledge
1	Oct	8	Bottesford Town	7-1	Botham,Gray3,Medcalf,Ellis,Blott	148			3	4		14			12	10		6	13		8	11	7		2	5	1			9		
QF	Mar	3	PICKERING TOWN	7-1	Blott2,Hogg2,Hartas,Thompson,Medcalf	425			3	4		6		11	9	12		14			8		13	7	2	5	1			10		
SF	Apr	2	HALL ROAD RANGERS	5-1	Hartas,Hogg2,Griffin,Phillips(pen)	441			3	4		8	7	13	9			12			14	6		11	2	5	1			10		
F1		16	NostellMW	1-1	Gray	378			2	4		6	7	12	9			13			8	3		11		5	1			10		
F2		28	NOSTELL MW	1-2	Gray	559		2	5	4		6	7		9						8	3		11			1			10		

North Riding Senior Cup

							Bramley	Wood	Kemp	Hartas	Widdowson	Ellis	Griffin	Thompson	Blott	Medcalf	Morton	Hepples	Guthrie	Danforth	Phillips	Botham	Hartley	Hogg	Hoyle	Waltham	A Reid	Farthing	T Reid	Gray	Spencer	Routledge
2	Nov	26	Stokesley SC	3-4	Thompson, Gray, Hartley	210		13	2	5		6		11	9			8			12	3	7	10		4	1			14		

Friendlies

Jul	12	Hutton Cranswick	4-4	Medcalf,Thompson,Ellis,Hogg	224
	19	Frickley Athletic	0-2		212
	26	Bridlington Town	1-2	Medcalf	298
	29	Pickering Town	0-1		283
Aug	2	Winterton Rangers	2-3	Ellis, Plant (og)	110
	5	BRODSWORTH WELFARE	2-0	Blott, Ellis	155

Scarborough Athletic FC: 2008-09

Back(L to R) Darren France(asst manager), Waltham, Hoyle, Gray, Ellis, Reid, Hartas, Kemp, Brian France(manager), Exley(coach)
Front(L to R) Hepples, Botham, Connor Avison(mascot), Blott, Thompson,Hankey(physio)

2008-09

1st in Teesside League Division Two

Scarborough Town

No	Month	Day	Opponent	Score	Scorers	Att	Clark	Ramm	Craig	Perry	Hickin	Rose	Clough	Barber	Patterson	Brooksby	Hawkes	C Cook	Danby	Greening	Jones	Thomas	N Cook	Brown	Gildea
1	Aug	13	Teesside Athletic	5-0	Hawkes 3, Patterson 2	67	1	2	3	4	5	6	7	8	9	10	11		13	14			12		
2		16	Great Ayton United	1-1	Greening	82	1	2	3	4	5	6	7	8	9	10	11			13	12				
3		23	Acklam Steelworks	3-2	Brooksby, Thoomas, Greening	63	1	7	3	4	5	6	12	8	2	10	11		14	13		9			
4		27	Redcar Rugby Club	2-2	Hawkes, Brooksby	48	1	7	3	4	5	6	12	8	2	10	11		13			9			
5		30	GRANGETOWN YCC	3-0	Perry, Clough, Rose	223	1	7	3	4	5	6	12	8	2	10	11			13		9	14		
6	Sep	1	Norton & Stockton	2-1	Rose, Thomas	95	1	7	3	4	5	6		8	2	10	11		12	13		9	14		
7		27	WHINNEY BANKS YCC	9-0	Patterson, Brooksby 2, Thomas 3,	139	1	7	3	4	5	6	12	8	2	10	11		14			9	13		
8	Oct	11	ST MARY'S COLLEGE	1-0	Ramm	130	1	2	3	4	5	6	11	8		10	12	13	14			9	7		
9		18	South Bank St Peter's	3-1	Clough 2, Patterson	32	1	2	3	4	5	6	12	8	7		10	11	13			9			
10	Nov	1	BILLINGHAM KADER	5-1	Ramm2(pens),Clough,Patterson,Barber	106	1	2	3	4	5	6	12	8	7	10	13	11				9	14		
11		15	BILLINGHAM TOWN	9-1	Thomas 3, Brooksby, Rose,	131	1	2	3	4	5	6	12	8	7	10	11	13				9	14		
12	Dec	6	SOUTH BANK ST PETER'S	4-0	Ramm, Hawkes, Clough, Greening	103	1	2	3	4	5		10	8	7		11	6	14	12		9	13		
13		20	GREAT AYTON UNITED	2-0	Thomas, Clough	184	1	6	3		4		7		8	10	11	5	2	12		9	13	14	
14	Jan	24	St Mary's College	4-1	Ramm, Thomas, Clough, Hawkes	87	1	2	3	4	5		6	8	7	10	11	12		14		9	13		
15		31	COULBY NEWHAM	5-1	Hickin, Greening 3(1pen), Barber	115	1		3	4	5	6	12	8	7	10		2	14	11		9	13		
16	Feb	21	Billingham Kader	3-1	Greening 2 (pens),Barber	37	1		3	4	5	6	12	8	7	10	13		2	11		9	14		
17		28	ACKLAM STEELWORKS	3-0	Greening (pen),Clough, Ramm	80	1	2	3	4		6	12	8	7	10	14			11		9	13		5
18	Mar	7	Coulby Newham	1-1	Gildea	44	1	2	3	4		6		8	7	10	12		13	11		9	14		5
19		21	NORTON & STOCKTON	0-0		97	1	2	3	4		6		8	7	10	11		14	13		9	12		5
20		28	Grangetown YCC	7-0	Ramm 2, Brooksby, Greening,	35	1	2	3	4	13	6			7	10	11		12	14		9	8		5
21	Apr	18	TEESSIDE ATHLETIC	3-1	Thomas, Danby, Hawkes	91	1	2	3		4	6		8	7	10	11		12	13		9		14	5
22		25	Whinney Banks YCC	2-0	Thomas, Greening	50	1	2	3	4		6		8	7	10	11		13	12		9	14		5
23	May	2	REDCAR RUGBY CLUB	12-0	Barber 2, Patterson,Thomas 3,	235	1	2	3	4	13			8	7	10	11		14	12		9	6		5

additional goalscorers:
v Whinney Banks — Perry, Clough, Ramm (pen)
v Billingham Town — Clough 3, Hawkes
v Grangetown YCC — Danby 2, Thomas
v Redcar Rugby Club — Brooksby 2, N Cook, Greening 2, Danby

	Clark	Ramm	Craig	Perry	Hickin	Rose	Clough	Barber	Patterson	Brooksby	Hawkes	C Cook	Danby	Greening	Jones	Thomas	N Cook	Brown	Gildea
Apps	23	21	23	21	17	19	6	21	22	21	17	5	2	4	0	21	3	0	7
Subs					2		10				5	3	15	13	1		15	2	
Goals		9		2	1	3	12	5	6	8	8		4	13		16	1		1

MacMillan Bowl

Month	Day	Opponent	Score	Scorers	Att	Clark	Ramm	Craig	Perry	Hickin	Rose	Clough	Barber	Patterson	Brooksby	Hawkes	C Cook	Danby	Greening	Jones	Thomas	N Cook	Brown	Gildea
Sep	13	SOUTH BANK ST PETER'S	3-1	Hawkes, Ramm (pen), Brooksby	143	1	7	3	4	5	6	12	8	2	10	11			13	14	9			
Nov	8	GUISBOROUGH QUOIT CLUB	7-2	Thomas 2, Clough, Patterson,	99	1	2	3	4	5	6	12	8	7	10	11		14	13		9			
Jan	17	NUNTHORPE ATHLETIC	1-2	Ramm	126	1	2	3	4	5		12	8	7	10	11	6		13		9			

additional goalscorers:
v Guisborough Quoit — Craig, Greening, Barber

Alex Burness Plate

Month	Day	Opponent	Score	Scorers	Att	Clark	Ramm	Craig	Perry	Hickin	Rose	Clough	Barber	Patterson	Brooksby	Hawkes	C Cook	Danby	Greening	Jones	Thomas	N Cook	Brown	Gildea
Oct	4	REDCAR RUGBY CLUB	2-0	Ramm (pen), Clough	118	1	2	3	4	5	6	7	8		10		11	14	12		9	13		
Nov	29	GREAT AYTON UTD	10-0	Brooksby 2, Hawkes 4, Thomas 2,	87	1	2	3	4		6		8	7	10	11	5	13	12		9	14		

additional goalscorers:
v Great Ayton Utd — Patterson, Greening

North Riding Senior Cup

Month	Day	Opponent	Score	Scorers	Att	Clark	Ramm	Craig	Perry	Hickin	Rose	Clough	Barber	Patterson	Brooksby	Hawkes	C Cook	Danby	Greening	Jones	Thomas	N Cook	Brown	Gildea
Oct	25	GRANGETOWN BC	1-2	Hawkes	86	1	2	3	4	5	6	12	8	7		10	11	13			9	14		

Friendlies

Month	Day	Opponent	Score	Scorers	Att
Jul	12	Hall Road Rangers	3-1	Brooksby 2, Ramm (pen)	46
Aug	2	Hutton Cranswick Utd.	2-1	Clough, Greening	55
Mar	14	Barton Town Old Boys	2-2	Thomas, Barber	60

Scarborough Town FC: 2008-09

Back (L to R) Danby, Gildea, Cook, Thomas, Hawkes, Clough, Perry, Barber, Hickin
Front (L to R) Clark, Craig, Rose, Ramm, Patterson, Greening, Brooksby

SCARBOROUGH ATHLETIC
PLAYER STATS 2007-08

	Apps	Goals
Tom BARKER	1 (3)	1
Ryan BLOTT	21 (2)	20(1pen)
Graham BOTHAM	24 (1)	2
Anthony BOWSLEY	8 (3)	1
Dave BRAMLEY	33	-
Lee CAPPLEMAN	0 (2)	-
Shaun CHADBURN	0 (2)	-
Ryan DAVIES	12 (7)	-
Jon ELLWOOD	2	-
Craig EVANS	14 (4)	-
Danny EXLEY	4 (1)	1
Martyn FERREY	2	-
Mark GRIFFIN	32 (2)	7
Joel HARTLEY	2 (3)	-
Gary HEPPLES	17 (7)	4
Craig HOGG	23 (13)	14
Chris HYAM	9	-
Dave KEMP	26 (2)	2
Matty KENNETT	6	2
Joe LIGHTOWLER	3 (2)	1
Richard MEDCALF	18 (4)	5
Kevin MILNER	6 (2)	-
Ryan MORTON	11 (2)	2
Andy NEIL	0 (3)	-
Darren PHILLIPS	3	-
Scott PHILLIPS	30 (3)	19(8pens)
Rob PINDER	4 (7)	2
Glenn POWLEY	5	-
Alex REVELEY	1 (6)	-
Craig SMETHURST	2 (2)	-
Mike TATE	0 (1)	-
Dave THOMPSON	24 (2)	2

SCARBOROUGH ATHLETIC
PLAYER STATS 2008-09

	Apps	Goals
Ryan BLOTT	46 (3)	42(2pens)
Graham BOTHAM	39 (5)	7
Dave BRAMLEY	11	-
Phil DANFORTH	2	-
Rob ELLIS	34 (9)	10
Danny FARTHING	3	-
Danny GRAY	20 (15)	22
Mark GRIFFIN	29 (14)	7(1pen)
Richard GUTHRIE	0 (5)	-
Dave HARTAS	50	7
Joel HARTLEY	23 (7)	3
Gary HEPPLES	19 (20)	2
Craig HOGG	20 (15)	15
Rob HOYLE	30 (5)	1(pen)
Dave KEMP	46 (1)	4
Richard MEDCALF	22 (15)	11
Ryan MORTON	3	-
Scott PHILLIPS	43 (7)	18(10pens)
Arran REID	40	-
Tom REID	1	-
Paul ROUTLEDGE	0 (5)	3
Matty SPENCER	0 (1)	-
Dave THOMPSON	31 (7)	7
Jamie WALTHAM	38	2
Liam WIDDOWSON	1 (3)	-
Carl WOOD	9 (7)	-

SCARBOROUGH TOWN
PLAYER STATS 2008-09

	Apps	Goals
Mark BARBER	27	6
Wayne BROOKSBY	26	11
Matty BROWN	0 (2)	-
Rob CLARK	29	-
Darren CLOUGH	7 (14)	14
Carl COOK	9 (3)	-
Nathan COOK	3 (18)	1
Dean CRAIG	29	1
Joe DANBY	2 (19)	4
Liam GILDEA	7	1
Josh GREENING	4 (18)	15(4pens)
Robbie HAWKES	22 (5)	14
Tom HICKIN	22 (2)	1
Marcus JONES	0 (2)	-
Jamie PATTERSON	27	8
Matt PERRY	27	2
Joel RAMM	27	12(5pens)
Georgie ROSE	24	3
Neil THOMAS	27	20

Scarborough Athletic FC: 2009-10

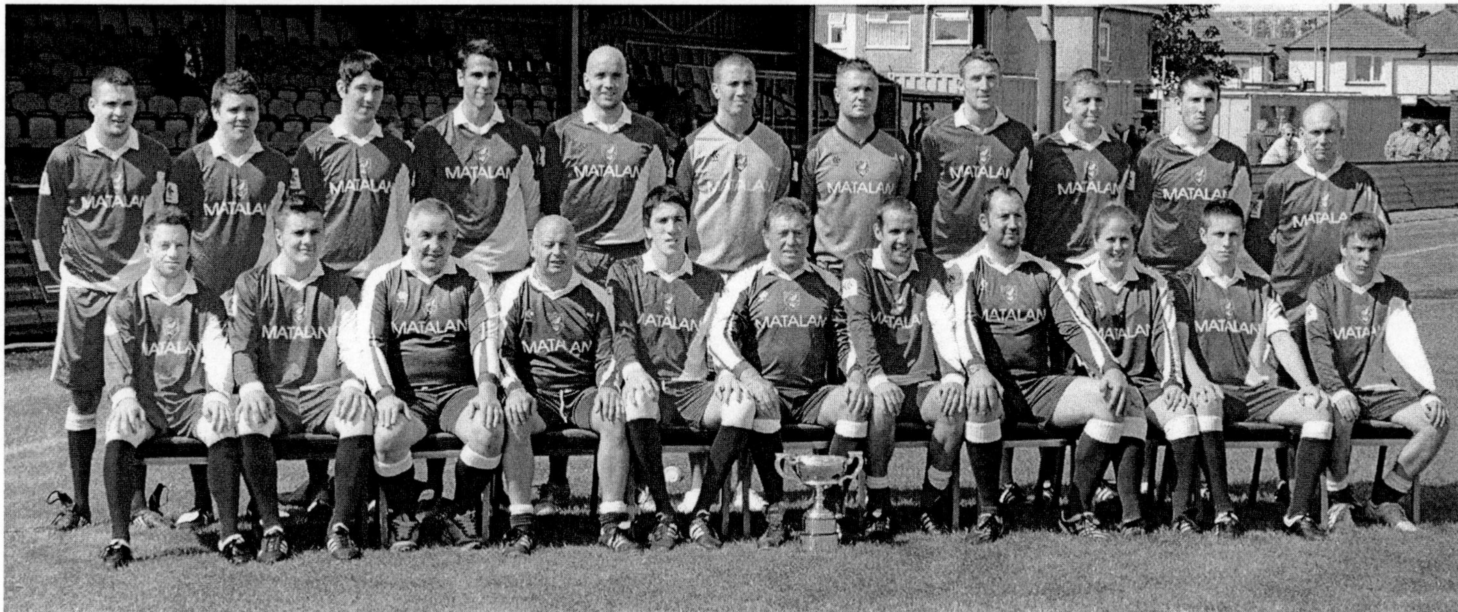

Back(L to R) Kemp, Griffin, Hogg, Hartas, Jamie Waltham, Arran Reid, Bramley, Gray, Logan, Miller, Hepples
Front(L to R) Hartley, Evans, Brian Waltham(physio), Exley(coach), Brian France(manager), Dawes(kit man), Hankey(physio), Callum Reid, Routledge

Scarborough Town FC: 2009-10

Back (L to R) Ramm, Thomas, Gildea, C.Cook, Danby, Clark, Waterfield, Jenkinson, N.Cook, Craig, Greening
Front (L to R) Patterson, Hawkes, Rose, Brown, Barber, Brooksby.

Final League Tables: 1986-87 to 2008-09

1986-87 GM Vauxhall Conference

	P	W	D	L	F	A	Pts
Scarborough	42	27	10	5	64	33	91
Barnet	42	25	10	7	86	39	85
Maidstone United	42	21	10	11	71	48	73
Enfield	42	21	7	14	66	47	70
Altrincham	42	18	15	9	66	53	69
Boston United	42	21	6	15	82	74	69
Sutton United	42	19	11	12	81	51	68
Runcorn	42	18	13	11	71	58	67
Telford United	42	18	10	14	69	59	64
Bath City	42	17	12	13	63	62	63
Cheltenham Town	42	16	13	13	64	50	61
Kidderminster Harriers	42	17	4	21	77	81	55
Stafford Rangers	42	14	11	17	58	60	53
Weymouth	42	13	12	17	68	77	51
Dagenham	42	14	7	21	56	72	49
Kettering Town	42	12	11	19	54	66	47
Northwich Victoria	42	10	14	18	53	69	44
Nuneaton Borough	42	10	14	18	48	73	44
Wealdstone	42	11	10	21	50	70	43
Welling United	42	10	10	22	61	84	40
Frickley Athletic	42	7	11	24	47	82	32
Gateshead	42	6	13	23	48	95	31

1987-88 Barclays Football League Division

Wolverhampton Wandererers	46	27	9	10	82	43	90
Cardiff City	46	24	13	9	66	41	85
Bolton Wanderers	46	22	12	12	66	42	78
Scunthorpe United	46	20	17	9	76	51	77
Torquay United	46	21	14	11	66	41	77
Swansea City	46	20	10	16	62	56	70
Peterborough United	46	20	10	16	52	53	70
Leyton Orient	46	19	12	15	85	63	69
Colchester United	46	19	10	17	47	51	67
Burnley	46	20	7	19	57	62	67
Wrexham	46	20	6	20	69	58	66
Scarborough	46	17	14	15	56	48	65
Darlington	46	18	11	17	71	69	65
Tranmere Rovers	46	19	9	18	61	53	64(-2pts)
Cambridge United	46	16	13	17	50	52	61
Hartlepool United	46	15	14	17	50	57	59
Crewe Alexandra	46	13	19	14	57	53	58
Halifax Town	46	14	14	18	54	59	55(-1pt)
Hereford United	46	14	12	20	41	59	54
Stockport County	46	12	15	19	44	58	51
Rochdale	46	11	15	20	47	76	48
Exeter City	46	11	13	22	53	68	46
Carlisle United	46	12	8	26	57	86	44
Newport County	46	6	7	33	35105		25

1988-89 Barclays Football League Division 4

Rotherham United	46	22	16	8	76	35	82
Tranmere Rovers	46	21	17	8	62	43	80
Crewe Alexandra	46	21	15	10	67	48	78
Scunthorpe United	46	21	14	11	77	57	77
Scarborough	46	21	14	11	67	52	77
Leyton Orient	46	21	12	13	86	50	75
Wrexham	46	19	14	13	77	63	71
Cambridge United	46	18	14	14	71	62	68
Grimsby Town	46	17	15	14	65	59	66
Lincoln City	46	18	10	18	64	60	64
York City	46	17	13	16	62	63	64
Carlisle United	46	15	15	16	53	52	60
Exeter City	46	18	6	22	65	68	60
Torquay United	46	17	8	21	45	60	59
Hereford United	46	14	16	16	66	72	58
Burnley	46	14	13	19	52	61	55
Peterborough United	46	14	12	20	52	64	54
Rochdale	46	13	14	19	56	82	53
Hartlepool United	46	14	10	22	50	78	52
Stockport County	46	10	21	15	54	52	51
Halifax Town	46	13	11	22	69	75	50
Colchester United	46	12	14	20	60	78	50
Doncaster Rovers	46	13	10	23	49	78	49
Darlington	46	8	18	20	53	76	42

1989-90 Barclays Football League Division 4

	P	W	D	L	F	A	Pts
Exeter City	46	28	5	13	83	48	89
Grimsby Town	46	22	13	11	70	47	79
Southend United	46	22	9	15	61	48	75
Stockport County	46	21	11	14	68	62	74
Maidstone United	46	22	7	17	77	61	73
Cambridge United	46	21	10	15	76	66	73
Chesterfield	46	19	14	13	63	50	71
Carlisle United	46	21	8	17	61	60	71
Peterborough United	46	17	17	12	59	46	68
Lincoln City	46	18	14	14	48	48	68
Scunthorpe United	46	17	15	14	69	54	66
Rochdale	46	20	6	20	52	55	66
York City	46	16	16	14	55	53	64
Gillingham	46	17	11	18	46	48	62
Torquay United	46	15	12	19	53	66	57
Burnley	46	14	14	18	45	55	56
Hereford United	46	15	10	21	56	62	55
Scarborough	46	15	10	21	60	73	55
Hartlepool United	46	15	10	21	66	88	55
Doncaster Rovers	46	14	9	23	53	60	51
Wrexham	46	13	12	21	51	67	51
Aldershot	46	12	14	20	49	69	50
Halifax Town	46	12	13	21	57	65	49
Colchester United	46	11	10	25	48	75	43

1990-91 Barclays Football League Division 4

Darlington	46	22	17	7	68	38	83
Stockport County	46	23	13	10	84	47	82
Hartlepool United	46	24	10	12	67	48	82
Peterborough United	46	21	17	8	67	45	80
Blackpool	46	23	10	13	78	47	79
Burnley	46	23	10	13	70	51	79
Torquay United	46	18	18	10	63	47	72
Scunthorpe United	46	20	11	15	71	62	71
Scarborough	46	19	12	15	59	56	69
Northampton Town	46	18	13	15	57	58	67
Doncaster Rovers	46	17	14	15	56	46	65
Rochdale	46	15	17	14	50	53	62
Cardiff City	46	15	15	16	43	54	60
Lincoln City	46	14	17	15	50	61	59
Gillingham	46	12	18	16	57	60	54
Walsall	46	12	17	17	48	51	53
Hereford United	46	13	14	19	53	58	53
Chesterfield	46	13	14	19	47	62	53
Maidstone United	46	13	12	21	66	71	51
Carlisle United	46	13	9	24	47	89	48
York City	46	11	13	22	45	57	46
Halifax Town	46	12	10	24	59	79	46
Aldershot	46	10	11	25	61	101	41
Wrexham	46	10	10	26	48	73	40

1991-92 Barclays Football League Division 4

Burnley	42	25	8	9	79	43	83
Rotherham United	42	22	11	9	70	37	77
Mansfield Town	42	23	8	11	75	53	77
Blackpool	42	22	10	10	71	45	76
Scunthorpe United	42	21	9	12	64	59	72
Crewe Alexandra	42	20	10	12	66	51	70
Barnet	42	21	6	15	81	61	69
Rochdale	42	18	13	11	57	53	67
Cardiff City	42	17	15	10	66	53	66
Lincoln City	42	17	11	14	50	44	62
Gillingham	42	15	12	15	63	53	57
Scarborough	42	15	12	15	64	68	57
Chesterfield	42	14	11	17	49	61	53
Wrexham	42	14	9	19	52	73	51
Walsall	42	12	13	15	48	58	49
Northampton Town	42	11	13	18	46	57	46
Hereford United	42	12	8	22	44	57	44
Maidstone United	42	8	18	16	45	56	42
York City	42	8	16	18	42	58	40
Halifax Town	42	10	8	24	34	75	38
Doncaster Rovers	42	9	8	25	40	65	35
Carlisle United	42	7	13	22	41	67	34

(Aldershot resigned from the League 25 March -record expunged)

1992-93 Barclays Football League Division 3

	P	W	D	L	F	A	Pts
Cardiff City	42	25	8	9	77	47	83
Wrexham	42	23	11	8	75	52	80
Barnet	42	23	10	9	66	48	79
York City	42	21	12	9	72	45	75
Walsall	42	22	7	13	76	61	73
Crewe Alexandra	42	21	7	14	75	56	70
Bury	42	18	9	15	63	55	63
Lincoln City	42	18	9	15	57	53	63
Shrewsbury Town	42	17	11	14	57	52	62
Colchester United	42	18	5	19	67	76	59
Rochdale	42	16	10	16	70	70	58
Chesterfield	42	15	11	16	59	63	56
Scarborough	42	15	9	18	66	71	54
Scunthorpe United	42	14	12	16	57	54	54
Darlington	42	12	14	16	48	53	50
Doncaster Rovers	42	11	14	17	42	57	47
Hereford United	42	10	15	17	47	60	45
Carlisle United	42	11	11	20	51	65	44
Torquay United	42	12	7	23	45	67	43
Northampton Town	42	11	8	23	48	74	41
Gillingham	42	9	13	20	48	64	40
Halifax Town	42	9	9	24	45	68	36

1993-94 Endsleigh Football League Division 3

Shrewsbury Town	42	22	13	7	63	39	79
Chester City	42	21	11	10	69	46	74
Crewe Alexandra	42	21	10	11	80	61	73
Wycombe Wanderers	42	19	13	10	67	53	70
Preston North End	42	18	13	11	79	60	67
Torquay United	42	17	16	9	64	56	67
Carlisle United	42	18	10	14	57	42	64
Chesterfield	42	16	14	12	55	48	62
Rochdale	42	16	12	14	63	51	60
Walsall	42	17	9	16	48	53	60
Scunthorpe United	42	15	14	13	64	56	59
Mansfield Town	42	15	10	17	53	62	55
Bury	42	14	11	17	55	56	53
Scarborough	42	15	8	19	55	61	53
Doncaster Rovers	42	14	10	18	44	57	52
Gillingham	42	12	15	15	44	51	51
Colchester United	42	13	10	19	56	71	49
Lincoln City	42	12	11	19	52	63	47
Wigan Athletic	42	11	12	19	51	70	45
Hereford United	42	12	6	24	60	79	42
Darlington	42	10	11	21	42	64	41
Northampton Town	42	9	11	22	44	66	38

1994-95 Endsleigh Football League Division 3

Carlisle United	42	27	10	5	67	36	91
Walsall	42	24	11	7	75	40	83
Chesterfield	42	23	12	7	62	37	81
Bury	42	23	11	8	73	36	80
Preston North End	42	19	10	13	58	41	67
Mansfield Town	42	18	11	13	84	59	65
Scunthorpe United	42	18	8	16	68	63	62
Fulham	42	16	14	12	60	54	62
Doncaster Rovers	42	17	10	15	58	43	61
Colchester United	42	16	10	16	56	64	58
Barnet	42	15	11	16	56	63	56
Lincoln City	42	15	11	16	54	55	56
Torquay United	42	14	13	15	54	57	55
Wigan Athletic	42	14	10	18	53	60	52
Rochdale	42	12	14	16	44	67	50
Hereford United	42	12	13	17	45	62	49
Northampton Town	42	10	14	18	45	67	44
Hartlepool United	42	11	10	21	43	69	43
Gillingham	42	10	11	21	46	64	41
Darlington	42	11	8	23	43	57	41
Scarborough	42	8	10	24	49	70	34
Exeter City	42	8	10	24	36	70	34

1995-96 Endsleigh Football League Division 3

	P	W	D	L	F	A	Pt
Preston North End	46	23	17	6	78	38	86
Gillingham	46	22	17	7	49	20	83
Bury	46	22	13	11	66	46	79
Plymouth Argyle	46	22	12	12	68	49	78
Darlington	46	20	18	8	60	42	78
Hereford United	46	20	14	12	65	47	74
Colchester United	46	18	18	10	61	51	72
Chester City	46	18	16	12	72	53	70
Barnet	46	18	16	12	65	45	70
Wigan Athletic	46	20	10	16	62	56	70
Northampton Town	46	18	13	15	51	44	67
Scunthorpe United	46	15	15	16	67	61	60
Doncaster Rovers	46	16	11	19	49	60	59
Exeter City	46	13	18	15	46	53	57
Rochdale	46	14	13	19	57	61	55
Cambridge United	46	14	12	20	61	71	54
Fulham	46	12	17	17	57	63	53
Lincoln City	46	13	14	19	57	73	53
Mansfield Town	46	11	20	15	54	64	53
Hartlepool United	46	12	13	21	47	57	49
Leyton Orient	46	12	11	23	44	63	47
Cardiff City	46	11	12	23	41	64	45
Scarborough	46	8	16	22	39	69	40
Torquay United	46	5	14	27	30	84	29

1996-97 Nationwide Football League Division 3

Wigan Athletic	46	26	9	11	84	51	87
Fulham	46	25	12	9	72	38	87
Carlisle United	46	24	12	10	67	44	84
Northampton Town	46	20	12	14	67	44	72
Swansea City	46	21	8	17	62	58	71
Chester City	46	18	16	12	55	43	70
Cardiff City	46	20	9	17	56	54	69
Colchester United	46	17	17	12	62	51	68
Lincoln City	46	18	12	16	70	69	66
Cambridge United	46	18	11	17	53	59	65
Mansfield Town	46	16	16	14	47	45	64
Scarborough	46	16	15	15	65	68	63
Scunthorpe United	46	18	9	19	59	62	63
Rochdale	46	14	16	16	68	68	58
Barnet	46	14	16	16	46	51	58
Leyton Orient	46	15	12	19	50	58	57
Hull City	46	13	18	15	44	50	57
Darlington	46	14	10	22	64	78	52
Doncaster Rovers	46	14	10	22	52	66	52
Hartlepool United	46	14	9	23	53	66	51
Torquay United	46	13	11	22	46	62	50
Exeter City	46	12	12	22	48	73	48
Brighton & Hove Albion	46	13	10	23	53	70	47(-2pts)
Hereford United	46	11	14	21	50	65	47

1997-98 Nationwide Football League Division 3

Notts County	46	29	12	5	82	43	99
Macclesfield Town	46	23	13	10	63	44	82
Lincoln City	46	20	15	11	60	51	75
Colchester United	46	21	11	14	72	60	74
Torquay United	46	21	11	14	68	59	74
Scarborough	46	19	15	12	67	58	72
Barnet	46	19	13	14	61	51	70
Scunthorpe United	46	19	12	15	56	52	69
Rotherham United	46	16	19	11	67	61	67
Peterborough United	46	18	13	15	63	51	67
Leyton Orient	46	19	12	15	62	47	66(-3pts)
Mansfield Town	46	16	17	13	64	55	65
Shrewsbury Town	46	16	13	17	61	62	61
Chester City	46	17	10	19	60	61	61
Exeter City	46	15	15	16	68	63	60
Cambridge United	46	14	18	14	63	57	60
Hartlepool United	46	12	23	11	61	53	59
Rochdale	46	17	7	22	56	55	58
Darlington	46	14	12	20	56	72	54
Swansea City	46	13	11	22	49	62	50
Cardiff City	46	9	23	14	48	52	50
Hull City	46	11	8	27	56	83	41
Brighton & Hove Albion	46	6	17	23	38	66	35
Doncaster Rovers	46	4	8	34	30	113	20

1998-99 Nationwide Football League Division 3

	P	W	D	L	F	A	Pts
Brentford	46	26	7	13	79	56	85
Cambridge United	46	23	12	11	78	48	81
Cardiff City	46	22	14	10	60	39	80
Scunthorpe United	46	22	8	16	69	58	74
Rotherham United	46	20	13	13	79	61	73
Leyton Orient	46	19	15	12	68	59	72
Swansea City	46	19	14	13	56	48	71
Mansfield Town	46	19	10	17	60	58	67
Peterborough United	46	18	12	16	72	56	66
Halifax Town	46	17	15	14	58	56	66
Darlington	46	18	11	17	69	58	65
Exeter City	46	17	12	17	47	50	63
Plymouth Argyle	46	17	10	19	58	54	61
Chester City	46	13	18	15	57	66	57
Shrewsbury Town	46	14	14	18	52	63	56
Barnet	46	14	13	19	54	71	55
Brighton & Hove Albion	46	16	7	23	49	66	55
Southend United	46	14	12	20	52	58	54
Rochdale	46	13	15	18	42	55	54
Torquay United	46	12	17	17	47	58	53
Hull City	46	14	11	21	44	62	53
Hartlepool United	46	13	12	21	52	65	51
Carlisle United	46	11	16	19	43	53	49
Scarborough	46	14	6	26	50	77	48

1999-2000 Nationwide Conference

Kidderminster Harriers	42	26	7	9	75	40	85
Rushden & Diamonds	42	21	13	8	71	42	76
Morecambe	42	18	16	8	70	48	70
Scarborough	42	19	12	11	60	35	69
Kingstonian	42	20	7	15	58	44	67
Dover Athletic	42	18	12	12	65	56	66
Yeovil Town	42	18	10	14	60	63	64
Hereford United	42	15	14	13	61	52	59
Southport	42	15	13	14	55	56	58
Stevenage Borough	42	16	9	17	60	54	57
Hayes	42	16	8	18	57	58	56
Doncaster Rovers	42	15	9	18	46	48	54
Kettering Town	42	12	16	14	44	50	52
Woking	42	13	13	16	45	53	52
Nuneaton Borough	42	12	15	15	49	53	51
Telford United	42	14	9	19	56	66	51
Hednesford Town	42	15	6	21	45	68	51
Northwich Victoria	42	13	12	17	53	78	51
Forest Green Rovers	42	13	8	21	54	63	47
Welling United	42	13	8	21	54	66	47
Altrincham	42	9	19	14	51	60	46
Sutton United	42	8	10	24	39	75	34

2000-01 Nationwide Conference

Rushden & Diamonds	42	25	11	6	78	36	86
Yeovil Town	42	24	8	10	73	50	80
Dagenham & Redbridge	42	23	8	11	71	54	77
Southport	42	20	9	13	58	46	69
Leigh RMI	42	19	11	12	63	57	68
Telford United	42	19	8	15	51	51	65
Stevenage Borough	42	15	18	9	71	61	63
Chester City	42	16	14	12	49	43	62
Doncaster Rovers	42	15	13	14	47	43	58
Scarborough	42	14	16	12	56	54	58
Hereford United	42	14	15	13	60	46	57
Boston United	42	13	17	12	74	63	56
Nuneaton Borough	42	13	15	14	60	60	54
Woking	42	13	15	14	52	57	54
Dover Athletic	42	14	11	17	54	56	53
Forest Green Rovers	42	11	15	16	43	54	48
Northwich Victoria	42	11	13	18	49	67	46
Hayes	42	12	10	20	44	71	46
Morecambe	42	11	12	19	64	66	45
Kettering Town	42	11	10	21	46	62	43
Kingstonian	42	8	10	24	47	73	34
Hednesford Town	42	5	13	24	46	86	28

2001-02 Nationwide Conference

	P	W	D	L	F	A	Pts
Boston United	42	25	9	8	84	42	84
Dagenham & Redbridge	42	24	12	6	70	47	84
Yeovil Town	42	19	13	10	66	53	70
Doncaster Rovers	42	18	13	11	68	46	67
Barnet	42	19	10	13	64	48	67
Morecambe	42	17	11	14	63	67	62
Farnborough Town	42	18	7	17	66	54	61
Margate	42	14	16	12	59	53	58
Telford United	42	14	15	13	63	58	57
Nuneaton Borough	42	16	9	17	57	57	57
Stevenage Borough	42	15	10	17	57	60	55
Scarborough	42	14	14	14	55	63	55(-1pt)
Northwich Victoria	42	16	7	19	57	70	55
Chester City	42	15	9	18	54	51	54
Southport	42	13	14	15	53	49	53
Leigh RMI	42	15	8	19	56	58	53
Hereford United	42	14	10	18	50	53	52
Forest Green Rovers	42	12	15	15	54	76	51
Woking	42	13	9	20	59	70	48
Hayes	42	13	5	24	53	80	44
Stalybridge Celtic	42	11	10	21	40	69	43
Dover Athletic	42	11	6	25	41	65	39

2002-03 Nationwide Conference

Yeovil Town	42	28	11	3	100	37	95
Morecambe	42	23	9	10	86	42	78
Doncaster Rovers	42	22	12	8	73	47	78
Chester City	42	21	12	9	59	31	75
Dagenham & Redbridge	42	21	9	12	71	59	72
Hereford United	42	19	7	16	64	51	64
Scarborough	42	18	10	14	63	54	64
Halifax Town	42	18	10	14	50	51	64
Forest Green Rovers	42	17	8	17	61	62	59
Margate	42	15	11	16	60	66	56
Barnet	42	13	14	15	65	68	53
Stevenage Borough	42	14	10	18	61	55	52
Farnborough Town	42	13	12	17	57	56	51
Northwich Victoria	42	13	12	17	66	72	51
Telford United	42	14	7	21	54	69	49
Burton Albion	42	13	10	19	52	77	49
Gravesend & Northfleet	42	12	12	18	62	73	48
Leigh RMI	42	14	6	22	44	71	48
Woking	42	11	14	17	52	81	47
Nuneaton Borough	42	13	7	22	51	78	46
Southport	42	11	12	19	54	69	45
Kettering Town	42	8	7	27	37	73	31

2003-04 Nationwide Conference

Chester City	42	27	11	4	85	34	92
Hereford United	42	28	7	7	103	44	91
Shrewsbury Town	42	20	14	8	67	42	74
Barnet	42	19	14	9	60	46	71
Aldershot Town	42	20	10	12	80	67	70
Exeter City	42	19	12	11	71	57	69
Morecambe	42	20	7	15	66	66	67
Stevenage Borough	42	18	9	15	58	52	63
Woking	42	15	16	11	65	52	61
Accrington Stanley	42	15	13	14	68	61	58
Gravesend & Northfleet	42	14	15	13	69	66	57
Telford United	42	15	10	17	49	51	55
Dagenham & Redbridge	42	15	9	18	59	64	54
Burton Albion	42	15	7	20	57	59	51(-1pt)
Scarborough	42	12	15	15	51	54	51
Margate	42	14	9	19	56	64	51
Tamworth	42	13	10	19	49	68	49
Forest Green Rovers	42	12	12	18	58	80	48
Halifax Town	42	12	8	22	43	65	44
Farnborough Town	42	10	9	23	53	74	39
Leigh RMI	42	7	8	27	46	97	29
Northwich Victoria	42	4	11	27	30	80	23

2004-05 Nationwide Conference

	P	W	D	L	F	A	Pts
Barnet	42	26	8	8	90	44	86
Hereford United	42	21	11	10	68	41	74
Carlisle United	42	20	13	9	74	37	73
Aldershot Town	42	21	10	11	68	52	73
Stevenage Borough	42	22	6	14	65	52	73
Exeter City	42	20	11	11	71	50	71
Morecambe	42	19	14	9	69	50	71
Woking	42	18	14	10	58	45	68
Halifax Town	42	19	9	14	74	56	66
Accrington Stanley	42	18	11	13	72	58	65
Dagenham & Redbridge	42	19	8	15	68	60	65
Crawley Town	42	16	9	17	50	50	57
Scarborough	42	14	14	14	60	46	56
Gravesend & Northfleet	42	13	11	18	58	64	50
Tamworth	42	14	11	17	53	63	50 *
Burton Albion	42	13	11	18	50	66	50
York City	42	11	10	21	39	66	43
Canvey Island	42	9	15	18	53	65	42
Northwich Victoria	42	14	10	18	58	72	42 #
Forest Green Rovers	42	6	15	21	41	81	33
Farnborough Town	42	6	11	25	35	89	29
Leigh RMI	42	4	6	32	31	98	18

* 3 points deducted. # 10 points deducted

2005-06 Nationwide Conference

	P	W	D	L	F	A	Pts
Accrington Stanley	42	28	7	7	76	45	91
Hereford United	42	22	14	6	59	33	80
Grays Athletic	42	21	13	8	94	55	76
Halifax Town	42	21	12	9	55	40	75
Morecambe	42	22	8	12	68	41	74
Stevenage Borough	42	19	12	11	62	47	69
Exeter City	42	18	9	15	65	48	63
York City	42	17	12	13	63	48	63
Burton Albion	42	16	12	14	50	52	60
Dagenham & Redbridge	42	16	10	16	63	59	58
Woking	42	14	14	14	58	47	56
Cambridge United	42	15	10	17	51	57	55
Aldershot Town	42	16	6	20	61	74	54
Canvey Island	42	13	12	17	47	58	51
Kidderminster Harriers	42	13	11	18	39	55	50
Gravesend & Northfleet	42	13	10	19	45	57	49
Crawley Town	42	12	11	19	48	55	47
Southport	42	10	10	22	36	68	40
Forest Green Rovers	42	8	14	20	49	62	38
Tamworth	42	8	14	20	32	63	38
Scarborough	42	9	10	23	40	66	37
Altrincham	42	10	11	21	40	71	23 *

* 18 points deducted

2006-07 Conference North

	P	W	D	L	F	A	Pts
Droylesden	42	23	9	10	85	55	78
Kettering Town	42	20	13	9	75	58	73
Workington	42	20	10	12	61	46	70
Hinkley United	42	19	12	11	68	54	69
Farsley Celtic	42	19	11	12	58	51	68
Harrogate Town	42	18	13	11	58	41	67
Blyth Spartans	42	19	9	14	57	49	66
Hyde United	42	18	11	13	79	62	65
Worcester City	42	16	14	12	67	54	62
Nuneaton Borough	42	15	15	12	54	45	60
Moor Green	42	16	11	15	53	51	59
Gainsborough Trinity	42	15	11	16	51	57	56
Hucknall Town	42	15	9	18	69	69	54
Alfreton Town	42	14	12	16	44	50	54
Vauxhall Motors	42	12	15	15	62	64	51
Barrow	42	12	14	16	47	48	50
Leigh RMI	42	13	10	19	47	61	49
Stalybridge Celtic	42	13	10	19	64	81	49
Redditch United	42	11	15	16	61	68	48
Scarborough	42	13	16	13	50	45	45 *
Worksop Town	42	12	9	21	44	62	45
Lancaster City	42	2	5	35	27	110	1 *

* 10 points deducted

2007-08 Northern Counties East League Division 1

	P	W	D	L	F	A	Pts
Dinnington Town	32	24	6	2	88	40	78
Hall Road Rangers	32	22	1	9	65	42	67
Bottesford Town	32	19	5	8	62	40	62
Rainworth MW	32	16	9	7	60	38	57
Scarborough Athletic	32	18	7	7	80	45	55 *
Gedling Town	32	16	7	9	70	45	55
Leeds Met Carnegie	32	17	4	11	67	45	55
Staveley MW	32	14	4	14	49	53	46
Barton Town OB	32	13	9	10	82	62	45 #
Teversal	32	10	12	10	58	66	42
AFC Emley	32	10	8	14	59	66	38
Tadcaster Albion	32	9	7	16	48	66	34
Borrowash Victoria	32	8	6	18	49	76	30
Yorkshire Amateur	32	7	8	17	37	67	29
Worsbrough Bridge	32	7	6	19	40	67	27
Rossington Main	32	7	3	22	47	87	24
Pontefract Collieries	32	1	6	25	29	85	9

* 6 points deducted # 3 points deucted

2008-09 Northern Counties East League Division 1

Scarborough Athletic	36	29	5	2	121	24	92
Rainworth MW	36	23	9	4	90	42	78
Askern Villa	36	21	9	6	65	34	72
Staveley MW	36	20	8	8	77	43	68
Barton Town OB	36	20	7	9	76	53	67
Bottesford Town	36	20	2	14	77	62	62
Leeds Carnegie	36	17	10	9	79	41	61
AFC Emley	36	17	9	10	59	48	60
Pontefract Collieries	36	16	5	15	62	56	53
Hemsworth MW	36	13	11	12	57	52	50
Rossington Main	36	12	7	17	53	67	43
Appleby Frodingham	36	11	9	16	58	79	42
Grimsby Borough	36	11	7	18	52	68	40
Teversal	36	12	3	21	59	86	39
Brighouse Town	36	9	8	19	55	73	35
Worsbrough Bridge	36	9	5	22	45	86	32
Tadcaster Albion	36	9	4	23	47	94	31
Yorkshire Amateur	36	7	8	21	42	77	29
Glasshoughton Welfare	36	0	6	30	29	118	6

2008-09 Teesside League Division 2

Scarborough Town	20	16	4	0	72	11	52
South Bank St Peters	20	16	1	3	71	41	49
Whinney Banks YCC	20	14	1	5	71	36	43
Coulby Newham	20	11	3	6	47	32	36
Redcar Rugby Club	20	8	4	8	44	61	28
Great Ayton United	20	7	5	8	38	35	26
Acklam Steelworks	20	7	2	11	44	47	20 *
Norton & Stockton Res	20	5	3	12	31	47	18
Teesside Athletic Res	20	5	2	13	24	50	17
St Mary's College	20	3	3	14	25	46	12
Grangetown YCC	20	3	2	15	23	84	11

* 3 points deducted

(Billingham Kader, Billingham Town Res and Coble Ennis Square, all withdrew during the season, and their records were deleted)

Player of the Year Awards: 1970 to 2009

Sponsored by the Scarborough Evening News,
and decided on votes cast by supporters at the end of each season.

SCARBOROUGH FC

1970 Harry Dunn
1971 Jeff Barmby
1972 Ted Smethurst
1973 Colin Appleton
1974 Harry Dunn
1975 Tony Aveyard
1976 John Woodall
1977 Billy Ayre
1978 Dave Chapman
1979 Gerry Donoghue
1980 Neil Sellers
1981 Neil Sellers
1982 Ian Smith
1983 Kenny Dennis
1984 Bryan Magee
1985 Marshall Burke
1986 Neil Thompson
1987 Kevin Blackwell
1988 Alan Kamara
1989 Gary Brook
1990 Alan Kamara
1991 Ian Ironside
1992 Tommy Mooney
1993 Darren Foreman
1994 Shaun Murray
1995 Jason White
1996 Stuart Hicks
1996 Stuart Hicks
1997 Jason Rockett
1998 Gary Bennett
1999 Jamie Hoyland
2000 Steve Brodie
2001 Paul Ellender
2002 Andy Woods
2003 David Pounder
2004 Mark Hotte
2005 Chris Senior
2006 Michael Coulson
2007 Denny Ingram

SCARBOROUGH ATHLETIC

2008 Scott Phillips
2009 Dave Hartas

SCARBOROUGH TOWN

2009 Wayne Brooksby

~ Advanced Subscribers ~

Scarborough Athletic FC
Trevor Bull
Peter Tomkys, Beverley
Don Fewster
John Horsley, Beverley
Alan Moffatt, York
Bill Hunter
Geoffrey Smith
S. Blaydes, Hunmanby
Derek Megginson
Stuart Canvin
Ben Naylor
Joe Davis, Chicago, USA
Dave Metcalf
John & Judith Birley
Nigel Wood
Sean Hunter
Dave Stoneleigh, Leicester
James C. Fisher, Skelmorlie
John Atkinson
Roger Hopkin
Eric Pickup
Christopher Hoggarth
Paul Andrews
Sandra Troughton
Mark Hobson
James Hunter
Tony Stockdale, Allerston
Scott Pringle, Edinburgh
Clive Harvey, York
David Reynolds, York
Ian Whittaker, Leeds
Martin Sykes, Hunmanby
Walter Sowersby
Mike Price, Welsh Seadog
Len Taylor, Filey
Mark Alcorn
Gary & Gavin Wilson
Richard Adamson
Phil Buckton, York
Jim Turner, Beverley
Mohammed Yogi, Norwich
Stephen Goodall, Middlesbrough
Adam Faulkner, Skipton
David Faulkner, Skipton
Jack Thompson, Stockport
Dominic Garfield.
James Toal
Andrew Toal
Gordon Toal
Karl Bardsley
Iain Stanton, London E18
David Uffindall, Ripon
Don Widdows, Sheffield
Kim Johnson, Chatham, Kent
Gary Stewart, York
Jonathan Wood
Anthony Gough
Adam & Neil Daniel
Alan Mason, Luton, Beds
Bernard Morris, Leeds
Brian Clark, Driffield
Peter Holmes, Liskeard
Nigel Smith, Alfreton
Sheffield Seadogs
Barrie Watson
Rachael Dermott
Stuart Fairbridge, Middlesbrough
R.S. Bernard
Dave Nunn, York
Neil Fletcher, Hucknall
Joseph Kennedy, Newport, Salop
Max Cope, Newark
Rob Bernard, Willesden Seadog
Kenny Carr, Pickering
Paul Dayes - shed faithful
Kevin Russell Hardwick
Brian Hill, Leeds
Ian Ridley, Penrith
Jason & Greg Lyndon, Gillingham
Craig Harte, Leeds
Craig Tyreman, Whitby
Martin Burrows, Leeds
Dr Andrew Davidson
Phil Rumsey, Harrogate
Trevor Garfield, Weston-Super-Mare
Justin Garfield
Tony Scott
Steve Colley
Hugh Bellamy
Paul Harper
Norman Bellamy
Gavin Barker
Matthew Flinton

The Athletic Ground in 2008...
Derelict and abandoned!

What does the future hold ?

After several years of lurching from one financial crisis to another, Scarborough Football Club - once the best non-League club in the country - finally collapsed under a mountain of debt on 20 June 2007. Just over two years later, and there is the situation of not one, but two vibrant, successful ,Scarborough clubs now competing at the lower levels of the football pyramid. After all the years of doom and gloom, local football supporters are now enjoying their sport again, watching entertaining, attacking football, and attending matches with smiles on their faces.

The two new clubs have both enjoyed success since their formations, and both won their respective league titles for the 2008-09 season. As this book went to print, both were again riding high in their leagues, Athletic in the Northern Counties East League Premier Division, and Town in the Wearside League. Unfortunately the ground situation is still unclear, with no suitable stadium yet available in Scarborough, so both the new clubs could well have their ambitions thwarted by the lack of facilities in town.

The two clubs are both well run, by keen, enthusiastic supporters, who just want to contribute to the success of their club, and help out behind the scenes without any financial gain. Football in Scarborough is making headlines for all the right reasons once again (results on the pitch, not boardroom changes or financial difficulties), and both Scarborough Athletic and Scarborough Town are attracting attention for their achievements on the football field.

But, what does the future hold for senior football in the town? With a population of around 55,000, is Scarborough big enough to support two senior clubs at a fairly high level of non-League football? Both clubs have their roots in the old Scarborough FC, and the followers of the two clubs were, in the main, fellow supporters of the same club just two years ago. Is there not a way that the two could once again come together for the greater good of senior football on the East Yorkshire Coast?

At present there is still a degree of mistrust between certain people involved with the two clubs, and it is difficult to see any coming together in the immediate future. Scarborough Athletic, although currently exiled 17-miles down the coast in Bridlington, at present have the bigger fan base, while Scarborough Town at least have a home ground in Scarborough, even if it is little more than a fenced off school pitch at the moment. Town also have the highly acclaimed School of Excellence under their wing, and are therefore guaranteed a steady conveyor belt of local talent in the coming years. Both clubs have excellent coaches, good, hard working committee's and a loyal hardcore of supporters that is the envy of all the rival clubs in their respective leagues.

Scarborough football is currently at a crossroads, and it looks as if the two clubs are going to take different paths and continue along their separate ways. What a pity that the two cannot put their differences aside, and work together in the years ahead to get a unified Scarborough club back to the top levels of semi-professional football.

UNITY IS STRENGTH

~Yore Publications ~

Established in 1991 by Dave Twydell, Yore Publication, have become the leading publishers of Football League club histories. Of the thirty plus published to date, including the successful Scarborough FC History 1879 - 1998 (now out of print). Most are large page quality hardbacks containing well illustrated and written histories. A number of Football League Who's Who books have also been produced. A slightly new venture is the more extensive coverage of non-League clubs, together with this book, also published in 2009 is 'We Are 'Ayes' (Centenary History of Hayes F.C.) The 'Gone But Not Forgotten' series (published twice yearly continuously since 1992), contain written and illustrated (abbreviated) histories of defunct English non-League clubs and/or former grounds, whilst The Rejected F.C. series consist of the compilation histories of former Football League clubs (several clubs per book) - written and illustrated, with some statistics; plus a much acclaimed 90 minute DVD.

Unusual titles include 'The Lesser Stadiums Of The World', 'Denied F.C.' (English clubs' election struggles to gain League status), 'The Ultimate Directory of English and Scottish Football League Grounds' (extensive details of every ground - 314 in total) and 'Football Through The Turnstiles... Again' (First published in 1992, updated in 2002 - the history of English football relating to attendance figures, including the seasonal average for every club from 1888).

We only publish football books - normally of an historic nature -
for which two free Newsletters are available each year.
For your first copy, please send a S.A.E. to:
Yore Publications, 12 The Furrows, Harefield, Middx. UB9 6AT.
(Also see our Web site on: www.yore.demon.co.uk or look for 'Yore Publications')